SCENES FROM TANGLEWOOD

Andrew L. Pincus

SCENES FROM

TANGLEWOOD

Boston

NORTHEASTERN UNIVERSITY PRESS

Northeastern University Press

Library of Congress Cataloging-in-Publication Data
Pincus, Andrew L., 1930–
Scenes from Tanglewood / Andrew L. Pincus.
p. cm.
Includes index.
ISBN 1-55553-049-4 (alk. paper)—
ISBN 1-55553-054-0 (pbk. : alk. paper)
I. Tanglewood Music Center. II. Tanglewood (Music Festival)
III. Boston Symphony Orchestra. IV. Title.
ML200.8.B5P56 1989
780'.7'97441—dc19   89-2856
                                      CIP
                                      MN

Designed by David Ford.

Composed in Stone Serif by Eastern Typesetting Co.,
South Windsor, Connecticut. Printed and bound by
Kingsport Press, Kingsport, Tennessee. The paper is Glatfelter
Offset, an acid-free sheet.

MANUFACTURED IN THE UNITED STATES OF AMERICA
94 93 92 91 90 89   5 4 3 2 1

Tanglewood is my blood and tears—

and my greatest joy.

—Serge Koussevitzky

CONTENTS

FOREWORD

M Y ASSOCIATION with the Boston Symphony Orchestra began when Charles Munch, then the orchestra's music director, invited me to become a student at the Tanglewood Music Center. Since that time, Tanglewood has always held a special place in my heart. Little did I imagine then, back in 1960, that someday I would follow in the illustrious footsteps of Charles Munch and Serge Koussevitzky.

Now, as the BSO's music director, I am in the role of teacher to the Tanglewood Music Center students. Having the opportunity to work with these young performers is one of my most cherished Tanglewood experiences. In describing the Tanglewood Music Center and the many other facets of Tanglewood, this book shows how the members of the Boston Symphony Orchestra and other fine musicians meet intense artistic challenges. It captures the essence of Tanglewood — not just as a magnificent physical setting in the beautiful surroundings of the Berkshires, but as a community of people joined in the common goal of making music at the highest level. We must all work hard, and there are many pressures — but there are many rewards, too.

This book conveys how unique and magical the Tanglewood experience can be. I hope that it will also create a special place for Tanglewood in your heart.

SEIJI OZAWA

PREFACE

I BEGAN COVERING Tanglewood as the music critic of the *Berkshire Eagle* in 1975. The festival activities quickly became a source of endless interest. What seized me was not just the music but the process by which several hundred human beings — musicians, teachers, students, administrators, volunteers, and others, all of different backgrounds and temperaments —gather in the country each summer to stage a music festival for a national audience in the hundreds of thousands. The interaction between the parent Boston Symphony Orchestra and its school, the Tanglewood Music Center, and between musicians and listeners, posed further fascinating questions. These finally included a question of critical importance for the arts in America: how far should a symphony orchestra — or any institution — go in making great art digestible for a broad public?

Tanglewood thus became a microcosm for a look at the role of music in a cultural democracy. Putting it in everyday terms, I wanted to find out why people play and listen to music, and why they come to this particular place to do it. My method in these "scenes" has remained that of a practicing journalist. I have poked my nose in strange places, asked presumptuous questions, and tried to come upon musicians from unexpected angles — to surprise them, and the reader, by going beyond the picnics and holiday air on the lawn. Over a half-century Tanglewood has grown from the plaything of well-heeled arts patrons into an institution with a tradition of greatness. The successes (and failures) can tell us a great deal about the uses (and abuses) of music.

My material from 1975 on comes largely from my own reporting, listening, and observation. For other material I have drawn on Herbert Kupferberg's excellent 1976 history, *Tanglewood,* and on other sources as noted in the text. I am grateful to the editors of the *Berkshire Eagle* for permission to adapt work that first appeared in the *Eagle* and its magazine, *Berkshires Week.* I am also indebted to the BSO staff, particularly Daniel R. Gustin and Caroline Smedvig, for their assistance, and to all the musicians who knowingly or unknowingly became protagonists in this story. I hope that in helping me to tell it, they have contributed to an understanding of how a music festival — and thereby the art of music — works.

Lenox, Massachusetts
September 1988

SCENES FROM TANGLEWOOD

Chapter I

THE IDEA OF A FESTIVAL

*T*HE STONY SOIL of New England will receive only certain crops. One of them is music festivals. Summer comes and music resounds from peripatetic chamber series amid mountain and island hamlets, resounds from the internationally known chamber concerts and school at Marlboro, Vermont — resounds from every form, style, and mix up to the pop, symphonic, and jazz offerings at the Great Woods performing arts complex south of Boston. Amid these centers of refreshment and uplift, the granddaddy and king is Tanglewood.

In one sense the Berkshires of western Massachusetts are a natural setting for a music festival. During the nineteenth and early twentieth centuries, the region, with its unspoiled lakes and hills, was a home to Nathaniel Hawthorne, Herman Melville, Fanny Kemble, Edith Wharton, Oliver Wendell Holmes, and a succession of wealthy families, including the Vanderbilts, Westinghouses, and Carnegies, who summered on grand estates. Indeed, Lenox ranked with Newport as an industrial barons' resort. Hawthorne, living in a cottage on the present Tanglewood grounds, wrote his *Tanglewood Tales* there and thus gave not only an estate but also a festival its name. But in another sense the Lenox location lessened the prospects for success. The year-round residents of the area worked in paper, textile, and electrical-equipment mills, and the very remoteness that made the area a watering place for the rich made it less accessible to the larger concertgoing audience necessary to sustain a festival. And the time was the 1930s, in the depths of the depression. Who would pay to found or hear symphonic concerts in the wilderness when millions could not put food on the table?

3

Serge Koussevitzky in the 1930s.

Nevertheless, it was into this soil that a group of Berkshire arts patrons and Serge Koussevitzky, the Boston Symphony Orchestra's music director from 1924 until 1949, dropped the seed that eventually became the Tanglewood festival. Now one of the world's preeminent music festivals, offering fifty concerts by internationally known artists over a span of two months each summer, Tanglewood needed grit and luck as much as artistic vision to get started. And it began neither with the BSO nor on the 210 acres of lawn, gardens, meadows, and woods the world now knows as Tanglewood.

Members of the New York Philharmonic-Symphony Orchestra and assorted other New York musicians, under Henry Hadley, played the first two seasons of summer symphonic concerts in the Berkshires in 1934 and 1935. The organizers were a committee of summer and year-round Berkshire residents, mostly women. Their president and guiding spirit was Miss Gertrude Robinson Smith, a

Miss Gertrude Robinson Smith in 1955.

determined New Yorker and part-time Berkshirite who declared: "It is high time that America had its own Salzburg, and we are taking a step in that direction. The people of the Berkshires are prepared to receive and serve visitors from all over the United States."

Already three themes that were to run through the festival were evident. One was the idea of an American Salzburg, a glittering symphonic festival tucked away in the mountains. Another was the welcome from "the people of the Berkshires," a chancy affair both then and now, dividing Berkshirites who provide rooms and services from ordinary residents who want no part of the summer infestation. Finally, there was the paradox of a New Yorker, and the many New Yorkers on her committee, inviting "visitors from all over the United States" to the Berkshires. Although these visitors came in growing numbers, it is a curious fact of summer life that the Berkshires, equidistant from New York and Boston, continue to draw summer residents and visitors primarily from New York and its environs.

The first two seasons' concerts took place in a riding ring about three miles south of today's Tanglewood. The first year, the players sat in a plywood shell while the audience risked the elements on wooden benches. In 1935 a tent put shelter over everyone's head. Both seasons attracted large, enthusiastic, and often stylish audiences — as many as 3,500 listeners at a concert — and even turned an unexpected profit. But Miss Robinson Smith and the committee found Hadley's programming of classical tidbits pedestrian and felt a need for something more durable than a pick-up orchestra if they were to create a new Salzburg. Ailing, and recognizing the problem, Hadley bowed out.

It was then that the festival committee turned to Koussevitzky and the BSO, though as only one of several possibilities, to carry on the series. Koussevitzky was enthusiastic, the orchestra's trustees assented despite some misgivings, and in 1936 the BSO played its first Berkshire season, consisting of three concerts spread over a single weekend. The site now was Holmwood, a five-hundred-acre estate with a mansion and long, rolling lawns, about three miles east of Tanglewood, and the audience, which numbered about five thousand at each concert, shared a large tent with the orchestra. With the celebrated Koussevitzky reigning over so pioneering a venture, listeners came from distant points in the United States and abroad, fulfilling the Robinson Smith prophecy. National newspaper and radio coverage came with them.

Not content with music in a tent, however, Koussevitzky began pressing almost immediately for a permanent concert pavilion on a permanent site. The BSO trustees resisted the expense, and non-musical Berkshire residents — many of them — resisted the outsiders and their citified ways. Then a miracle happened. Mrs. Gorham Brooks, a Boston resident and BSO aficionado, and Miss Mary Aspinwall Tappan, her elderly aunt, offered the BSO their unoccupied estate, named Tanglewood, after Hawthorne's tales, as a home for the festival. The gift of a house and land straddling the Lenox-Stockbridge line was gratefully accepted. On August 5, 1937, in yet another tent, Koussevitzky conducted the BSO in an all-Beethoven program that launched the Tanglewood of today. The inaugural season consisted of two weekends of three concerts each.

Koussevitzky's enthusiasm for Tanglewood sprang from deeper sources than a mere sojourn in the country. Back in his native Russia he had dreamed of what he later described as "an Academy of Music and Art." It was to be "a permanent institution, a Center where the greatest living composers would teach the art of composition, the

A young Leonard Bernstein, left, helps Serge Koussevitzky celebrate a birthday. Bernstein's fellow conducting student from 1940, Lukas Foss, is at right.

greatest virtuosi, the art of perfect performance, the greatest conductors, the mystery of conducting orchestras and choruses." Unable to realize this vision in revolutionary Russia despite wealth from his marriage to Natalie Ushkov, the daughter of a tea merchant, he saw possibilities in Tanglewood beyond the festival committee's imaginings.

The first step, however, was construction of a concert pavilion. It was planned for 1939, but the project was delayed because of the expense. Suddenly the idea received help from an unexpected quarter — a thunderstorm, perhaps the most famous in Berkshire history. Even a tent provided the audience no protection. During an all-Wagner program on the opening night of the second 1937 weekend, a Rhine not of Wagner's making spattered and mired the concertgoers in all their finery. When the intermission came and Koussevitzky sat gloomily in his dressing room, Miss Robinson Smith seized the opportunity to mount the stage and appeal to the dripping audience for money to build a music shed. By the time the concert let out, she had raised $30,000 of the $100,000 she needed. The rest followed quickly.

At Koussevitzky's recommendation the distinguished architect Eliel Saarinen was hired to design the building. His plans proved too ambitious for the festival's budget, however, and a Berkshire engineer, Joseph Franz, modified them to complete the job at $90,000, $10,000 below the limit. The resulting "shed" — a name it has retained to this day — was a hangar-like structure open on three sides, fanning out in a broad crescent from the wooden stage. It had an earthen floor, good acoustics, and seats for six thousand under cover, with space for many thousands more on the surrounding lawns. Despite modifications over the years, including acoustical "clouds" over the stage to improve the sound and new, wider chairs that reduced the seating capacity to five thousand, the auditorium remains much as it was at the beginning. For the inaugural concert on August 4, 1938, Koussevitzky conducted Beethoven's Ninth Symphony. The work has been a Tanglewood staple for special occasions ever since.

Two years later Koussevitzky realized the other half of his dream. Over the doubts and objections of some trustees, the Berkshire (now Tanglewood) Music Center opened for an inaugural six-week session with 312 students — many of them on scholarships — and a distinguished faculty that included Aaron Copland as its chairman,

Paul Hindemith as a composer, Gregor Piatigorsky in charge of chamber music, and Herbert Graf and Boris Goldovsky running an opera program. Among those 312 students was a gifted pianist and conductor from Lawrence, Massachusetts, recently out of Harvard. His name was Leonard Bernstein. Koussevitzky had found not only his school but his protégé.

"Little did I think," Koussevitzky said that summer, "that my own early dream of a Music and Art Center in Moscow, in the heart of Russia, would find its realization in the heart of New England a quarter of a century later. Indeed, miracles cannot be accounted for."

The idea of a festival goes back to the Olympic Games and even earlier, when ritual celebrations with music and dance honored the gods, often in a plea for good crops or some other happy event. Both the religious and the competitive strains remained parts of early Christian, medieval, and Renaissance festivals. In church use, music and pageantry accompanied feasts, processions, and other celebrations, much as they do today. Perhaps the best-known embodiment of the competition is the Welsh eisteddfod, which began in the Middle Ages as a contest among musicians and poets and evolved into today's choral festivals, making the Welsh hills ring with music. And every opera lover knows Wagner's *Meistersinger,* which shows the master singers of medieval Nuremberg vying to see who can make the finest song.

The eighteenth and nineteenth centuries in Europe were a time of great choral festivals, as befits a period when composers like Bach, Handel, and Mendelssohn were producing epic choral works that remain the heart of the repertoire today. In the United States the festival movement began in the late nineteenth century with choral gatherings on the European model — as in Europe, sometimes the bigger the better. The annual Bach festival in Bethlehem, Pennsylvania, and other major festivals in Chautauqua, New York, and Ann Arbor, Michigan, date from this time. But Massachusetts led the way. The Worcester Festival, founded in 1858, launched the movement, and in 1869 the Great National Peace Jubilee in Boston amassed a chorus of ten thousand and an orchestra of one thousand.

With the rise of the symphony orchestra and easier travel and communications, the face of festivals changed again in the twentieth century. Some festivals continued the tradition of honoring a composer — Wagner at Bayreuth, for instance, or Mozart at Salzburg, or Britten at Aldeburgh in England. Others, such as Marlboro in Vermont and Prades in France, drew their inspiration from the presence of a great performer — Rudolf Serkin at Marlboro, Pablo Casals at Prades. In 1934 the Glyndebourne Festival began its series of elegant, intimate productions of operas, especially Mozart's, on an English country estate. But the new model became the international festival built around a symphony orchestra, often in tandem with opera, chamber music, or both. Salzburg was the leader and model, as Gertrude Robinson Smith recognized.

Travelers today can attend a virtually continuous olympiad of music festivals in cities and villages throughout the United States and Europe. Some, like Marlboro, remain small, specializing in a specific composer or genre, such as contemporary, chamber, or choral music. But the most famous take place in summer and offer a common repertoire of standard symphonic, operatic, and chamber works performed by a standard cadre of circuit-riding international conductors, soloists, and even orchestras. Settings, languages, and occasional premières or novelties make a difference, and each festival will draw on its own country's musicians, if only because of availability and cost. But the basic fare in Salzburg and Strasbourg is much the same, that in Edinburgh close to Tanglewood's.

Tanglewood was not the first symphonic festival in the United States. Concerts under the stars (or city lights) took place as early as 1918 at Lewisohn Stadium in New York, where the New York Philharmonic for many years was the presiding orchestra. Ravinia Park in Chicago, where the Chicago Symphony Orchestra now plays, began even earlier, opening with opera in 1911 and adding symphonic concerts in the 1930s. Hollywood Bowl, the summer home of the Los Angeles Philharmonic, began its symphonic series in 1922. Philadelphia's Robin Hood Dell, with the Philadelphia Orchestra, followed in 1930. Yet all these alfresco events took place in urban settings, with trucks, trains, or planes providing a noisy counterpoint to the masters. None of the series, moreover, offered a school in conjunction with the performances. Koussevitzky was the first to take a great orchestra to the country, play music amid a setting of lakes and hills, and build a major school around the concerts.

In the years since, Tanglewood has provided an example, and often a model, for other cities, orchestras, and promoters. The Cleveland Orchestra now has its Blossom Festival outside Cleveland; the National Symphony Orchestra plays at Wolf Trap near Washington. The Philadelphia Orchestra spends a month each summer at the Saratoga Performing Arts Center, a ninety-minute drive from Tanglewood. The Pittsburgh Orchestra holds forth at Great Woods, the latest entrant, opened in 1986 at the opposite end of Massachusetts and sometimes called "the Tanglewood of the east."

Amid this musical plenitude Tanglewood remains unique. Now as at the beginning, it is the only festival where the orchestra is part of a community of musicians, studying, teaching, and performing in an idyllic setting removed from the pressures of city and campus life. The Los Angeles Philharmonic's summer institute, patterned on the Tanglewood Music Center, comes closest to the Tanglewood model, but the activities center on a university campus to which faculty members from the orchestra commute. The Aspen Festival in Colorado has spectacular mountain scenery and a school larger than Tanglewood's, but only a student-faculty orchestra. The Cleveland Orchestra, on the other hand, is in a class with the BSO, but the school associated with Blossom is run by and primarily at Kent State University, twelve miles away. Saratoga has no school at all and is, in fact, an arts supermarket where symphonic music, opera, rock, folk, dance, and theater jostle. Great Woods's attempts at a school have been fitful.

These performances before swarms of devotees have come a long way from the Olympics. Yet some traces remain at Tanglewood. Although prizes are awarded to outstanding students at summer's end, the competitive strain has largely died out and the Music Center emphasizes cooperation and collegiality. In the orchestra, for instance, players rotate positions to assure as many students as possible a chance at the first — as well as last — chair. But at its best Tanglewood has an air of both joyful and solemn ceremony as the crowds gather before the altar of great music. In its celebration of art amid nature, the festival in the Berkshire Hills, on the ground where Hawthorne lived, evokes some of the sense of great mysteries that must have moved the ancients.

If Tanglewood was not the first outdoor symphonic festival in the United States, neither was it the first summer cultural attraction in the Berkshires. In 1918 Mrs. Elizabeth Sprague Coolidge, later a patron of the music program at the Library of Congress, founded a chamber music festival and school at South Mountain in Pittsfield. Ten years later the Berkshire Playhouse opened in Stockbridge, with Eva Le Gallienne and her company presenting her play *The Cradle Song.* In 1933 Ted Shawn established the Jacob's Pillow Dance Festival for his company of male dancers on his farm in Lee. Like Tanglewood in its turn, these smaller festivals, all within a fifteen-mile radius, attracted both summer and year-round Berkshirites as well as more distant pilgrims to art in the country. Some of the rustic, pioneering 1930s flavor remains in the barnlike construction, open to heat waves, drafts, and breezes — and sometimes bats and mosquitoes — that all four places have carefully maintained amid changing times, comforts, and audiences.

And times have changed. At Tanglewood in the beginning women wore evening dresses, men white or black jackets. The lawn crowd, which can range up to ten thousand today and is so conspicuously a part of the scene, at first numbered only in the hundreds, and old-timers recall seeing women strolling under parasols in the gardens. The audience, according to other veterans, included more young people than can be seen in the predominantly gray-haired Shed gatherings of today, and Tanglewood actually served as a singles scene for meeting and dating through the postwar years. The idea of dressing up remained so fixed that in the late 1940s women arriving in shorts or slacks received wraparound skirts on loan at the gates, with a request to cover up. The experiment in decency sputtered on for several years but was doomed from the start. As fast as management could buy the skirts, which displayed the name "Tanglewood," the recipients carried them off as souvenirs. The *New York Herald Tribune,* observing that the garments came in only two sizes — medium and large — editorialized wryly: "Obviously there are more cellos at Tanglewood than piccolos."

Before Tanglewood could expand into a summer-long festival with crowds in casual attire, however, it had to weather World War II like the rest of the country. With the opening of the Music Center in 1940, the bso summer season was extended from two to three weeks. The following year, in addition, brought the opening of the Theater–Concert Hall, which was then equipped, with flies and a pit, for the productions of the Graf-Goldovsky opera program. But with Pearl Harbor and gas rationing, the bso's trustees refused to approve a 1942 season.

In the end Koussevitzky paid for the season himself and staged concerts without the BSO. Using his own money and gifts from friends, he kept the Music Center open for a full six-week term, during which the student orchestra presented the three weekends of concerts in the Shed. As the war deepened in 1943, even Koussevitzky could not mount a festival but had to content himself with chamber concerts in the Lenox Library as a Red Cross benefit. In 1944 and 1945, however, he succeeded in bringing out a chamber-sized BSO to play two weekends of concerts, featuring works by Bach and Mozart, in the Theater–Concert Hall. The programs kept the festival spark alive and provided the inspiration for two opening weekends of small-orchestra concerts that became a fixture of later seasons.

Victory in Europe and the Pacific enabled Tanglewood to return to full operation in 1946. The BSO resumed a three-week season in the Shed. At the Music Center Leonard Bernstein, now back as Koussevitzky's assistant, led a mixed cast of student and professional singers in the American première of Benjamin Britten's opera *Peter Grimes*, one of many Koussevitzky coups.

Despite growing audiences (and traffic jams) the next Tanglewood milestones were less happy ones. In 1948 Koussevitzky announced his decision to retire the following year, when he would be seventy-five. The move was partly an attempt to force the appointment of Bernstein as his successor, but the trustees considered the jazz-playing, Broadway-wise pianist and conductor too young and brash to occupy an eminence that had belonged only to sage Europeans. They turned instead to a Frenchman, Charles Munch.

For two years Koussevitzky held a kind of emeritus status at Tanglewood, still active and revered but no longer master in his own house. The final Tanglewood concert of the 1950 season, which he conducted, proved his last either at Tanglewood or with the BSO. He died in Boston on June 4, 1951, before he could conduct Goldovsky's opera students that summer in Tchaikovsky's *Pique Dame*, a project that had occupied him during the winter.

For Tanglewood the Munch years meant both marching onward and standing still. The BSO season grew to four weeks in 1954 and continued to expand until it reached eight weeks in 1962, Munch's farewell year. The Music Center session went to eight weeks in the same year. In 1958 the Fromm Music Foundation began its support for a series of contemporary-music concerts that were formalized six years later as the Festival of Contemporary Music, a week-long festival within a festival. Munch gave many glittering performances, notably in his specialty, French music. But the excitement of the early years, when Koussevitzky would regularly sprinkle new works — many by Tanglewood composers like Copland, Hindemith, Honegger, and Messiaen — in among audience favorites, wore off. Munch, moreover, was not the inspired teacher Koussevitzky had been, and the Music Center languished under his attitude of laissez faire and benign neglect. Bernstein became the de facto head of the conducting program for a time but, especially after he took command of the New York Philharmonic in 1958, his appearances became fewer and fewer.

The changes were reflected in conducting styles. Harry Ellis Dickson, a retired BSO violinist and the associate conductor laureate of the Boston Pops, remembers the Koussevitzky era as one in which "almost every rehearsal was a nightmare, every concert a thrilling experience." In his 1969 book of BSO reminiscences, *"Gentlemen, More Dolce Please,"* Dickson goes on: "Those were the days when it was expected of conductors to be tyrannical and temperamental, and Koussevitzky was no exception. During his reign there were in the BSO one hundred and five players and one hundred and six ulcers. (One man had two.)"

Also from the early years Dickson recalls a "hot and sticky" August afternoon when Leopold Stokowski was the guest conductor and the musicians had received permission to play in their shirtsleeves. "But Stokowski," Dickson says, "walked onstage attired in a heavy black cutaway coat, afternoon trousers, pearl-gray vest, Windsor tie, and high wing collar. He looked like a character from the pages of Charles Dickens." If shorts and even bathing suits have taken over the lawn today, the tieless white tunic and slacks favored by Seiji Ozawa, the BSO's current music director, set a sartorial standard on the podium.

The BSO enjoyed playing under the charming, easygoing Munch, one of whose endearing traits was that he disliked rehearsals and often cut them short or dropped them entirely. Zubin Mehta, a member of the 1958 conducting class along with Claudio Abbado, found Munch no more attentive to student rehearsals. In the bi-

Seiji Ozawa as a student with his mentor, Charles Munch (right), and Eleazar de Carvalho, a member of the Tanglewood conducting staff.

ography *Zubin* (1978) by Martin Bookspan and Ross Yockey, Mehta recalls:

> He would sometimes come to rehearsals and just sit there, and every now and then he would scream at us or at the members of the orchestra. Claudio he ignored completely, but he did say something to me once. He yelled at me, "Put your feet together!" That was the only instruction he ever gave me.

In 1962 Erich Leinsdorf succeeded Munch, bringing a reform agenda to Tanglewood. One of his first moves was to abolish the opera department, headed by Goldovsky since 1946, and to conduct opera himself with both the BSO and students. Unlike Munch, Leinsdorf also plunged into the activities of the Music Center, guiding it to a renaissance in his roles as a leader, teacher, and performer. He was also responsible for adding a training program at the high school level, the Boston University Tanglewood Institute, to the Music Center's offerings. With the BSO his Tanglewood seasons often had a unifying theme — a Prokofiev cycle in 1963, a Richard

Strauss retrospective for the Strauss centennial in 1964, the romantic concerto in 1966.

But Leinsdorf and the BSO, it turned out, were not a match made in heaven. The orchestra that had thrilled to performances by the hot-blooded Koussevitzky and the elegant Munch found the cool, meticulous Leinsdorf too clinical and even Prussian for its taste, and he and the management and trustees wrangled endlessly about everything from rehearsal schedules to the music director's workload. He was no more enamored of the orchestra than it was of him. He called it flabby and considered management too weak-kneed to make the necessary changes. Tanglewood in many ways prospered under Leinsdorf, but everyone, including Leinsdorf himself, heaved a sigh of gratitude when he departed the BSO with a performance of the Beethoven Ninth on the final day of Tanglewood in 1969.

Leinsdorf's successor was William Steinberg, the seventy-year-old, ailing director of the Pittsburgh Symphony. Steinberg made it clear from the start that he had no interest in Tanglewood and would appear only as a guest conductor. To avoid a vacuum at the top like that in the Munch years, the trustees named a triumvirate of Ozawa, Bernstein, and Gunther Schuller to run the festival, with Ozawa the overall Tanglewood music director. Michael Steinberg, then the music critic of the *Boston Globe*, later the BSO's program annotator, liked the idea that Tanglewood would "be run by three professional swingers."

Ozawa, it became clear in time, was a swinger in appearances only. Nevertheless, the appointments ushered in the modern era at Tanglewood. Schuller, a composer, conductor, author, and educator who was president of the New England Conservatory, had been the nominal head of the Music Center for the last few years under Leinsdorf. He now became its leader in fact — a role he continued to play until his resignation in 1984 in an angry break with the BSO and Ozawa. Bernstein, who had recently ended his eleven-year tenure with the New York Philharmonic, stepped into the position of music adviser, his first formal connection with the festival since 1955.

For Ozawa, the winner of the 1960 Koussevitzky Prize at the Music Center and the director-designate of the San Francisco Symphony, the stakes were even higher. Building on an impressive record as a conductor and administrator, he became the BSO's music adviser in

A large audience watches Seiji Ozawa conduct the BSO, Tanglewood Festival Chorus, and four soloists in a choral work.

1972. (The position constitutes a polite way of saying the music director cannot or will not handle all the program planning and administrative detail himself and needs an assistant.) In 1973, as Steinberg's health failed, Ozawa succeeded him as the BSO's director.

Tanglewood under Ozawa has continued the Yankee tradition of making haste slowly — or, as the French might put it, the more things have changed, the more they have stayed the same. A Tanglewood graduate himself (and a Munch protégé), he took a personal interest in the operation of the Music Center, where he regularly leads the student orchestra at least once a season and coaches conducting students. Opera also became an early concern, first with an experimental three-year Music Theater Program using students, then, in 1980 — to the delight of audiences but largely the derision of critics — with a series of semi-staged productions by the BSO in the Shed. By the late 1980s planning had begun for an expanded opera program, either student or professional, in a new theater to replace the crumbling older one that Koussevitzky had built.

The Tanglewood season, meanwhile, continued to grow in size and diversity. The pivotal year was 1978, when three major changes took place. One was a move to a nine-week season with the introduction of a pre-BSO weekend of chamber music sponsored by the Boston Symphony Chamber Players. Along with that came the inauguration of a midweek recital series, largely by celebrity artists, and the abolition of the two opening weekends of Bach-Mozart concerts played by a half-sized BSO. For the first time the full complement of BSO players would be in residence at Tanglewood all eight weeks. To carve out time in the schedule, the orchestra cut two weeks from the players' spring Pops season in Boston. (A second Pops orchestra, made up of freelancers, lengthened its season by a corresponding two weeks.) Chamber-orchestra programs would remain on the Tanglewood calendar, but now they were scattered through the season.

In 1985, dropping the opening weekend of chamber music, Tanglewood moved to a ten-week BSO season. The change was an experiment, partly to see if — as merchants and innkeepers said — there was an audience for a longer season. But players complained of the length of the summer commitment, and the crowds did not come before July Fourth, the traditional opening of the high Berkshire season. The ten-week season dropped back to nine BSO weeks in 1986, only to be revived in 1988 with the return of an overture weekend of chamber music.

One after another during this period, season attendance records were exceeded. The BSO meanwhile embarked on a program of property acquisition to enhance and protect Tanglewood's holdings. In 1979 the orchestra bought Seranak, Koussevitzky's old mansion and 170-acre estate high on a hillside a few hundred yards up the road from the Main Gate. Vacant since the death of Koussevitzky's second wife, Olga, the year before, the house provided a student composers' residence, seminar facilities, and a social center for receptions, dinners, and a patrons' supper club. In the same year Nelson J. Darling, Jr., then the BSO's president, bought a ten-acre farm adjoining Tanglewood on the west. Now only the festival's eastern flank remained open to development if the property should go on the market. In 1987 the BSO sealed off that flank as well with the acquisition of

The terrace at Seranak.

Highwood, an estate containing another mansion (or "cottage," as the wealthy modestly call their Berkshire retreats) on another 120 acres. The property became a possible site for the new theater and additional parking, as well as a new home for social and fund-raising events.

As a place, Tanglewood has changed so little over the years that Koussevitzky would know it at a glance. The only major construction since 1937, other than the Theater–Concert Hall, is a glassy new backstage area for the Shed, built in 1981 to replace the rotting original offices and dressing rooms. (There is still no air conditioning except in the conductor's Green Room.) The sweeping lawn, the stately oaks and spruces, the views past Hawthorne's cottage to the lake and wooded hills — all of it remains pristine, even as second-home colonies and malls rise all around.

But if little has changed physically, Koussevitzky would be astonished by the proliferation of activity. During the BSO's nine weeks in residence it will play twenty-five or more concerts, each with a different program — or, to put it another way, as many programs as the orchestra plays in a seven-month subscription season during the winter in Boston. Those programs will include the annual semi-staged opera, major choral works like the Beethoven Ninth, and a Pops-at-Tanglewood evening. In most seasons one visiting orchestra will spell the BSO for a night, and one star soloist, such as Leontyne Price or Wynton Marsalis (both Tanglewood graduates), will give a

Aerial view of Tanglewood, with the Shed at 1, the Main Gate at 2, the Theater–Concert Hall at 3, and the Main House, headquarters of the Music Center, at 4.

recital in the Shed. Before each Friday night concert a Weekend Prelude will present one or more of the weekend's guest artists, or a BSO ensemble, in an hour-long interlude for concertgoers and picnickers arriving early.

Across the lawn in the Theater–Concert Hall, about fifteen other recitals and the Festival of Contemporary Music will take place. The recitalists will range from celebrities like Alfred Brendel, Jessye Norman, and Yo-Yo Ma to string quartets — the Juilliard, Vermeer, and Kronos are among recent visitors — and BSO ensembles and faculty members. On the nights when the professionals are not playing, the students will take over with vocal, chamber, or orchestral concerts. The student orchestral programs provide some of the summer's most electric music. The chemistry between the fired-up young players, who range in age from eighteen to thirty, and senior conductors like Ozawa and Bernstein, can produce results that often elude the students' BSO elders, burdened as they are with revolving-door repertoire and guest conductors. And when these older students are not performing, the high-schoolers in the Boston University Tanglewood Institute are — often, too, with results beyond their years.

Since 1968 Tanglewood has also toyed with rock (or, as they are now called, "Popular Artists") concerts, the idea being to get a younger audience into the habit of attending a music festival. For a time, especially after a Jackson Browne program in 1978 attracted a throng of 21,370 — still a Tanglewood record — and left a trail of noise, litter, and slumbering youth along quiet Berkshire roads, Tanglewood seemed on its way toward becoming a minor league Woodstock. But public outrage and second thoughts within the BSO itself forced a reassessment. Now the concerts, when they are held at all, average about three a season, those offering mostly soft rock and folk. Still, Koussevitzky, who could barely abide the Pops, would bemoan what had become of his beloved Tanglewood.

What has primarily become of Tanglewood is what Gertrude Robinson Smith and her cohort of ladies wanted to make of it: a place for relaxed listening — sometimes elegant, sometimes informal — to the time-honored symphonic classics. The warhorses do not always run as dazzlingly as they did in Koussevitzky's day. But, then, neither are conditions what they were in Koussevitzky's day:

a non-union orchestra playing a three-week season before an audience whose expectations of great music had not been conditioned by superstars and television.

It is striking to read in Moses Smith's 1947 biography of Koussevitzky that because of the conductor's neglect of form, tempo, "line," and other means of expression, "the beauty of tone and richness of color that Koussevitzky draws from his orchestra often end in monotony rather than variety of expression." Much the same objection, on grounds of facility rather than tone and color, is raised against Ozawa by his severest critics. Ozawa, of course, is not Koussevitzky. But the jet age, of course, is not that of the steamship. A big difference at Tanglewood today is that the pressures of preparing and presenting twenty-five programs in nine weeks, with conductors and soloists shuttling in and out every week, sometimes tarnish even smoothness of ensemble, and audiences seem neither to notice nor to care as long as a famous musician is onstage.

Still, culture in the Berkshires has flourished as Tanglewood has flourished. In music alone a virtual industry has sprung up in Tanglewood's shadow. Many smaller festivals have come and gone, but among those that now share the summer audience are the Berkshire Opera Company, the Berkshire Choral Institute, the Aston Magna early-music festival, Berkshire Friends of Baroque Music, the Curtisville Consortium, the West Stockbridge Concert Society, and a variety of chamber series in the adjoining counties of Massachusetts, Connecticut, and New York, not to omit South Mountain, Tanglewood's predecessor. All these have enriched not only culture but also Berkshire businesses and services, which have learned to love Tanglewood now, even if they did not before.

On July 8, 1940, as war was ravaging Europe, Koussevitzky said in his speech opening the Music Center: "There is hope for humanity, and all those who believe in the value and inheritance of culture and art should stand in the front ranks. If ever there was a time to speak of music, it is now in the New World." The belief in the cleansing power of music seems as apt today as it was then. Whatever Tanglewood's failings, it has kept Koussevitzky's faith alive in a New World whose shape he could not have foreseen.

Chapter II

INSIDERS

$\mathbb{T}$ANGLEWOOD IS many things to many people, but backstage it is a place of powerful, sometimes clashing personalities and interests. Atop the pyramid of insiders, of course, is the Boston Symphony's music director, Seiji Ozawa. A man of apparent paradoxes, he is a foreigner by birth who feels an intense loyalty to Tanglewood, a nice guy with a mystical streak, and a conductor who had to overcome a longtime sense of inadequacy with the BSO — a problem he does not face with orchestras he guest-conducts.

Immediately below Ozawa ranks the concertmaster, now Malcolm Lowe. Formerly a concertmaster in Canada, Lowe came to the BSO chair through an injury that forced him to give up the violin for a year. His predecessor, Joseph Silverstein, presents another paradox. A commanding figure at Tanglewood for two decades, he left the BSO to pursue a career as a conductor and violin soloist. Yet despite plans for him to stay on at Tanglewood as a teacher and perhaps a performer, he has faded from the scene except as a listener.

One of the many hats Silverstein wore was that of assistant conductor. When he departed, it took two assistant conductors to replace him. One of the pair, Carl St. Clair, had a harrowing baptism under fire at Tanglewood when the scheduled conductor, Gennady Rozhdestvensky, came down with a virus and St. Clair replaced him at two concerts without benefit of rehearsal. St. Clair's heroics recalled the debuts of two earlier Tanglewood conducting stalwarts, Leonard Bernstein and Michael Tilson Thomas, under similar circumstances.

Still other BSO insiders work backstage in management. One of the most important if least conspicuous of these is Costa Pilavachi, a Canadian who holds the title of artistic administrator. In consultation with Ozawa he chooses the music that listeners will hear and the conductors and soloists who will play it.

Life among insiders is rarely what it seems to the crowds of five thousand, ten thousand, or more relaxing with Beethoven or Tchaikovsky. What kind of SOS is issued, for instance, when a conductor cannot go on at the last minute, and what kind of butterflies does his substitute get in the stomach? What are the built-in sources of tension between a music director and his players? And what about business considerations? In spite of rising ticket prices, Tanglewood runs an annual deficit approaching $1 million. Rain can spell a loss of up to $75,000 for a single concert. Such situations produce a delicate balancing act in programming. Orchestra members meanwhile find relief from concert life by running a bed and breakfast, playing golf or tennis, gardening, or playing more music. Every three years negotiations for a new musicians' union contract pit players against management. Other players pursue sidelines as conductors. Sometimes romance blooms in the ranks.

Like automobiles on an assembly line, the product is music. But art, of course, is more than steel and rubber. When everything is going right — when programming and performance combine in a special time and place — Tanglewood can evoke a force of religious intensity. One such concert occurred on the final day of the 1986 season, when Ozawa and his singers and players commemorated the destruction of Hiroshima with a twentieth-century composer's plea for peace.

*   *   *   *   *

Ever since the Boston Symphony Orchestra made Tanglewood its summer home in 1937, the Berkshires have been a haven for music lovers. They come for the concerts in the summer, fall in love with the hills and villages, and return again and again, often to become homeowning summer or year-round residents.

As Tanglewood opened its forty-second summer in 1979, the Berkshires gained another such resident. He was not quite the usual tourist. In fact, he had first come to Tanglewood as a student in 1960, speaking almost no English and having, by his own admission, "not enough money to buy a can of beer." Yet he went quickly on to build an international career as a conductor, which took him back to his childhood Japan and his adopted Berkshires season after season.

After years of renting summer places, Seiji Ozawa, the BSO's thirteenth music director — heir to Koussevitzky, Munch, Leinsdorf, and Steinberg — put down roots in a white, barn-style house on a hillside overlooking far-flung valleys and hills in three directions. With his Japanese-Russian wife Vera, and their daughter Seira, born in 1971, and son Yukiyoshi, born three years later, he began buying apples at a nearby orchard, schussing at a family ski area near Pittsfield, and shopping in the village stores as other Berkshirites do.

Because of the musical associations and the natural beauty of the surroundings, Ozawa said in his improving English, "I still have a very close feeling here. I still feel this is my first in America and am grateful my kids can have this kind of nature and life."

Former BSO concertmaster Joseph Silverstein, who played under Ozawa for twelve years before moving on to take up a conducting career of his own, put it in a different light. His strongest impression as an Ozawa watcher, he said, was a "picture of Seiji arriving at Tanglewood for an 8:30 concert fresh from an afternoon of water skiing, accompanied by the family, greeting everyone cheerfully, looking relaxed, quickly changing clothes and, without a moment's pause for quiet reflection, walking out on the stage to conduct a work of great complexity from memory without fault."

Much has happened to Ozawa since those innocent years. Criticism grew barbed, not just in the papers but within the orchestra itself. Vera and the children went back to Japan to live for ten months each year. Silverstein and other key players left, some for retirement but others out of frustration. Honest about his failings — more so than a music director ordinarily is or perhaps ought to be — Ozawa admits his share of the blame for the difficulties. But Tanglewood was the beginning. And, by one of those coincidences that occasionally give the *grande dame* of American music festivals an air of both tradition and change, two events on an August weekend in 1977 show why Tanglewood remains a key.

First, on a chilly Friday night Ozawa led the BSO in a performance of Hector Berlioz's *Requiem*, using the all but megalomaniac forces the French composer specifies — some 450 players and singers. The next morning, after a year's search by the family for a suitable place, a bulldozer broke ground for the house on the hillside about a mile west — three miles by winding country roads — of Tanglewood. The common thread in the two events was Charles Munch, Ozawa's mentor and predecessor fifteen years before on the BSO podium. It was Munch who attracted Ozawa, then twenty-five, to Tanglewood as a student, and it was Munch for whom Ozawa turned the Berlioz *Requiem,* with its ringing public utterances by four offstage brass bands, into a personal service for the dead.

The Berlioz work holds intimate associations for Ozawa. Munch, who died in 1968, six years after retiring from the BSO, made a specialty of it. To honor the Frenchman's memory Ozawa conducted in formal black dress instead of the customary Tanglewood whites, and had a picture of Munch placed in the Shed's Green Room during the concert. (In the darkness the black garb also helped to limn Ozawa for the offstage brass bands against the whites of the onstage chorus and orchestra.) So strong was the sense of communion, Ozawa said, that he felt Munch heard the performance.

It was very emotional for me [Ozawa recalled]. Physically, I was very tired. Mentally, not just very tired but empty. The feeling is like a funeral. A dear man close to me is gone.

My father always said to me music must be closest to serving God. He was a Buddhist but my mother is a Christian. So God in my house is very wide. And my father really believed God is one but there are many kinds of ways of serving God.

I agree now. I didn't agree then. We have so much beautiful music — the Berlioz *Requiem,* the Mozart *Requiem,* the Brahms *Requiem,* the Fauré *Requiem,* the Bruckner *Te Deum:* all that music connecting to God is really close to serving God. So, after a sad feeling, this little part of my mind is very happy, satisfied. Maestro Munch is there. I still believe that Maestro Munch listened to this, and many of my colleagues in the orchestra feel the same who were close with Maestro Munch.

Ozawa is one of a generation of conductors, also including Zubin Mehta, Lorin Maazel (both Tanglewood graduates), James Levine, and André Previn, who succeeded to major American podiums in the late 1960s and 1970s. Whether native or foreign-born, these conductors have little in common except a lack of the traditional European upbringing and apprenticeship that characterized the previous generation. Yet in Ozawa's case the Munch connection provides a link with the past and involves a relationship as much like that of father and son as mentor and protégé. The intimacy is akin to that which developed twenty years earlier between Leonard Bernstein and Serge Koussevitzky — except that it fell to Ozawa to carry on the orchestra's tradition, while Koussevitzky never succeeded in his desire to have Bernstein named his successor.

Charles Munch, Serge Koussevitzky, Pierre Monteux, Karl Muck: above the podium Ozawa inherited hovered the ghosts of giants from the half-century 1912 to 1962. As he himself says, the idea of his becoming their successor was "beyond my wildest dream" when he was "a poor Chinaboy Japanese," born in Manchuria and growing up in Japan.

The third of four sons of a Japanese dentist, Ozawa became attracted to Western music through an elder brother, who played the organ in the Christian church in Japan to which the mother sent the four boys. Young Seiji studied both Oriental and Western music and, at the age of sixteen, entered the Toho School of Music in Tokyo as a piano student. Always a lover of sports, he broke both index fingers during a rugby game. That put an end to any piano career. He turned instead to the study of composition and conducting under Hideo Saito, another father figure. After early successes in Japan, Ozawa left for Europe in 1959 at Saito's suggestion. While traveling around the continent on a motorscooter and supporting himself as a motorscooter salesman, he entered the International Competition of Orchestra Conductors at Besançon, France. There he won first prize.

Munch, who was guest-conducting in Europe that summer, happened to be in the audience at Besançon. So were others who recognized the unknown Japanese youth's potential, most notably Lorin Maazel, who was on the jury, and Piltti Heiskanen, a music-loving Finnish diplomat. They arranged for Ozawa to meet Munch. At the introduction, Ozawa asked to study with the BSO director. Munch said he did not take private students but suggested that Ozawa come to Tanglewood the following summer to study. Ozawa did, again walking off with the top honor, the Koussevitzky Prize.

From Tanglewood the trail led to study with Herbert von Karajan at the Berlin Philharmonic, an assistantship with Bernstein at the New York Philharmonic, and the directorships, from 1964 to 1969, of Chicago's outdoor Ravinia Festival and the Toronto Symphony. Beginning in 1964, guest-conducting appearances with the BSO became increasingly frequent. In 1970, needing a director for the

Seiji Ozawa leads a performance during his student year.

festival at Tanglewood, the BSO turned naturally to the young Tanglewood graduate with five years of experience at running Ravinia. That December Ozawa became director of the San Francisco Symphony as well.

The next and biggest step came in 1973. When the BSO saw it would need a music director to replace William Steinberg upon his retirement that year, it turned again to Ozawa. Thus, at the age of thirty-eight, still weak in English but brilliant in musical promise, he became the jet-age conductor of two major American orchestras. So things continued — not without inevitable conflicts and frictions — until 1976. Finding two jobs on opposite coasts too much of a drain, Ozawa gave up San Francisco, except for guest appearances, to devote himself to Boston.

At the BSO the lithe, slender conductor with the flowing gestures and black hair established himself as an export as durable as the Toyota. (By 1979 the former motorscooter kid was driving a Mercedes sedan and a newly delivered, custom-built, air-conditioned Chevrolet van.) He took over an orchestra that, while

still solidly in the front rank of American symphonies, was somewhat dispirited and run down after seven years under the respected
but generally unpopular Erich Leinsdorf and four under the ailing
Steinberg. After a decline during the Leinsdorf-Steinberg years,
attendance now edged close to the sold-out seasons of the
Koussevitzky-Munch era. Tanglewood, similarly, began a series of
record attendance years.

The orchestra, increasingly American as the Koussevitzky and
Munch appointees from Europe died or retired, began playing with
a precision and sheen like that Koussevitzky had drawn from it.
Despite some grumbling among younger members who would have
liked to do more solo work or advance faster, and regrets among
older members that the esprit of the Koussevitzky days was gone,
pride reappeared in the playing. The honeymoon was on.

Conductors are like college presidents and corporate executives
in modern America in having a life expectancy of no more than
about ten years on the job. By the late 1970s the pack was after
Ozawa, led by the press. Critics, both in Boston and on national
publications, derided his programming as pedestrian, his performances as slick and impersonal. ("Bland in Boston," blared the
headline over a review in *New York* magazine.) Some of the Boston-
Cambridge intelligentsia, centering on Harvard, pooh-poohed
Symphony Hall as a wasteland. Orchestra members also began complaining of performances wanting in style and substance. Behind
the scenes — and later, in a couple of cases, in print — players called
for his head.

Ozawa, meanwhile, stepped up his guest conducting, particularly
in opera, a field largely new to him. (The interest in opera was to
find an outlet at Tanglewood in the series of semi-staged BSO productions that began with *Tosca* in 1980.) The 1978-79 season appears to have been a turning point. Ozawa took on a limited number
of opera engagements, usually involving one production a year. He
began in Paris and Tokyo, later adding La Scala in Milan and Covent
Garden in London. At the same time Vera and he decided to educate
the children in Japan to give them the option of being Japanese as
adults. She would live most of the year with them in Tokyo, where
she was a children's clothing designer (and former model) for Hanae
Mori. Henceforth the noisy family times in the Berkshire house
would be confined to summers.

Seiji Ozawa and his wife, Vera (center), talk with the Japanese clothing designer Hanae Mori at a Seranak reception. Hanae Mori designs Ozawa's conducting clothes, including the white tunic and matching trousers he wears here. Mrs. Ozawa, formerly a Hanae Mori model, designs children's clothing for her.

The turmoil came to a head during the BSO's post-Tanglewood tour of major European festivals in 1979 — the first time the orchestra had ever left Tanglewood before the end of the season. At a party Ozawa gave for the orchestra near Salzburg, the first stop on the eight-city trip, he made a remarkable confession. First, he apologized for having been absent much of the past year. Then he promised to study harder to become a better conductor, and to rededicate himself to the BSO.

Explaining why he had spent so much time conducting opera outside Boston, Ozawa said, according to press reports from Austria, "I didn't know Puccini, Rossini, so I had to study opera in order to grow as a conductor." Before, he added, "I thought I was the famous conductor, going from city to city. No more. I want to be with you. I hope you can help me."

In the emotional speech Ozawa admitted he had been upset over the changes at home. It had been difficult to concentrate on music, despite the decision to send the children to school in Japan. The family's absence during the previous winter, while he remained in Boston, had been a physical and emotional drain. Besides his own travel back and forth to Tokyo to visit, there were telephone calls and "so many problems, worrying about schooling. Every night it was talk, talk, talk." Now, Ozawa told the players, all that was behind him. "I have made the decision," he said. "My music life is you."

The orchestra cheered the talk, but the problems and complaints persisted. The twenty-two weeks a year Ozawa spends with the BSO — six of those weeks at Tanglewood — are as much as, or more than, his counterparts at the other "big six" American orchestras put in. And while he still does one opera a year in Europe, he gradually cut back on his guest conducting with orchestras, as he had promised in Salzburg. Yet it was not until Tanglewood 1987 that a new pattern in his music making emerged with consistency.

He had always excelled in massive vocal-orchestral works in which he could exercise a field marshal's powers over the performing forces: the Berlioz *Requiem,* for instance, or Bach's *St. Matthew Passion,* or Schoenberg's *Gurrelieder.* Everyone agreed on that. Now a more spacious, probing style emerged in Schumann, Mahler, Strauss — the very romantics who had always seemed most foreign to him. At his home on the mountain, with Vera, the children, and the housekeeper setting up a happy babble in the background, he made another confession. He said that, from his student year at Tanglewood onward, he had stood in such awe of the BSO — Munch's BSO — that he had not dared to assert himself as he did when guest conducting in Berlin, Paris, or Tokyo. He became "timid," "shy," "hesitating," or "mild" — still troubled by English, he could not find the exact word — in asking his own orchestra to follow him into battle.

Finally, having crossed the frontier of gray hair and fifty, he decided he would have to take command and give more depth to the music with his own players, too. He recalled something Karajan had once told him: "It took him [Karajan] twenty years to understand orchestra." Only after Karajan's third recorded cycle (of four) of the Beethoven symphonies could he say "he was really happy."

"It's not just one morning I wake up [and change]," Ozawa said. "It's come very slowly. You can't change those things by thinking, you know. Has to change by intuition. But also, orchestra is getting more serious, too. Boston Symphony is working harder and work is deeper now. I can smell that."

Players sensed the difference, too. Ralph Gomberg, who retired that summer after thirty-seven years as principal oboist, observed that Ozawa was "expressing his feelings more about the music, rather than worrying about remembering the music." Principal second violinist Marylou Speaker Churchill, who in a magazine article a year before had accused the conductor of superficiality, agreed that in the past he had "treated us as Munch's orchestra, the orchestra he knew as a student." Now, she said, "he truly cares about the orchestra" and showed the concern in both his conducting and a sensitivity to such things as new players' happiness.

Other players suggested other causes for the change. Some said former concertmaster Silverstein's departure in 1984 to head the Utah Symphony had removed a rival — and therefore an irritant and inhibition — for control of the orchestra. Others said the installation, early in 1987, of George H. Kidder as board president and Kenneth Haas as managing director gave Ozawa strong front-office support lacking in the previous administration. Ozawa himself credited the new team with freeing him and the players to concentrate on music rather than administrative problems. And he got a concertmaster of his own choosing in Malcolm Lowe, Silverstein's successor.

A year before at Tanglewood there had been a clue that change was in the wind. Ozawa's Beethoven with the BSO had grown over the years to be solid, clear, and a bit characterless, the details but not the big picture in focus. His performances with the student orchestra, meanwhile, had nearly always generated excitement, but often it was a surface excitement, artificially whipped up, like froth. But that summer, conducting the Music Center Orchestra in its opening concert, Ozawa had led a surely paced, subtly shaded, exhilarating Beethoven Seventh. It had that extra dimension that music lovers can recognize but never define.

Nobody can know exactly what is in a musician's mind in the heat of a performance. For all of Ozawa's friendliness with his BSO players — he is always "Seiji" to them, not "Mr. Ozawa" or "Maestro" — his charm can be like silk stretched over a frame of steel.

He is also known to be a somewhat erratic administrator, hard to pin down and given to last-minute decisions.

But it is a good guess that in that Beethoven Seventh with the student orchestra he felt free to assert and express himself in ways that he did not across the lawn with Munch's group. And, indeed, the students love playing for him (as they do for most of the BSO conductors who take turns on the Music Center podium). Like the veterans of the BSO, they value his clear, graphic gestures and courteous, efficient rehearsing. But, unlike their sometimes jaundiced seniors, the students can let themselves be swept along on the tide of Ozawa's enthusiasm without worry about how Koussevitzky or Bernstein or Colin Davis or any of a dozen other guest conductors might have done it.

The touch is also evident in Ozawa's coaching of student conductors, both in the Seranak seminar room and with the student orchestra. He does not put on an intellectual circus, as Bernstein does; he has neither the temperament nor the reading in Western literature. Nor does he talk about careers and orchestra life, as other guest teachers like Previn do. Simply, in his gestures, which include a gift of mimicry, and in his fractured English, he can transform a student's akwardnesses into a physical command of the orchestra, and sometimes into a closer emotional identification with the music as well.

One of a student's first impressions at Tanglewood — and of the conductor who runs it — is Ozawa's pep talk each year at the Music Center's opening exercises. He begins by recounting his own student year, when he arrived by bus from Boston knowing no one, little English, and sometimes less about music than his fellow students. (His roommate, he will say, was studying Mahler scores. "Mahler?" he will ask. "I didn't know anything about this Mahler guy.") He will urge the students to study hard and take advantage of the distinguished faculty, but also to enjoy swimming in Stockbridge Bowl and the beauties of the Berkshire country. Then there will be a personal reminiscence to suggest how the Berkshire summer, free of job and money pressures, can be a golden moment in a young musician's career.

In 1975 he talked about the importance of fathers — real and symbolic — in his life. The year before, his teacher in Japan, Saito, had died. The death followed his father's in 1970 (Munch had died only two years before that). The losses, Ozawa said, left him stunned and bewildered. He even doubted what music meant and why he went on conducting.

After talking it over with Leonard Bernstein and other friends, he realized that others had gone through similar experiences and "in music I had to go deeper." Going deeper, he explained, meant that "music is very personal and very much like philosophy," and "you have to adjust your exact feeling into each note." With that understanding he rededicated himself to his work.

When not conducting, rehearsing, auditioning, discussing artists and repertoire with the staff, meeting with players, giving interviews, dining with trustees, or greeting visiting dignitaries (including a steady stream of Japanese), Ozawa is often out playing tennis or golf, often in a Tanglewood or BSO T-shirt. Tennis is usually on the court at his house, but he also plays in the orchestra's annual tennis and golf tournaments. (It is no accident that the verb "play," with its sense of physical activity, applies equally to sports and music.) His frequent tennis partner is his personal manager, Ronald Wilford, whose country home is across the road from the Ozawas'.

There is also a fun-loving Ozawa whom audiences at Tanglewood see, unlike those at buttoned-up Symphony Hall. At Tanglewood on Parade each summer — a day-long affair half music and half carnival — he puts on an engineer's cap and plays choo-choo, waving to one and all, on the rubber-tired train that steams a mile and a half down the road from the center of Lenox to the festival grounds. One year he played the cuckoo whistle in a performance of Leopold Mozart's *Toy Symphony* at the evening concert. He had as much fun with his mugging and tweeting as the crowd did. He is good with children, too. His own will sit attentively with Vera in the conductor's box during concerts, and he says he does not mind interruptions by crying babies when he is conducting, a problem that can reach near-epidemic proportions. Tanglewood's informality, he says, provides a good atmosphere for families and for children to become comfortable with music.

Sometimes children respond. Once at a Music Center Orchestra concert, a boy in a Red Sox cap came up to him in the audience between numbers and asked for an autograph. Ozawa happily signed the program but, pointing to Bernstein, who was sitting in the next chair, asked, "What about him?"

"I don't know him," the boy said, and disappeared.

Many of Ozawa's best performances have been at Tanglewood. (Many of the worst, too. Besides his own limitations, he and other conductors are hemmed in by the necessity of preparing and presenting three concerts each weekend — a schedule that means only two rehearsals, and sometimes one, to a program.) Neither the orchestra nor the public has elevated him to the pantheon of great conductors like Koussevitzky or Bernstein. But, in his own way, he can seem in communion with the gods when doing those monumental sacred works like the Berlioz *Requiem* and the *St. Matthew Passion.* In scale and mood, these compositions go over especially well in the Shed, with its vast spaces and openness to the trees, lawn crowd, lake, and hills beyond. It is as if nature and music flow into one, each reinforcing the other.

On the other hand, there is something in the music itself that clearly speaks to the inner Ozawa. "God in my house," he said, apropos of Berlioz, "is very wide." And so it seems in the music making. Whatever it is in him that is sometimes guarded or merely efficient in other music, whatever trouble he might have with language, a mystical or devotional intensity suffuses all when he immerses himself — the score will stand unopened before him — in these masterworks. Ozawa is a man both simpler and more complex than his critics paint him. He is unpretentious in his approaches to people (including critics) and music yet elusive in his search for depths and meanings. And both sides of him become manifest at Tanglewood.

Outwardly cheerful through everything, Ozawa in 1987 began his fifteenth year as head of Koussevitzky's and Munch's BSO — among the "big six" conductors at that time, a reign exceeded only by Sir Georg Solti's nineteen years in Chicago. Taking stock in the country house as Vera and the children chattered in the next room, he said he wanted to make Tanglewood a "real festival" by programming more fresh repertoire and fewer repeats from the winter season and by attracting more European conductors and soloists. Audiences, he said, know these artists from recordings and expect to hear them at a festival with an international standing like Tanglewood.

As for himself, Ozawa said that with the changes in his attitude and the BSO operation

I want to think this is now a new era for me. New management came and I feel very good with management, and we're working very closely as orchestra members. And I personally feel very free that I can do anything — no box on my work. And certainly I know better about my group and they know me better — good way or bad way. And I know board of directors are very hot for future of Boston Symphony now. So I feel it's good to have a second start for me.

For years rumors have circulated that Ozawa will replace Karajan at the Berlin Philharmonic. It might yet work out that way. But the relationship between a music director and an orchestra, in all its complexity of need and abrasion, is like that in a marriage. Gripe as players might about Ozawa, most know, deep within, that there is no conductor — not even Bernstein, with his endless talk and ego, or Koussevitzky, with his temper and peculiarities of tempo and phrasing — without serious, perhaps crippling limitations.

Midway through his second decade with the BSO, Ozawa's tenure seemed strengthened rather than weakened. As in any other marriage, there were bad days and good days. But he needed the BSO and the BSO needed him. It was another insider, Joseph Silverstein, who became a casualty of the frustrations and pressures.

*   *   *

Why did Silverstein, after two decades as the BSO's concertmaster — the best concertmaster in the world, according to André Previn and many other musicians — decide to chuck it all and become the director of the Utah Symphony? Was it some Mormon instinct in him, reenacting the westward trek that took Brigham Young and his followers to the desert in the mid-nineteenth century? Was it ambition? Disenchantment with the BSO or an unspoken rivalry with Ozawa, as some players suggested? Boredom? All of these?

None of them, Silverstein said. It was a desire to get out from under an increasing burden of orchestral work and strike out on his own as a conductor and violin soloist. And he did not plan it that way; it just happened.

Over the past six or seven years [said the familiar Tanglewood performer, teacher, gourmand, and jogger as he prepared to begin his new life in

Utah] the whole shape of my musical life has changed quite a bit. The activities that I've had as a soloist and a conductor have multiplied well beyond what were my original expectations. Perhaps it's a backward way of making a career because, as you know, in this country once you establish yourself as a certain kind of something, it's very difficult to gain acceptance or credibility as something else.

He no longer chose, in other words, to "wear a shirt that said concertmaster–assistant conductor."

Silverstein, who was fifty-one in that year of decision, 1983, headed west the following year, ending a twenty-nine-year career with the BSO. For the last twenty-two of those years he had been concertmaster, and for the last thirteen years assistant conductor as well. By coincidence, he passed a distinguished colleague heading east. In 1982 Maurice Abravanel, who had built the Utah Symphony into a well-regarded, sometimes pioneering orchestra during his thirty-two years as its director, had come to Tanglewood for the summer to fill in as director of the Music Center while Gunther Schuller took a sabbatical. Abravanel became the guest who never left, returning in the summers afterward as a teacher, counselor, and fatherly presence. In Salt Lake City Silverstein became the successor to Abravanel's successor.

Silverstein had been playing in symphony orchestras since he turned professional at the age of seventeen. As more and more invitations to conduct and perform as a soloist with other orchestras came in, and as he had to turn more and more of them down, he had become increasingly restless in the BSO, he said. Nor was it just a matter of the demands on him as concertmaster. He did heavy duty as assistant conductor, leading occasional concerts of his own — including one each year at Tanglewood — and acting as a sort of orchestral fireman, on call whenever sickness, grounded planes, or other emergency struck the scheduled conductor. He also served as leader of the Boston Symphony Chamber Players, impresario for other BSO-sponsored chamber concerts in Boston and at Tanglewood, chairman of the faculty at Tanglewood, and general factotum for a variety of dealings with the musicians, trustees, and public. He enjoyed and found satisfaction in all these things. But that was not the point.

Joseph Silverstein conducts the BSO.

"Friends," he said, "have asked me, if I had my druthers over the past few years, what would I be doing? And I have said very frankly that I would love to be the music director of a good orchestra. And when I was asked were there any possibilities, I said, 'Well, I'm still waiting for the telephone to ring.'"

In the fall of 1982 the telephone jingled. The Utah Symphony was having difficulties with its music director, Varujan Kojian. Not artistic difficulties, mind you. Salt Lake City is Mormon country, and Kojian, who was in his third year as Abravanel's successor, had a lifestyle that . . . And would Silverstein . . . ?

Silverstein said of course he would be interested. A Utah search committee auditioned some of his concerts as guest conductor with the Baltimore and Houston symphonies. Interviews with the search committee and with Utah officialdom, from the lieutenant governor and the top brass of the legislature to the president of the chamber of commerce and the leaders of the Mormon church, followed. (The director of the Utah Symphony, explained Deputy Lieutenant Governor Brad E. Hainsworth, is "a personality in the state comparable to the governor and the presidents of the church.")

Eventually the field was narrowed to two candidates, Silverstein and Gerard Schwarz, the ex-trumpeter who heads New York's Mostly Mozart Festival and assorted other musical enterprises, and who is fifteen years Silverstein's junior. In January 1983 Utah opted for experience. It announced the appointment of Silverstein, first as part-time artistic director for a year while he played out his BSO contract. If that trial marriage worked out, he would become a full-time music director, beginning in September 1984. As soon as Tanglewood ended that summer, Silverstein left to guide his new band through a fifty-two-week season involving a total of about 250 performances in subscription, pops, school, tour, and other concerts as well as opera and ballet duty. He returned as permanent music director a year later.

Silverstein's departure set off ripples all the way to the back rows of the BSO brasses and basses. According to Previn (who recommended him for the Utah job), it was not opinion that Silverstein was the world's greatest concertmaster but "a fact, like 'Look! It's summer!'" Few in the BSO would have disputed that. But many resented his ubiquitousness as a conductor, soloist, chamber player, and public figure, as well as the columns of news space and hours of camera time he generated. No other orchestra member received such attention, or was quite so receptive to it. And, among his fellow violinists, a sizable minority coveted his job when he gave it up. Since only one could have it, that would mean disappointment, and perhaps bitterness, for some or all of those applicants. Indeed, within three years, two of the three violinists with whom he shared the front stands of his section would be gone, both because they were passed over for promotion.

If Silverstein was an iron man who rarely missed a concert, the new concertmaster was a dark horse. The BSO and Seiji Ozawa turned not to associate concertmaster Emanuel Borok, assistant concertmistress Cecylia Arzewski, or any of the half-dozen other orchestra members who sought the position, but to Malcolm Lowe, a thirty-one-year-old Canadian who had never before played in a big-league orchestra or under a big-league conductor.

Borok, a Soviet émigré known for his outspokenness about music and musicians, was discouraged by Ozawa from even applying. That was the last straw for him. In 1985, at the age of forty-one, he left to become concertmaster of the Dallas Symphony Orchestra. "Dallas!" he said, shaking his head in disbelief at the direction his career had taken since he left Moscow in 1973. "I could never imagine it in my life that I would go to Dallas!" But in cowboyland he received an offer he could not resist — a thirty-two-week season with a 50 percent increase in salary. There would also be, not incidentally, solo and chamber music opportunities such as only Silverstein enjoyed in Boston.

Arzewski, even more outspoken and openly hostile to Ozawa besides — she had "contempt written on her face practically under his nose," according to Helen Epstein in her book *Music Talks* — auditioned not only for Silverstein's job but also for Borok's when he followed Silverstein out the door. She won neither. And before either of those attempts, auditions for the concertmaster's jobs in Pittsburgh and Montreal brought the same frustrations. Sexism seemed an issue.

But was it? Although a man won the BSO concertmaster's job, it was by a unanimous or nearly unanimous vote — backstage reports differed — of the audition committee. And in two rounds of auditions for the associate's position — in effect, the number two job in the orchestra — Arzewski was one of three finalists both times. And both times, all three finalists were women.

In the first round Ozawa, who exercises veto power over orchestral appointments, found none of the finalists satisfactory and ordered new auditions. In the second round he chose Tamara Smirnova-Šajfar, former concertmistress of the Zagreb Philharmonic in Yugoslavia. Clearly, whatever fine musical differences there might have been among women players, he felt more comfortable with an outsider than with Arzewski. That was enough for her. At the age of thirty-eight she left to become associate concertmistress in Cleveland.

In a sense, Lowe had to give up the violin for a year so he could become the new concertmaster. The slender, soft-spoken Canadian does not talk about himself in terms of destiny. But the accident that led him to Boston and Silverstein's chair recalls Hamlet's prophecy to Horatio:

> There's a divinity that shapes our ends,
> Rough-hew them how we will.

Lowe was concertmaster of l'Orchestre Symphonique de Québec when, in the spring of 1982, he injured his hand while doing a yoga handstand. As he tells the story, he did not feel any pain at the time — just a slight immobility. Four mornings later the hand was immobile, useless.

> I went through a terrible time going to different doctors at that point for about five months [he said], and got some bad advice telling me to rest it. I woke up one morning and I couldn't even do the buttons up on my shirt, and I said, "Something is going on here and I don't like it."

What he did about it was to consult Gary Graffman, one of a small but distinguished band of pianists, including Tanglewood's Leon Fleisher, who have lost the use of a hand — and sometimes a career — through mysterious muscular afflictions. Graffman suggested that Lowe do what he had done: go to Massachusetts General Hospital in Boston for diagnosis and rehabilitation.

There was, it turned out, nothing mysterious about Lowe's affliction. He had torn the ligaments and tendons, and atrophy had set in. In the fall of 1982 he began a rehabilitation program at Massachusetts General. For more than a year he did not touch his instrument. Finally, in the summer of 1983, he felt strong enough to return to the concert stage. He played the solo part in Mozart's G Major Concerto with the Toronto Symphony under Andrew Davis. The performance, he said, went "very well."

> It was an exhilarating feeling [he recalled]. I felt freer than I had ever felt, or remember feeling, playing the violin. A year of not pursuing something that is so important to you really changes your perspective of many things. And I felt in a sense that it [the violin] was no longer as important as it was to me at one time, in a narrow way. And yet at the same time it was much more important in a very broad sense.

What Lowe put behind him was "a very selfish, habitual view of things," resulting from his training, his "perceptions of how much you have to work in order to achieve something," and "the limitations that are unconsciously imprinted in your mind by teachers and other influences." In their place he experienced "a renewed searching for what I wanted to say in music and in other areas of my life that I felt strongly about." His progress was so favorable during the next few months that he decided to audition for Silverstein's job. He beat out forty-one fellow auditioners, including six BSO members, to get it. In September 1984 he became the BSO's tenth concertmaster.

Lowe came to the BSO and the United States as an outsider. Born in the farm town of Hamiota, Manitoba, he began studies at two and a half with his parents, both professional musicians. When he was nine, the family moved to Regina, Saskatchewan, where, in a youth symphony, he promptly began a series of Canadian concertmasterships. After further study at the Regina Conservatory, the Meadowmount School of Music in upstate New York, and the Curtis Institute in Philadelphia, he became concertmaster of the Regina Symphony. He moved on to Quebec in 1977, remaining concertmaster there until his hand injury forced him out. Meanwhile, in 1980 he had won the auditions to become concertmaster of the Toronto Symphony but his contract in Quebec kept him where he was.

To win the BSO chair, Lowe and his fellow competitors had to play for an audition committee consisting of nineteen musicians, including the principal player of each section. There were three rounds of auditions. In the first the committee heard 29 violinists selected from the 46 applicants on the basis of tapes each had submitted. Four of those 29 made it into the semifinals. The committee invited 7 other candidates — either well-known violinists or runners-up from earlier BSO auditions — to participate in that round. Out of those 11, 4 survived into the finals, where Ozawa sat in for the first time. They were joined by the 6 BSO candidates, who, by contract, were allowed to skip the preliminaries. Borok, conspicuously, was not among them. Arzewski, of course, was.

Lowe's repertoire for the finals — the auditioners were allowed some leeway in their choice of concertos — included excerpts from the Mozart G Major Concerto and the Shostakovich Second Concerto, along with the big violin solos from Strauss's *Ein Heldenleben* and Beethoven's *Missa Solemnis.* He also played selections from the standard orchestral literature.

"It was one of our easier auditions," said BSO personnel manager William Moyer. Out of a highly qualified field, he said, "Malcolm proved to be the clear winner." Silverstein put it more pictorially. Lowe, he said, "took the audition committee by storm." James DePriest, Lowe's former conductor in Quebec, said, "I felt Malcolm was capable of being the concertmaster anywhere. He has the remarkable dual qualities of being a superb violinist and an affable person."

The paradox of a scarcely known thirty-one-year-old walking into one of the world's top orchestral positions, as successor to Silverstein, is heightened by Lowe's personality. Affable he is, but he has the gentleness and inwardness one often meets in those who go deeply into yoga. Yet he is also a strong golfer and once considered a career as a baseball player.

The paradox is not lost on Lowe. He knows a concertmaster must have the iron to make an orchestra follow him and he must sometimes step on egos. If a guest conductor began to founder, for instance, Silverstein had no hesitation about taking over the performance, leading the BSO with cues from his head, shoulders, and violin bow.

Situations like that demand tough action, Lowe agreed. "It has to be. There's sometimes only one alternative, and the orchestra and the people around you have to feel that about you — that you're deciding that that's the time and that you're taking the responsibility, and that your alternative is the one to take."

Quietly and steadily, despite intermittent illness, Lowe assumed his authority with the orchestra. For better or worse, there was not

Concertmaster Malcolm Lowe performs a solo with the BSO in the Shed.

the sense of total command — of one man being everywhere and doing everything at once — that there was with Silverstein, but there was not the occasional sense of push and shove, either. Lowe's less assertive, more introspective, but beautifully finished playing, like Silverstein's only in its avoidance of overt virtuosity, also brought a different color and personality to the concertmaster's solos and the Chamber Players' programs. Unlike Silverstein, too, Lowe has no conducting aspirations, and the BSO eventually had to designate a pair of assistant conductors to wear that hat the previous concertmaster wore.

Silverstein, meanwhile, has apparently thrived in the desert soil of Utah. He turns up regularly as a conductor or soloist, or sometimes both, with orchestras around the country (though not yet with the BSO). But things did not work out exactly according to the script at Tanglewood. He and his wife, Adrienne, keep their cottage near Stockbridge Bowl and show up faithfully every summer, a slimmer, even svelte Silverstein occasionally taking a turn as a teacher or soloist (again, not with the BSO). But his plan to stay on as chairman of the faculty ran aground on Tanglewood's needs and his own schedule, which came to include directing the orchestra at the Chautauqua festival in upstate New York, and Silverstein's most conspicuous appearances these days are as a member of the BSO audience in the Shed. Somehow the change of an era was summed up at a concert one night when a woman asked for his autograph. Refusing, Silverstein politely but firmly said, "I don't work here anymore."

*   *   *

Although part of an assistant conductor's job is to take over a concert on short notice if necessary, Carl St. Clair had no inkling of the ordeal ahead when he became one of the BSO's two assistants to replace Silverstein. His travails began with a telephone call at 6:43 on an August evening in 1986. He remembers the exact time showing in the green numbers on his digital clock because for him it was one of those moments, like a death in the family, when you know your whole life is about to be turned upside down.

Gennady Rozhdestvensky, who was to have led that night's BSO concert at Tanglewood, was sick. There was a good chance St. Clair would have to go on.

The thirty-four-year-old St. Clair, a slightly built, lightly bearded farm boy out of Texas, had never conducted a major symphony orchestra before. Until twelve years back he had never heard of Tanglewood and thought of Leonard Bernstein only as the composer of *West Side Story*. Yet here was Daniel R. Gustin, the BSO's acting general manager, on the phone, telling him he might have to take over Rozhdestvensky's concert without rehearsal — without, for that matter, ever before having stood in front of the BSO for any purpose whatever.

St. Clair, a bachelor, was supposed to have gone to a pre-concert party at six. As it happened, he took a nap in his rented house over the mountain from Tanglewood instead. On waking, he decided to look at the scores for the evening's concert, just in case. He was that night's "cover," or standby conductor, and when he is on duty he assumes that "every concert is go" until the scheduled conductor shows up.

At first when the phone rang, he thought, "This is a call from somebody at the party, going, 'Why aren't you here?'" On hearing

Gustin's voice telling him to get ready but not to get alarmed, he knew why he had decided to skip the party. Fate made him do it.

A little after seven Gustin was on the phone again.

"It's certain now," Gustin said. In an hour and a half St. Clair would go onstage in the Shed, before seven thousand people, to conduct two rarely played works by Tchaikovsky, each nearly an hour long. His soloist in the Piano Concerto no. 2 would be Viktoria Postnikova, Rozhdestvensky's wife, who came to the United States to perform with her husband. It was to have been the Russian conductor's first appearance in this country in seven years, marking a renewal of cultural exchanges that ceased with President Carter's boycott of the 1980 Moscow Olympics to protest the Soviet occupation of Afghanistan.

The other work on the program was act 2 of *The Nutcracker* — not the concert suite from the ballet, which everybody knows and conducts, but the complete act, which is seldom done in the concert hall. St. Clair had never conducted either piece before. In fact, he knew both only from having sat in on Rozhdestvensky's rehearsals that week.

Those two calls began a thirty-six-hour experience unlike anything Carl St. Clair had ever gone through before. He went without sleep, ran a fever, could not keep food down, and, after a day of squirming and wondering, had to take over Rozdestvensky's second BSO program the next night. Tossing and turning at 4 A.M. after the first concert, he listened to a tape of it for relief, worrying all the while what he would do if he had to take over the next program.

"If you can envision the way you would like to have your first concert with the Boston Symphony," he said, "I don't think this would have been it."

Difficult as it was, the road St. Clair took is one that has carried other young conductors to fame. BSO history holds two notable precedents. In 1943, one year out of Tanglewood, an unknown named Leonard Bernstein substituted for Bruno Walter with the New York Philharmonic at the last minute, with consequences all the world knows. In 1969 another recent Tanglewood graduate, Michael Tilson Thomas, took over from the ailing William Steinberg in the middle of a BSO concert in New York. Installed only a month before as the orchestra's assistant conductor — a predecessor to St.

Clair — Thomas went on to lead thirty-seven more BSO concerts that season, become associate conductor, and forge an international career.

St. Clair's life is bound up with Bernstein's through another accident. He was born into a farm family in the south Texas town of Hochheim (population fifty, more or less). His mother bought him a piano and started him on lessons for his sixth birthday — "not a very exciting gift" for a small-town Texas boy, he recalled, and for years he did not talk about it in front of friends. Trying his hand at composition, he wrote a few "stupid little pieces." He took up trumpet in the fifth grade and went on to study opera conducting at the University of Texas. From there he went to Southern Illinois University, and then the University of Michigan, to conduct and teach.

In a sense, the turning point came in 1985. St. Clair, still on the faculty at Michigan, was a conducting fellow that summer at Tanglewood. When Bernstein came to town for his two-week annual visit to teach and conduct, St. Clair was one of three student conductors he chose to share the Music Center Orchestra podium with him in an all-Copland program — an incredible experience, St. Clair said. The BSO noticed, of course, and when it held auditions that fall for a new assistant conductor it invited St. Clair to try out. Without a Silverstein in the wings, the orchestra wound up with not one but two assistant conductors. In January 1986 St. Clair and Pascal Verrot, a Frenchman, were chosen to share the job, taking turns on duty.

But St. Clair said the big moment really came in 1974, when he was home from college on Christmas vacation and getting ready to go to a Friday night country and western dance. (Even for a college kid studying opera conducting, country and western was the only show in town.) Waiting for friends to pick him up, he began fiddling with the television dial. A rebroadcast of a Tanglewood concert by Bernstein with the BSO popped up. Incredible as it seems, that was the first time, outside of a few recordings, that St. Clair had ever heard a symphony orchestra or known there was a Tanglewood.

Hypnotized by what he saw and heard on the tube, he finally had to send his friends on without him. "I've got to stay and watch this," he told them, his eyes glued to the screen.

So when Carl St. Clair rehearsed and conducted Copland with Leonard Bernstein as his mentor at Tangelwood eleven years later, he really did have a sense that fate was knocking. And when he climbed back onto the podium in the Shed a year after that to take over a BSO concert — well, it was not just Mr. Gustin banging on the door.

"I tell you, I can't understand it and I can't believe it," St. Clair said afterward, still shaking his head in disbelief. "I mean, it's so incredible that it's like a dream you couldn't dream. It isn't like back then I was thinking this is a goal, because basically I don't live my life that way." But it was "something very, very meant to happen."

A throat infection making the rounds of the BSO staff had felled the genial, fifty-five-year-old Rozhdestvensky. He recovered in time to lead the Music Center Orchestra, as scheduled, a few days later in a powerful performance of Shostakovich's Tenth Symphony. While recuperating, he sent St. Clair a letter saying he had listened to the broadcasts of his BSO programs and St. Clair had "carried both concerts off brilliantly."

St. Clair went into the experience without dreams of glory. While sitting in on Rozhdestvensky's rehearsals, he had carefully made notes in his scores about the Soviet conductor's tempos, phrasings, and other ideas about the music. As the standby conductor, he knew his first priority was not to create his own performance, but, as nearly as he could, to re-create the performance Rozhdestvensky would have given. Anything else, especially without rehearsal, would only pile confusion on top of confusion. His goal with the players was to "allow them to be the musicians that they are."

Working quickly in the time remaining before the concert, the BSO staff arranged a run-through of the second movement of the Tchaikovsky concerto, which Rozhdestvensky had chosen to perform in the uncut original version. The movement, a lyrical andante, contains extended solo passages for piano, violin, and cello, almost as in a triple concerto, and twenty minutes before the performance St. Clair met in the Shed's Green Room with Postnikova, concertmaster Malcolm Lowe, and first cellist Jules Eskin to go over the parts. To duplicate, as best he could, Rozhdestvensky's unusual habit of conducting from the floor, St. Clair arranged to use a low

podium. He called Rozhdestvensky at the house where he was staying and wished him a speedy recovery. Rozhdestvensky, in turn,
wished St. Clair luck and promised to stay tuned on the radio as
long as his strength held.

At 8:40 Gustin went onstage to announce that Rozhdestvensky
was sick and St. Clair would conduct in his place. In the dark the
crowd murmured its disappointment and regret. All that remained
was for St. Clair to walk out and make his BSO debut.

Was he nervous?

> One note and I was relaxed — one note, one sound, from that orchestra
> [St. Clair said]. I felt less nervous and I realized, "I'll just have to do my
> job and it'll be okay." The strongest thing you have in this situation is
> just to think of the music, not the situation, the circumstances, whatever.
> The power comes from thinking about the music.

The performance in both pieces got off to a shaky start but soon
picked up smoothness and momentum as the orchestra got used to
the new conductor's ways. After the initial disappointment the audience felt a sense of event — of excitement, even, and discovery.
Like Bernstein and Thomas before him, St. Clair not only saved the
concert but, with the BSO supporting him at every turn, took command and made the music live. When it was all over Postnikova
and St. Clair won tumultuous ovations from both the orchestra and
the audience. In the excitement the pianist warmly embraced her
conductor for the evening. The concert might not have been what
Rozhdestvensky would have made of it but it was clearly a success
in its own right.

Afterward the weary St. Clair joined Costa Pilavachi, the BSO's
artistic administrator, for dinner at Pilavachi's home. Then he went
home to try to sleep.

Sleep, however, was impossible. Listening to a tape of the concert
at 4 A.M. helped to calm his nerves, but he kept going over the
evening's events — "all of those things that go through your mind
a million times" — while waiting for a sleepless dawn. Finally he
got up and sat in on the BSO's open rehearsal Saturday morning; he
was also the cover for Christopher Hogwood, who was conducting,
and would have to take Hogwood's place at the Sunday afternoon
concert if Tanglewood suffered another casualty. Amid conferences
with Pilavachi and other BSO staff members, he awaited word on
Rozhdestvensky's condition.

Viktoria Postnikova and Carl St. Clair exchange congratulations after his
last-minute substitution for her husband, Gennady Rozhdestvensky.

Rozhdestvensky's second program was also all-Russian, consisting
of Prokofiev's Fifth Symphony and Shostakovich's First Piano Concerto — both fairly well known — and Shostakovich's *Bolt* ballet
suite, a rarity. At 5 P.M. on the stage of the Shed — again, just in
case — St. Clair had a run-through of the Shostakovich concerto
with Postnikova and the BSO principals who had important solo
parts. At the end of the rehearsal the doctor reported: Rozhdestvensky was worse, not better. St. Clair would have to go on again.

By then, his stomach was bad and he was feeling feverish. He
took a twenty-minute nap on a sofa in the Green Room. Staff members brought in a snack of hot tea, mineral water, bread, and pasta
without oil. Staffers also made sure his tuxedo was clean and pressed
and brought black socks to replace the everyday pair he had worn
from home. At his request, Gustav Meier, his friend and mentor at
Michigan, who heads Tanglewood's student conducting program,
came in for a quiet talk.

Again St. Clair went on and did the job. Again big ovations washed over him and Postnikova. Again dinner followed, now with Pilavachi and orchestra manager Anne Parsons at a restaurant. But on going home at 12:30 A.M. St. Clair was really sick and began throwing up. He dozed off around 5:30, felt "tenuous" all day Sunday, and finally on Monday ate food he could savor and keep down — pizza. Friends from out of town joined him at the restaurant. Acclaimed a hero, St. Clair could begin looking forward to the following summer, when he would have his first regularly scheduled BSO concert.

The "amazing feeling" that he took away from both stand-in appearances was of being surrounded by the BSO's sound.

> You know [he said of that sound], when you hear it from the audience, it's incredible. But when you're standing right in the center of that orchestra, when you're onstage with that instrument, it's more than you can imagine — just the ocean of sound that pours out. You sort of dream about what it's going to be like, but then you're right there and you only have a mental image of what it's going to be like until it happens.

Luck cheated St. Clair on only one count. Where Bernstein and Thomas had the good fortune to make their unplanned debuts in New York, he made his in outermost Massachusetts, without a New York critic in sight. Unlike their triumphs, his made hardly a ripple, much less a splash, on the national scene. Like fate, the media can be capricious.

Undeterred, St. Clair that fall left his teaching position at Michigan, after eight years, to devote himself to his assistant's job in Boston, which also meant conducting the Boston Pops, Boston Symphony Chamber Players, and BSO youth concerts, among other duties. The next summer at Tanglewood he led that first BSO program of his own choosing — a successful mix of Mozart, Rachmaninoff, Barber, and Respighi. Fate, however, had one more trick to play. This time St. Clair himself was on the disabled list. He hobbled onto and off the stage with a cane, favoring a broken ankle, still not wholly mended, from a pre-Tanglewood basketball game.

By then, Rozhdestvensky, happy and healthy, had returned to and gone home from the BSO conducting ranks. But it would not have mattered if he had still been around to repay a favor. Carl St. Clair, bum leg and all, wasn't giving up his podium to anybody. At least for this one night he was no longer a cover, no longer a claimant on fate, but a BSO conductor in his own right.

                        *   *   *

St. Clair's dinner with Costa Pilavachi was more than a friendly gathering of Tanglewood insiders. Pilavachi is the man responsible for picking the conductors, soloists, and repertoire that the BSO's audiences in Boston and at Tanglewood hear. He is St. Clair's colleague, but, more than that, it is part of his job to get conductors on and off the stage — happily and healthily if possible but by hook or crook if not.

A major symphony orchestra is a corporation whose product happens to be music. At the executive level there are a president, board of trustees, and board chairman. In the BSO the chief operating officer is the managing director, now Kenneth Haas. Immediately below him on the table of organization are five department heads. On the administrative side four are responsible for orchestra management, corporate business and finance, promotion, and development.

Pilavachi is the artistic administrator. In layman's terms that means he is Seiji Ozawa's right-hand man in the planning of concert programs. He calls himself the BSO's "eyes and ears" in the search for talent. Ozawa, who has the final say on artists, is too busy to keep track of who's who in the concert world. Pilavachi does it for him and makes the arrangements with artists to mount a ten-week Tanglewood season. In his glass-walled office at a back corner of the Shed, he arranges for available conductors and soloists to perform programs according to their own and the BSO's tastes.

Then a thirty-five-year-old bachelor from Canada, Pilavachi succeeded to the artistic administrator's job in 1985. Curly-haired and wiry, he comes by his diplomatic demeanor rightly: he is the son of a Greek diplomat. He was born in London and moved with his family to Greece, Egypt, Washington, D.C., and then back to Greece before settling down in Canada at the age of fourteen. When his father was transferred back to Greece again in 1970, Costa stayed on in Ottawa to complete his education. He earned a bachelor's degree in political science and a graduate degree in public administration, both from Carleton University in Ottawa. Then music took over.

Costa Pilavachi.

As a boy Costa had studied the violin. But when he was about eighteen he became "really bored" with it "because I enjoyed the finished product much more than practicing." So he became a music buff, going to concerts and buying records. While still a student, he landed a job as manager of the classical department in a large record store. It was, he said, "the first and last time in my career that I will have that kind of daily contact with the actual consumer." In Toronto Pilavachi worked on the staff of the St. Lawrence Center, helping to present a celebrity concert series, and then moved on to become an artists' manager for a leading Canadian arts management firm. In his three years as an artists' representative, he traveled widely in America and Europe and got to know the presenters of concerts — managers of orchestras, arts centers, festivals, and the like. For the next two years he was back at the St. Lawrence Center as director of music. Then in 1981 he went to the National Arts Center in Ottawa to direct its music program, which includes a symphony orchestra, an opera festival, and chamber and recital series. In his fourth year on the job the BSO hired him away. It was his tenth anniversary in the music business. "So I've never really done anything else," he said. Here, partly in his words, is how Pilavachi does it for Tanglewood and the BSO.

The planning for a Tanglewood season begins two years in advance and involves a conscious effort to attract, if possible, crowds of 8,000 to 15,000 to programs mixing familiar classics with a sprinkling of oddities and rarities. Tanglewood consumes nearly a third of the BSO's annual budget — in 1986, a typical year, $6,750,900 out of $25 million. The Tanglewood deficit for that year, after an estimated $3.5 million in ticket sales, and $1 million in fund raising and income from other sources, was figured at $844,200, part of it for the Music Center. With seating for five thousand in the Shed and lawn space for thousands more, the BSO counts on a large attendance to make ends meet, or nearly meet. (The official attendance record for a classical music concert, set at Tanglewood on Parade in 1981, is 17,901.) The programming must therefore have wide popular appeal, even when an unfamiliar or contemporary work makes a brave appearance. It was easier, of course, in pre-stereo, pre-video days for Koussevitzky to play what he wanted to play, regardless of audience preferences for the tried and true. But Pilavachi, naturally, tries to achieve artistic integrity while casting a wide video net.

Rain is always a danger. Shed tickets, for reserved seats, are sold in advance, with no refund possible, but a virtually unlimited number of lawn tickets is available right up to the moment of the concert. Even a threat of rain can wash out the lawn crowd. The loss can run as high as $75,000 for a program featuring a star soloist with wide appeal.

Pilavachi and Ozawa start the planning by "sitting down and discussing which conductors, in the best of all possible worlds, Seiji would like to have as guests." Around the same time they decide on the summer's opera, which Ozawa will conduct. It is the work that requires the most painstaking selection of soloists and the most preparation time, including design of the costumes and sets.

Obviously, said Pilavachi, "there are certain major conductors whom we try to have each year." Some, like Herbert von Karajan, it would be a waste of time to try to get; they are busy elsewhere (Karajan at Salzburg, for example) or simply cannot be bothered in the summer. So Pilavachi concentrates on those who are available, like Charles Dutoit and Leonard Bernstein, both Tanglewood regulars. Out of a total of about twelve conductors in a typical summer, three or four may be making debuts. The veterans will range from Bernstein, whose association goes back to the 1940s, to early-music specialists relatively new to the American symphonic scene, like Christopher Hogwood and Trevor Pinnock.

With commitments from most of the guest conductors, the next major step is to divide the concert dates, roughly, among Ozawa and them. At the same time, Pilavachi and Ozawa try to pin down a date for the opera. Those decisions provide a ground plan for the rest of the season.

It is now winter, about twenty months before the season. At this point "Seiji will discuss what other major works he will want." These are works requiring extra rehearsal and "very specific performers." For the Verdi *Requiem,* for example, "there are very, very few major singers" who can perform "at the level we would want for the Boston Symphony." That limits not only the choice of soloists but the dates when it is possible to schedule a performance.

Pilavachi now begins lining up the season's soloists, finding out from the managers, and sometimes from the artists themselves, who is available. Again he starts with the "hard-to-get people, who are very busy and, because of their quality and renown, will give luster to the festival — and naturally sell tickets as well." Because these artists are much in demand, "we have to give them every opportunity to find a date in the schedule that works," ideally with conductors who want to work with them, and with whom they want to work.

Other considerations include the midweek recital series in the Theater–Concert Hall and possibilities at the Music Center. Pianist Alfred Brendel, for example, is engaged as a BSO soloist. "We think, Alfred Brendel would be a perfect artist for the recital series." More negotiations take place, and he has a recital date. Cellist Yo-Yo Ma, pianist Emanuel Ax, and other BSO artists who fit in are also signed as recitalists. "Then we think, how can we include them in a kind of mini-residency at the Music Center?" Pilavachi talks to the staff, offering his roster of conductors and soloists. It is arranged that conductors like Bernstein and Rozhdestvensky will work with the student orchestra and conductors, preparing and leading a concert. Instrumentalists like Ma will give master classes, sometimes just a single session but in other cases, such as Ma's, as part of a longer term in residence.

It is now April, with fifteen months remaining till opening. Although most conductors have been engaged, "we also keep our options open until quite late because there are always interesting young conductors whom we want to bring to Tanglewood for a debut with the Boston Symphony." And so around now an Esa-Pekka Salonen or Semyon Bychkov fills a slot on the schedule. Tanglewood, according to Pilavachi, is a "great place" for debuts "because it has a huge audience and there is national publicity" through New York critics who come up for major debuts and pre-mières. And because of the intensive schedule "you get a very good idea very quickly" whether to reengage a conductor for a full-dress Symphony Hall debut.

Around this time Ozawa and Pilavachi also consider major anniversaries — a composer's centenary, for example — or other possible themes for the season. They likewise discuss what soloists or ensembles to bring in for Shed concerts on the nights (usually two a season) when the BSO does not play. These star appearances, a mid-1980s innovation, serve two purposes. One, obviously, is to lend variety and a splash of glamor. The other is more practical. A night off can give the BSO a breathing spell from its heavy rehearsal and performance schedule. Alternately, it can also provide extra rehearsal time for a major production like the opera. In recent years the special Shed attractions have included Itzhak Perlman and Leon-tyne Price in recitals, Wynton Marsalis and his ensemble in a pro-gram of jazz, and touring orchestras like the Israel Philharmonic and the Academy of St. Martin-in-the-Fields.

Ozawa, meanwhile, keeps his schedule flexible during the open-ing and closing weeks so he can take on an extra concert if necessary. Some guest conductors are also willing to juggle dates. If conflicts arise, another way out is to trade artists for a week with Ravinia, Blossom, or other festivals. Ravinia and Blossom, of course, are free to call upon Tanglewood for similar favors.

Soloists add glitter, but not every program must have a soloist. An all-Beethoven or all-Brahms program under a well-known con-ductor like Ozawa or Kurt Masur, for example, will sell well even without a Perlman or Brendel playing a concerto. "But Seiji wants to work with some of the great soloists of the world because it's wonderful, it's fulfilling." And so Perlman turns up regularly, play-ing the Beethoven, Brahms, or Mendelssohn violin concerto, usually under Ozawa. Other soloists are teamed with Ozawa or other conductors.

It's a matter of mixing and balancing and planning each weekend and each concert with an eye to quality, to freshness, and never forgetting that if you don't attract lots of people, it's not going to be that successful as an event [said Pilavachi]. You have to keep an eye on the box office all the time at Tanglewood. It's important (a) because if we don't sell tickets, we can't continue — we'll have serious budget problems — and (b) because there's nothing more depressing than a hall of five thousand seats which isn't full.

It is now fall; the season is nine months away. Pilavachi is still on the phone with guest conductors, "going back and forth — for months, frankly" — about repertoire satisfactory to both them and Ozawa, who will have his own preferences. Conductors are also concerned about rehearsal time. A new conductor is especially concerned because he wants to "make a good impression on the critics, the public, the orchestra, the management, Seiji, everybody." The BSO tries see that a "debut conductor gets his way as much as possible."

Along with the public's appetite for hits, the two-rehearsal limit for most programs at Tanglewood tends to discourage adventurous programming. If a conductor wants to do a new or unfamiliar work — even an unfamiliar work from an early era, such as a lesser-known Haydn symphony or Scriabin's *Poem of Ecstasy* — he must combine it with staples like a Beethoven symphony to carve out enough rehearsal time. (A single program played three or four times in a week in Boston, by contrast, gets four rehearsals.) Repeats between winter and summer seasons allow some flexibility; a new or large-scale work performed in Boston can be "reheated" at Tanglewood. Ozawa, on the other hand, is committed to varying the Tanglewood repertoire. He believes it is necessary to create a festival atmosphere. In the end, what is desirable must somehow be reconciled with what is possible and what today's audience will buy.

For twenty months Pilavachi has been working at the schedule, plugging holes with artists and works to be performed. By February the work is largely done. It is now time for the promotion and development offices to get out the season's announcements and offer tickets for sale, first to Tanglewood Friends (donors of $50 or more) and then to the general public. The BSO will have committed itself to spending about $650,000 for guest artists. Ozawa will have approved each work to be played and each artist to play it, not just in BSO programs but in each chamber recital. There might be last-minute cancellations and changes — Rozhdestvensky might come down with a throat infection, for instance — and there might be a few "to be announceds" on the schedule. But, as in a good restaurant, the menu will be as varied and full as possible.

Pilavachi's day is not over when the last telephone call has been made, just as the orchestra's work is not done when the rehearsal ends. In addition to the hours on the phone and in meetings, and the correspondence and contracts to keep the "bureaucracy" going, he must be at the concerts as host and hand holder for the guest artists, if only to be sure they are comfortable in their hotel rooms. "That's a very basic thing," he said. "I am the basic contact. They see me as the person who has prepared their contract and been responsible for their engagement, although, of course, it's always Seiji who ultimately decides yes or no. The other thing is that it's important for me to hear the orchestra and how they operate under different conductors and how a piece works, how a program works." For those reasons Pilavachi will attend every orchestral concert at Tanglewood, including those by the student orchestra. In Symphony Hall he will attend at least two programs in each series of three or four. He will also be watching for new conductors among both Tanglewood students and professionals on the world concert circuit. It is his job as the BSO's scout for talent.

Like sight-reading or improvisation, the programming process involves a certain amount of educated guesswork and trial and error. In an average season one or two conductors who look good on paper or somebody else's podium fail to produce. It may be that they cannot work within the two-rehearsal limit. Or perhaps the chemistry with the orchestra is not right. Such conductors — and soloists who falter — will generally not be invited back. Programming can also create mismatches or lower, rather than raise, players' interest. One of Tanglewood's besetting problems, in fact, is an air of routine that hangs over many concerts, not because there are villains in the wings but simply because orchestra musicians, like anyone else, find it difficult to fly to the heights of inspiration three times a week, nine weeks in a row, night after night, conductor after conductor, soloist after soloist, through heat, cold, rain, thunderstorms, and high humidity, with sore fingers and backs, like clocks set to go off at twenty-four-hour intervals.

Pilavachi likens his job to a game of checkers, each move affecting others in ways that are sometimes impossible to predict. He says he is more surprised than anyone when the twenty-five BSO concerts and fifteen to twenty others actually take place, mostly as planned. Like musicians themselves, he is capable of being hurt by criticisms and disappointments, as he was one year when critics complained of a bland Tanglewood season. But, ever the diplomat, he does not complain in turn. Backstage he is planning the next season — and the next, and the next.

*   *   *

To B & B or not to B & B: that was the question.

Like other Berkshire home buyers, Ronald Barron and his wife, Ina Wilhelm, found just the place they wanted, but also found the price a bit steep. Barron, however, is not just any Berkshire home buyer. He is the BSO's principal trombonist, and busy much of the time blowing his horn.

All the same, Barron became the orchestra's only member with a bed and breakfast sideline. The couple bought the two-hundred-year-old colonial mansion with a swimming pool and eight acres just two miles west of Tanglewood. With a spot of help from their three children, then aged seven to ten, they reopened it as Échezeaux, where they extended a country greeting to BSO guests and other visitors.

Nearly half of the BSO's one hundred players own summer places in the Berkshires. Once before Barron had been one of them. Tired of a homeowner's headaches, he finally sold that house and tried renting, as many other players do. Some renters find cottages, houses, or halves of houses to which they return summer after summer. Barron was not so lucky, and wearying of the nomadic life, he and his wife drove out to the Berkshires one March day to go house hunting. Over Lenox Mountain from Tanglewood, only a couple of miles from Seiji Ozawa's mountain retreat, the agent showed them the house of their dreams.

Too much, the couple said of the price.

Then open a B & B to help pay the bills, the agent suggested.

"We'd never really done anything like this before," Barron recalled. "But I've done a lot of entertaining, cooking for ten or twelve, so we decided to do it as a way of justifying the cost of the property."

Welcoming party at Échézeaux includes principal trombonist Ronald Barron, his wife, Ina Wilhelm, her son, Teddy Collatos, and Max.

The Barrons are wine buffs, and Échézeaux is the name of a stupendous 1949 red burgundy they discovered. For innkeepers who keep a well-stocked wine cellar, that seemed a fitting name for a B & B. The inn opened with four guest rooms in the main house and two longer-term rental units in a separate building. For both the family and the guests, Barron said, the advantages include the quick hop over the mountain to Tanglewood, the pool, the country setting, and room for children to do what children do.

Échézeaux is a family affair. Wilhelm does the shopping. Barron mows the lawn and handles heavy maintenance. The children keep up the pool and bake muffins and pastries for breakfast. The whole gang pitches in to clean rooms and make beds. The kids get a "weekly salary" — an allowance, Barron explained — for doing their share. Guests help themselves at breakfast but the Barrons try to be around to make folks feel at home. It is one BSO family's way of dealing with the need to keep up two homes, one winter and one summer.

The Tanglewood season, with its heavy concentration of music and its shuttle of guest artists in and out, transports BSO members into a different home, social, and musical milieu. The number of player services each week — concerts and rehearsals, as specified in the musicians' union contract — is the same as in Boston. But a whole orchestra is uprooted and moved to a land where vacations are business, and business often blurs into vacationing.

Some players love the Berkshires, bring their families with them, and cannot wait to kick off their shoes. Others — about ten — go back to families or other interests in Boston in their free time. (Because of the concert schedule Tanglewood's weekends are Mondays and Tuesdays.) A few skip town to play recitals. Principal clarinetist Harold Wright heads up to work his farm in Marlboro, Vermont, where Rudolf Serkin's music festival reigns. Others cook, garden, go sailing or swimming at Stockbridge Bowl, play golf or tennis, entertain — the BSO party season is intense — or get married.

Cupid hit the bull's-eye for Patricia McCarty, the assistant principal violist, and Ronald Wilkison — then a violinist, soon to become a violist.

"No, it wasn't fog-shrouded eyes across the orchestra," laughed Wilkison about the irresistible attraction of the viola section, to which he moved a month after the wedding. A switch-hitter on violin and viola, he had filled in as a violist before and, five months before getting married, auditioned for and won the third chair in the viola section. That means he sits in the second row, just behind his wife. When principal violist Burton Fine is off, or when McCarty moves up to become first violist of the Boston Pops, Wilkison also moves up. That gives the BSO, right in the front row, its only husband-wife team who are stand partners.

They were married at Seranak at the end of the 1982 season.

A couple of seasons earlier Margo Garrett, a pianist–vocal coach on the Music Center faculty, accompanied principal horn player Charles Kavalovski in a Weekend Prelude recital in the Shed. In time romance bloomed. They were married just before the 1987 season. Principal cellist Jules Eskin and violinist Aza Raykhtsaum are another BSO couple. So are Martha Babcock, the assistant principal cellist, and violinist Harvey Seigel.

Contract negotiations, a less harmonious business, occupy other players. The Tanglewood season ends the BSO's contract year. Every three years, the Players Committee, made up of five orchestra members, and three or four top members of management sit down between Tanglewood concerts and rehearsals to try to come to agreement on pay, vacations, work schedules, fringe benefits, and other such issues. "Ritual fang-baring time," Burton Fine has called it. Managing director Kenneth Haas describes it as a "triennial gnashing of teeth." The contract the negotiators eventually agree on will run for three years and determine not only bread-and-butter issues but also the length and format of those three seasons.

In 1986, the year Ronald Barron became an innkeeper, he was also Players Committee chairman and chief fang-barer for the musicians. That also happened to be a year when two months of talks at Tanglewood ended in deadlock and the orchestra went into the Boston season without a contract. The players continued to work under the old agreement, but threw up a picket line outside Symphony Hall on opening night and handed out leaflets to concertgoers arriving for the black-tie gala. The impasse went to the brink of a strike, which would have been the first since the BSO, in 1942, became the last of the country's major orchestras to join the American Federation of Musicians. Four weeks into the season, by a vote of 63 to 38, the players ratified a contract providing for a base salary of $48,360 and nine weeks of vacation.

The agreement also marked the end of the ten-week BSO season at Tanglewood. The old eight-week season, introduced during Charles Munch's last year, 1962, was extended by two weeks in 1985 to give the players more time with Beethoven and the like and less with the Pops during its spring-summer season in Boston. But ten weeks was too long, both sides agreed after trying it for two years.

The real issue, however, was the Pops. This venerable Boston institution, in a league with the Red Sox, Bruins, and Celtics, is the BSO minus its first-chair members, who tour as the Boston Symphony Chamber Players during Pops season. Pops players have never made any secret of their distaste for such gems as Leroy Anderson tunes and hits from the great movies. Indeed, Pops director John Williams once quit — only to return upon receiving the necessary apologies — when a paper airplane sailed by during a rehearsal of one of his own movie-music pieces. On the one hand, the players wanted less Pops. At the same time, they refused to cede the Boston Pops role and name to the separate Boston Pops Esplanade Orchestra, a band of freelancers who happily play the Pops concerts when the BSO is on vacation or at Tanglewood. In the new contract the players took back one of the two weeks of Pops concerts they had surrendered in going to ten weeks at Tanglewood. And so the Tanglewood season became nine weeks.

Nothing, however, so absorbs a musician's spare time as music. With management's encouragement most BSO members pursue sidelines as recitalists, chamber players, or both. Especially for string players massed in sections of ten to fourteen, this kind of intimate music making provides a chance to break out of the lockstep imposed by a conductor's demands. Management support comes in two forms: generous time-off policies (including sabbaticals) for performance, and Prelude recitals before BSO concerts at Tanglewood and in Boston. At Tanglewood the weekly Preludes, which present both BSO chamber groups and visiting artists, are a Friday evening institution, begun by Erich Leinsdorf. The original intent was to give concertgoers more driving time from the city by delaying the start of the main BSO concert from 8:30 to 9 P.M. and offering an entertainment in the interim. Soon the Preludes became an attraction in their own right, providing two concerts with an hour between for dinner on the lawn.

The Boston Symphony Chamber Players, who play in Tanglewood's recital series and Festival of Contemporary Music (usually not with the full complement, however), are the busiest and most visible BSO chamber ensemble. Eight or so other established groups are active within the orchestra. These ensembles, which tend to come and go over the years and change members from time to time, are mostly duos, trios, and quartets, but also include the larger contemporary-music group Collage, made up of both BSO members and friends from outside, and the Curtisville Consortium, a Tanglewood group with a taste for unusual repertoire. (The members can be unusual, too. For many years former BSO personnel manager William Moyer, an ex-trombonist who helped to found the Curtisville group, played the recorder in it.) The WUZ, a jazz combo, is a favorite at Tanglewood on Parade, parties, and other informal events. Other ensembles get together for specific performances; Russian-émigré string players, for instance, will occasionally organize and perform a Russian program. In an average summer the

Prelude series will present three or four BSO ensembles, usually in music commenting on that on the main BSO program.

Chamber music began as music performed for pleasure in the home. Sometimes for BSO players (though more in winter than in summer) it is still that. But sometimes what started out as fun takes a serious turn.

For four years violist Mark Ludwig was content to mix his BSO work at Tanglewood with chamber soirees with his family and friends at his rented summer home. The cast of characters at those musicales included his parents and younger brother Michael, a violin student already embarked upon a concert career. They drove over on summer weekends from Saratoga Springs, New York, where Mark's and Michael's father, Irving, a violinist, played in the Philadelphia Orchestra at the Performing Arts Center. At other times fellow BSO members, including assorted wind players and first cellist Jules Eskin, Ludwig's cousin, would drop in to make up quartets and quintets. Friends and neighbors came by to listen.

It was a "nice mixture" of music and musicians, Ludwig said — so nice it seemed a shame to let it end when Tanglewood did. Why not, he reasoned, give a concert series as an addition to the Berkshires' winter calendar, when music is less plentiful?

At twenty-nine Ludwig was already a seasoned chamber player. After coming to Boston from the Kansas City Philharmonic, where he was the co-principal violist, he became a member of the Brattle String Quartet, a BSO ensemble. The quartet played a memorable Prelude recital in 1984 at Tanglewood. It was memorable because a towering thunderstorm drowned it out. Soon after that the Brattle disbanded, though not because of the weather. Conflicting schedules made it impossible for the four players to continue getting together. Ludwig joined two other BSO string quartets, the Cambridge and the Hawthorne. He also continued to play recitals and other chamber engagements in Philadelphia and Boston and around New England.

Now he remembered a slide show he had attended in the Congregational church in Richmond, the rural town where he had his summer home (and where Barron opened his B & B that same year). The recently built church, traditional in design but with modern touches, seemed perfect for chamber music. So Ludwig approached the pastor, the Reverend Jed David Watson (who does double duty during the summer as a Tanglewood usher), and the church trustees. They gave approval for use of the building. A concert series was born.

For the Richmond Performance Series's first season, Ludwig built three programs around himself, brother Michael, BSO cellist Sato Knudsen, and other veterans of the Ludwig summer chamber music society. The church was not quite as ideal as he had thought. Sound bounced around its polished wooden surfaces like pingpong balls. Nevertheless, the series caught on and brought the BSO to the Berkshires in the winter.

The BSO also harbors within its ranks a trio with a loftier ambition — conducting. These veteran string players do not aspire (openly, at least) to replace Seiji Ozawa. Rather, like their chamber player colleagues, they feel that orchestra work alone is not the answer.

Max Hobart, one of the BSO's two assistant concertmasters, is director of the Civic Symphony Orchestra of Boston and the North Shore Philharmonic, community groups made up largely of skilled amateurs. His fellow baton wielders are violinist Ronald Knudsen (Sato Knudsen's father), who leads the Newton Symphony Orchestra, a community group just outside Boston, and cellist Ronald Feldman, director of the professional Worcester Orchestra. All three studied conducting while in a conservatory but graduated into a player's career, meanwhile conducting occasional student or chamber ensembles. As they worked under various conductors, however, they grew increasingly restless. Sometimes they felt they could do the job just as well as the man they were taking orders from. After a decade of mounting frustration, each decided to act.

Feldman said:

I've wanted to conduct ever since I got in the orchestra. A lot of it has to do with listening to other musicians and what they have to say, and getting so disgusted with how things get left out during rehearsals and seeing how the music suffers. After a while I wanted to pick up a baton, work off all the frustrations, and do the music justice in my own way.

Knudsen put it differently:

I find it's all too easy to sit in an orchestra as a player over the years and go on automatic pilot. So this is stimulating because I can learn from all these conductors that pass in front of us. I can learn the good and the bad. It maintains an inquiring mind, and that's all that's important.

Hobart agreed:

It makes me a better musician and ultimately a better player in the orchestra. I'm more aware of everything else going on in the orchestra. I think playing first violin, you tend to be a little narrow and one-sided. Things I had never heard before as a violinist I am hearing and enjoying.

Hobart, who joined the BSO in 1965, eventually got to guest-conduct the Pops and now leads it in two or three programs a year. As the Pops's assistant concertmaster, he had to take over the podium without rehearsal when John Williams came down with the flu a few hours before the 1987 Pops-at-Tanglewood concert. Like Carl St. Clair on his night of tears, Hobart found that "as soon as I got over my nerves and the shock of the situation, I began enjoying it." He got onto such a roll that he opened one score, found he barely recognized it, but kept skimming along, even while asking himself, *What is this piece?*

Knudsen began conducting community orchestras while playing in the Detroit Symphony. Like Hobart, he joined the BSO in 1965. He inherited the Newton Symphony, one of greater Boston's leading community groups, when Michel Sasson, a former BSO violinist who then conducted it, left to pursue a conducting career in Europe.

Feldman, a BSO member since 1967, was a novice at conducting when he took charge of the New England Philharmonic, a Cambridge-based community group. Two years before, however, he had begun playing first cello in the Worcester Orchestra at the invitation of Joseph Silverstein, then its director (another of the many hats the former BSO concertmaster wore). When Silverstein gave up Worcester in 1987 to concentrate on his career in Salt Lake City, Feldman succeeded him. By then he had also become the conductor for Extension Works, a Boston new-music consortium.

The conducting trio used to be a quartet but Lawrence Wolfe, the assistant principal double bassist, could not make a go of it. So now the BSO harbors an aspiring composer within its ranks.

In the early 1980s, wanting "to grow as a musician," Wolfe went out and founded his own radio orchestra. But after one concert over WGBH-FM, Public Radio's flagship station in New England, the chamber ensemble ran out of money. A musician but no fund raiser,

Wolfe turned to composing instead. Over the next few years he turned out fifty songs and other work mixing popular and classical idioms. His conducting career had a brief resurgence, though. On the occasion of Donald Duck's fiftieth birthday, he led a freelance orchestra in two anniversary concerts in Symphony Hall.

"It really put me on the map," he said, sarcasm thick. "It worked out so well that now Disney does it himself without me."

Despite the holiday crowds it is a long way from Disney World to Tanglewood, as Wolfe discovered. Just how far became evident on the final day of the 1986 season.

*   *   *

The final weekend in 1986 began with one of the coldest nights Tanglewood ever shivered through. It is a rare night when Itzhak Perlman plays badly, but it is a rare night when the temperature falls to 45° at an outdoor concert. Sweaters, furs, and electric heaters broke out onstage as players sought warmth for themselves and their fragile instruments. Garb in the audience was even more arctic — fur-lined parkas, mittens, blankets, and, on the lawn, sleeping bags. With Ozawa on the podium for one of his favorite soloists, listeners understood Perlman's plight as he fumbled, frigid-fingered, through the Brahms Violin Concerto.

On the next night the thermometer got up to 55°, and Perlman wanted to try again. This time, however, he was not on the bill. The Israel Philharmonic, under its music director Zubin Mehta, was in town on an American tour, the first orchestra from abroad to play at Tanglewood. When it came time for Mehta to make his entrance, who should appear, unannounced, but Perlman?

The Israeli-born violinist walked up to a waiting microphone on his crutches and told the delighted crowd that since he and the Philharmonic were visiting on the same weekend, he had gone to see his old friend Zubin for a little chat. And, Perlman said, he told the Maestro, "I'm here and I'm gonna play something!"

Play it he did. It was the Bruch G Minor Concerto, in which he made up for his troubles of the night before, and for some of the Israelis' troubles during an in-and-out evening of music.

For weather the summer of 1986 had been one of the most dismal in Tanglewood history. For nine weeks players, students, and audiences had slogged through seemingly endless rain and chill.

It was precisely the sort of weather that unbalances Tanglewood's books. Attendance, particularly on the lawn, fell. By some fancy of Berkshire gods, though, the sun seems always to smile on the last day of Tanglewood. And that is what happened on the final Sunday of this longest Tanglewood season, the last of the two that ran to ten weeks each. On a bright afternoon with just an edge of autumn in the air, an audience officially figured at 8,229 — medium-sized by Tanglewood standards — came to hear Benjamin Britten's *War Requiem*, given under Ozawa's direction.

The *War Requiem* and the Israelis: were the gods trying to say something? Here were the musical emissaries of a nation that, in its brief existence, had survived by war and the threat of war. Here, the next day, was a twentieth-century masterpiece by an English pacifist warning that two world wars have provided no answer to anything — that "they who love the greater love lay down their life; they do not hate."

The *War Requiem* had had its American première in 1963 at Tanglewood in the first of six BSO performances that Erich Leinsdorf led that year. The work then fell out of the BSO's repertoire. In 1985 Ozawa revived it to commemorate the fortieth anniversary of the end of World War II. Before Tanglewood he had led performances with orchestras in Tokyo and Berlin. (A projected Hiroshima performance could not be arranged.) Other BSO performances — "reheated" from Tanglewood, to use Costa Pilavachi's term — followed that fall in Boston.

There was another Tanglewood connection. Because of his convictions Britten remained in the United States from 1939 to 1942 to avoid military conscription at home in Britain. In America he composed his opera *Peter Grimes* on a commission from Koussevitzky through the Koussevitzky Music Foundation. The work had its American première at Tanglewood in 1946, with Britten in attendance. The conductor was the young Leonard Bernstein, later an outspoken opponent of war.

Britten wrote the *Requiem* in 1961 for the consecration of the rebuilt Coventry Cathedral in England. The new edifice stands beside the ruins of the medieval cathedral destroyed by German bombs. Contrition before God, for the sin of war, was the message of the reconstruction. Carved amid the blackened ruins near the new cathedral's west door, an inscription says: *Father, forgive.*

The Latin Mass for the Dead from the Roman Catholic liturgy — the same text set by composers from the Middle Ages on — is one of three layers of music in Britten's plan. A traditional symphony orchestra and mixed chorus, with a soprano soloist, perform this service in Britten's distinctive idiom, at once acid and disjunct yet tonal and familiar. Woven through the mass are Britten's settings of bitterly antiwar poems by Wilfred Owen, the English poet who, at the age of twenty-four, died in battle in World War I a week before the 1918 armistice. These are sung in English by a tenor and a baritone — clearly, enemy soldiers on a field of battle — to the accompaniment of a chamber orchestra. A separate boy choir, set apart, chants parts of the Latin service, their young voices innocent and distant from the turbulence all around.

Britten's juxtapositions of sound, space, and text can jar listeners' expectations. In the *Offertorium*, for instance, the chorus builds to a powerful fugue — a fixture in traditional settings of the mass — as it recounts the promise, "to Abraham and his seed," that St. Michael will lead the faithful into the paths of light. At that point the tenor and baritone break in, to a jaunty instrumental accompaniment, in a duet describing Abraham's preparations for sacrificing Isaac. But in Owen's version Abraham, holding the knife, denies the angel's plea that he sacrifice the ram instead:

> But the old man would not so, but slew his son —
> And half the seed of Europe, one by one. . . .

The savage words, mingling with the boy choir's innocent offer of "sacrifices of prayer and praise" for the souls of the dead, resound like a curse on all mankind.

So here, before eight thousand people, in a concert pavilion open to the late summer lake, hills, skies, and sun, a Japanese conductor carries a plea for peace from the capitals of the World War II enemy to his adopted country. "God in my house," he had said, apropos of another requiem, "is very wide." And the beauties of the Berkshire country are many. These big requiems, oratorios, and tone poems are Ozawa's specialty, but on an afternoon like this, when a healing sun returns and everybody knows the final chord will begin a ten-month silence, there is an extra dimension. Music, nature, and peaceful concourse of human souls combine to create a greater whole — in Britten's phrase, "a greater love."

From the opening dirge in the orchestra, with its eerie sense of stillness within motion, Ozawa welded the three soloists (Carol Vaness, Thomas Moser, and Benjamin Luxon), two orchestras, and two choruses into a superbly responsive unit. To his left a chamber orchestra made up of first-chair BSO players accompanied the two male soloists in the settings of Owen's poems. Before him the main BSO group accompanied the soprano and Tanglewood Festival Chorus in the liturgical mass. Offstage to the left, on risers at the side of the Shed, the Boston Boy Choir intoned its untroubled hosannas.

The angry fanfares of the *Dies irae* resounded with splendor in the BSO brass. When those fanfares combined with the biting imprecations of the chorus, the music became a struggle for men's souls. But the *War Requiem* ends in sorrow and in peace, with two enemy soldiers, in "some profound dull tunnel," embracing in eternal sleep. After the groaning, grinding harmonies and babel-like shouting of the *Libera me*, the final duet was both an event of timeless beauty and an unspoken prayer for reconciliation. The audience fell into a stunned silence before the applause and shouts could begin. The ovations lasted late into the afternoon.

Nothing that preceded the *War Requiem* that season came up to its standard. As in most seasons, a few concerts were sub-par, a few excellent in other ways, with much in the middle. It helped, of course, that on the final day the weather cleared. It helped that, under Pilavachi's plan, the visiting Israelis spelled the BSO to give extra rehearsal to the *Requiem*. It helped that Ozawa was doing music he felt in his marrow, that his players and singers recognized and responded to his conviction. In the end all the Tanglewood elements came together. With this music in this performance, on this day, the earth somehow shifted on its axis.

Chapter III

HONORED GUESTS

$\mathcal{S}$OME TANGLEWOOD figures occupy places of honor as teachers, guest artists, or sometimes simply guests. Among the most distinguished of these are Phyllis Curtin and Maurice Abravanel. Both are teachers whose long performing careers — Curtin as a singer, Abravanel as a conductor — and personal qualities have turned them into institutions. Curtin has been associated with Tanglewood for more than four decades as a student, performer, and faculty member. Abravanel has been around for only a few years (and then only as a sort of minister without portfolio). Yet both have contributed so much, not only to Tanglewood but to American musical life, that they touch an entire festival through their presence.

Conductors also affect a festival. Erich Leinsdorf and Michael Tilson Thomas, for instance, were once major figures at Tanglewood, Leinsdorf as the BSO's music director, Thomas as a *Wunderkind* assistant and then associate conductor. Both disappeared from the scene under less than happy circumstances. A decade later both reappeared as honored guests. Despite the BSO's gesture to kiss and make up, some of the old tensions resurfaced, too. Klaus Tennstedt, on the other hand, made his bombshell American debut with the BSO and thus began a checkered Tanglewood career, which ended in bad blood with the orchestra. Among other guest conductors Colin Davis and André Previn became favorites for a time and then departed the podium, though more from being in demand elsewhere than from being in disfavor. Now Charles Dutoit's star is on the rise.

Among soloists, two of the most startling were a pair whom Leonard Bernstein brought for their BSO debuts, pianist Marek Drewnowski one year and violinist Midori the next. Drewnowski, a Pole whom Bernstein discovered while listening to the radio during a bout of insomnia, played a Brahms concerto under the Maestro and was never heard from again. Tanglewood, on the other hand, became the launching pad for a major career when the fourteen-year-old Midori needed three violins to get through Bernstein's own *Serenade* in a concert he conducted. The widely publicized incident, along with the doll-like Japanese-American fiddler's savoir-faire, made her a darling of musicians and the media alike.

Cellist Yo-Yo Ma's career as a Tanglewood guest took a different turn. Within a few years of his debut as a BSO soloist, he was so much a part of the family that he settled in as a faculty member. Teaching was part of a maturing process for him, a way of repaying a debt to his own teacher, who had recently died, and of passing on his knowledge to a new generation.

What can one say about Thomas D. Perry, Jr.? As the BSO's executive director, he came up with the idea of putting skirts around women in shorts — they promptly stole the skirts, of course — and wrote a famous memo granting certain well-known musicians vehicle rights under the category of "burdens." Now retired, he enjoys emeritus status as a member of the audience, where he remains a bearer of the Koussevitzky legacy and, unmistakably, an honored guest.

BSO insiders work in the orchestra year-round. Honored guests come for the summer, or part of the summer, and contribute their particular knowledge, skills, and foibles. That, too, was part of Koussevitzky's design.

*   *   *   *   *

There is a scene in Mozart's *Marriage of Figaro* where the Countess, trying to win back the affections of her skirt-chasing husband, contemplates the loss of her youth. *Dove sono i bei momenti, di dolcezza e di piacer?* she sings. "Where are they, the happy moments of sweetness and of pleasure?" It is one of the great moments in opera, always worth a tear and a brava if sung well.

For years the Countess was one of Phyllis Curtin's favorite roles. In the 1970s, still glamorous but gray-haired, as a Countess should be, she found herself cast in the role in a new and all too vivid way. She could no longer sing the part. The last time she tried, her voice, like a needle on a gas gauge, "lay right there on the dangerous side" toward empty. Those happy moments of sweetness and pleasure, she realized, were over.

Phyllis Curtin is one of Tanglewood's great ornaments, if someone so central to an organization over more than four decades can be described as an ornament. She carries the title "artist in residence." It does not begin to describe her contribution as a student, performer, and teacher. Star singers — visitors for a week like Kathleen Battle, Jessye Norman, and Elly Ameling — come and go at Tanglewood, sometimes giving a master class in which they display themselves before students like pearls in a showcase. Week after week, year after year, Curtin slogs through the everyday travails of the students in her celebrated seminar, showing them both the fundamentals of singing and the imagination that transforms facility into art.

Becoming the countess in real life, after a lifetime onstage as Salome, Fiordiligi, Violetta, Tosca, Rosalinda, the Countess, and dozens of other operatic heroines, did not exactly encourage discovery of the world through rose-colored glasses. Curtin recalls advice her teacher, Joseph Regneas, gave her: "Every singer must learn to die twice." One death, of course, involves the cessation of all body organs but the earlier death involves only one — the voice. For ten years Curtin cheated the Grim Reaper of his first claim by giving up opera and devoting herself to the song literature, always a love of hers. Then in 1984, after a particularly bad week of it at Tanglewood and at home, she traveled across the state to give a recital at the Castle Hill Festival in Ipswich, Massachusetts. Afterward Castle Hill's manager approached her to discuss a return engagement the following summer.

"You've just had it all," replied Curtin. With that, at the age of sixty-two — well beyond the time when most singers have called it quits, or should have called it quits — she began her formal retirement.

> It's really awful [she reflected]. I remember Melissa Hayden [the dancer] when she retired at about fifty. Everybody said, "But, my dear, why should you retire when you're dancing so beautifully?" But you feel things in your body that you realize are not going to change. Your best days you may feel just marvelous and all coordinated in the best possible way, but there just isn't the same resilience in the breathing mechanism on the refined virtuoso level that there was five years ago, let's say.

But if there is no alternative to sooner or later giving up singing — to dying the first death — there are other roles to play in life, and a redemptive one is that of teacher.

Phyllis Curtin was born Phyllis Smith in Clarksburg, West Virginia, to a mother who was a church music director and a father who was an amateur tenor. (Curtin is the name of her first husband, from whom she is divorced.) After graduating from Wellesley as a political science major, she first went to Tanglewood in 1946 as a student in Boris Goldovsky's opera department. That was the summer of the *Peter Grimes* première, with Bernstein conducting, and Curtin sang her first operatic role, as one of the "nieces," in it. Sarah Caldwell was Goldovsky's assistant in those days, and, in another seafaring production that summer, Curtin sang in the first opera Caldwell ever directed, Vaughan Williams's *Riders to the Sea*. She returned as a student in 1948 and 1951 to continue her work under Goldovsky, now taking major roles — Tatiana in Tchaikovsky's *Eugene Onegin* and Lisa in his *Pique Dame*.

Listening to her friends and fellow students, Curtin became aware of her limitations as a singer. But, instead of forcing her strengths to conceal her weaknesses as other singers might, she sought out her friends' teacher, Joseph Regneas. She was thirty-one and he was eighty-two — the first American to sing Hans Sachs, Curtin remembers. He changed not only her voice but her life. Within a few years she was singing as many as 150 performances a year. She reigned as the New York City Opera's prima donna — Salome was her signature role -- and regularly graced the stages of the Vienna State Opera, La Scala, the Teatro Colon in Buenos Aires, and the Metropolitan. Besides her Mozart, Italian, and French heroines, she became known for her willingness to tackle twentieth-century opera. She sang, among other roles, Ellen Orford in *Peter Grimes* and the title role in Carlisle Floyd's *Susannah*, which he composed for her.

Ned Rorem, the American composer, who first met Curtin as a fellow student at Tanglewood, once called her one of the few intelligent singers in the business. He was referring specifically to her sensitivity to texts and championing of the contemporary song literature. But Curtin's penetrating intelligence applied to all aspects of her career from the start. Besides opera and songs she learned the symphonic repertoire for voice, and for two decades she was a reigning American soprano with the country's major symphony orchestras. Many of those engagements were with the BSO at Tanglewood and in Boston. She sang at Tanglewood in the *War Requiem* première in 1963, in a 1970 concert performance of *Così fan tutte* under Ozawa, and, in two last-minute substitutions in the early 1970s (she was there and available), in Schoenberg's *Gurrelieder* under Ozawa and Beethoven's *Missa Solemnis* under Bernstein. All four performances rank among Tanglewood's great moments.

The *War Requiem* appearance was pivotal. Erich Leinsdorf, who was in his first season as director of the BSO, had just abolished Goldovsky's student opera program, which he considered too independent of the Music Center. After the Britten performance Curtin met with the dozen or so student singers. With the opera apparatus dismantled, they had little to do, other than small parts in some programs. After listening to their complaints she agreed to a request by Harry Kraut, then administrator of the Music Center, to give a master class. The experience proved so exhilarating on both sides that Curtin and the BSO agreed to make it a full eight-week feature of the next season. Thus the Phyllis Curtin Seminar was born.

Curtin brings to the seminar the glittering mien of a diva and the practical, homely touch of a mother (she has a married daughter, Claudia) and veteran trouper. While the students, on folding chairs before her, deck themselves out in jeans, running shoes, and the other artifacts of the day, she infallibly shows up — even on the hottest days — in impeccable eye shadow, lipstick, and suits or skirts and blouses, her silver tresses swept up, Countess-like, in a bun.

The seminars meet in a rustic barn or recital hall, depending on the available facilities. There are actually two groups of students. The vocal fellows, an elite corps numbering twelve, attend on full-tuition fellowships and get to sing their finished work in public in group recitals. The twenty-four or so seminar members, usually younger or less experienced, receive only classroom help and perform only among themselves. Although the groups meet on alternate mornings, informality prevails, and members of one group are

Phyllis Curtin instructs a voice student and the seminar on proper breathing and posture.

free to sit in on the other's classes. "Seminarians," as Curtin calls them, sometimes return in later summers as full-fledged vocal fellows.

On most days as many auditors as students are in attendance. The auditors may be instrumental or conducting fellows or even BSO members, come to learn how to shape a phrase, or visitors curious about Tanglewood's inner workings. (The classes are technically closed to the public, but no serious onlooker is ever turned away.) Occasionally one of Curtin's friends from her student days, such as Sherrill Milnes, will drop in.

The format of a master class (which is what the Curtin Seminar is) remains much the same anywhere. A singer will come forward, usually with a student accompanist, and perform an aria or song he or she has prepared. The teacher and fellow students greet the performance with applause and praise; at least in Curtin's hands, the class also serves as a support group in which everyone learns from everyone else's travails and triumphs. Then the hard work begins. For the next fifteen minutes to half-hour, Curtin corrects the student on posture, pronunciation, breathing, voice placement, understanding of the music — anything and everything that bears on communication between singer and audience. Touch is important. She places her hands on diaphragm, cheeks, mouth, chest to see how the student's muscles and breath are working. Conversely, students — men as well as women — must reach around from behind her to feel her diaphragm as she demonstrates how to take a breath and let out a pealing, firmly supported tone.

For one student Curtin may spend much or all of the lesson on "opening up space," as she calls it, to allow the voice to resonate in the hollows behind the eyes. For another student, more advanced, the help might go to the meaning of the music and words. As the student struggles, Curtin stops the class for a little talk.

What a wonderful gift! she will say, smiling radiantly. What a gift it is to be able to illuminate poetry through song! How many people are privileged to read poetry, much less devote their lives to it? Not work but art should shine through. The person in the song is in love, praying, dying, happy, sad. You must be that person. But you must remain yourself, too, in control, taking the music where you want it to go. She remembers once when, singing the title role in *Butterfly*, she became so caught up in an exchange with the little daughter that she broke down in the middle. Don't let that happen to you, she says. Use the emotion. Let the poetry dictate the rise and fall of the phrase, the nuances, the inflections. And don't play prima donna's tricks. Apropos of a student's difficulties with changes in her voice, Curtin will recall the time when she was pregnant with her daughter and her voice dropped in range. Yet she did some of her most beautiful programs then, she says, and even continued singing Salome "until the day came when I suddenly turned the same size all up and down."

Laughter and tears are frequent as students break through fears and limitations, reaching notes or depths of expression they had never dreamed were in them. A hard, grinding half-hour can end with the student, overcome, falling on Curtin's shoulder in gratitude and happiness — or sometimes in despair. The magic is audible, too. What began as labored or hesitant will end in, if not a polished performance, one that can be as moving as anything onstage because of the human drama of struggle and victory. After eight weeks of this a student can be transformed. Because of the competition many will not enjoy careers. But others, such as Sanford Sylvan, James Maddalena, and Susan Larson, who sing regularly in and around Boston, particularly with the *enfant terrible* opera director Peter Sellars, and Cheryl Studer, who has gone on to a career in Europe, owe their start to the Phyllis Curtin Seminar.

Being smart can be a handicap as well as a gift. Curtin's career at the Met was never as big as she would have liked. She says Rudolf Bing, the general manager in those days, liked her as a luncheon companion but "didn't have much use for American singers." Nor, one suspects, for singers who picked and chose so carefully among roles. And when, late in her career, she accepted a faculty position at Yale, she quickly found that concert presenters around the country assumed anyone who teaches is worn out as a singer. That, she says, is "really very odd," because nobody considers an instrumentalist who teaches any the worse for wear.

Richard Dyer, music critic of the *Boston Globe* and a long-time Curtin watcher, deftly summed up her career:

Nearly every famous singer is famous for a specialty, but Curtin was famous for doing it all, on a very high level of accomplishment, and often on very short notice. If she never reached the highest peaks of celebrity, she never really sought them — and she sang better, and lasted longer, than most of those who did.

Recalling Regneas's advice, Curtin told Dyer:

> I was in the bloom of my thirty-one pretty years when he said that to me, and I thought I understood. But there is really no way to prepare yourself for what it means. It has been a long process. I gave up Mozart a long time before anything else. My body told me I was never going to have the playfulness, the extra colors, the sparkle that Mozart requires — and Mozart was a particularly delicious ease and pride of mine. My God, do you know what that means, to give up Mozart?

Song recitals had always played an important part in Curtin's career — it was for that, after all, that Ned Rorem had praised her intelligence — and when she could no longer sing opera, she re-studied the song literature and found new rewards in that repertoire. Schumann's *Frauenliebe und -leben,* a work she had detested in earlier years, finding it "goopy and oversentimental," now gave her "more satisfaction than anything has in years." She also began giving a series of occasional Cole Porter evenings, sometimes in public but more often as cabaret-style benefits for favorite organizations. And, with her lower, darker voice, she could still make twentieth-century works like Shostakovich's songs and Schoenberg's *Pierrot Lunaire* scorching in their grief or mockery.

Knowing the day would come when she could no longer sing in public, Curtin went to Yale in 1974 to head the voice department in the School of Music. In 1979 she became, in addition, the master of Branford, one of Yale's undergraduate resident colleges (she was the first woman to hold such a position). She and her husband, the photojournalist Eugene Cook, who met her in 1952 while covering her for *Life* and married her two years later, moved into the master's baronial apartments at Branford. (Among friends the joke ran that if Phyllis was Branford's master, did that make Gene the mistress?) In 1983, after a three-year courtship, John Silber, president of Boston University, won her away from Yale to be the dean of his School for the Arts, and she and Cook moved to Boston. With her withdrawal from the stage the following year, the transition was complete. Curtin became a full-time teacher and administrator, at B.U. in the winter and at Tanglewood in the summer.

There were still a few darts left in Curtin's quiver. She continued to do her Cole Porter evenings, though less and less frequently, and at one point, until the Russians said *nyet,* she contemplated coming out of retirement to give a pair of recitals in Moscow. She also proved an adroit fund raiser, running a campaign to upgrade B.U.'s School for the Arts.

But fate also had a few darts for Phyllis Curtin. One of them took the life of her beloved Gene. A week before the end of Tanglewood in 1986, with no warning, he died of a ruptured aorta. Burdened by paperwork and cares, Curtin would go home alone at night to the dean's mansion just outside Boston or to the country house near Tanglewood and long for the joys of being a singer, long to be Rosalinda, say, in *Fledermaus,* "a delicious role" of hers, chasing up and down scales, in the *Watch Duet,* singing it *staccatissimo,*

> when you run all over the stage singing it, and I always could. And she should be sexy, and she should be charming, and she should be witty, and all of those things, and you have to be easy in the singing to be all of those things, and it has to show in the music. . . .

Or Salome, where you must convince the audience you are a teen-aged sexpot bent on killing the holy man you wanted to kiss. Or the Countess, where Curtin could "spin endlessly lovely lines" in Mozart's endlessly lovely music. . . .

As every opera lover knows, the Countess gets the Count back in the opera and everything comes out happily in the end. Life sometimes does not have happy endings; but Curtin has remained true to her first love, music, and it has remained true to her. In concert and opera programs around the world, the bios of a new generation of singers boast that, wherever they have come from and whatever they have done, they were once members of the Phyllis Curtin Seminar at Tanglewood.

*   *   *

Nearly fifty years ago, Maurice Abravanel said, harking back to his earliest days in the United States, "My general practitioner said to me, showing me a metabolism chart, 'You must go to a psychoanalyst. You have an inferiority complex *that* big. You are headed for a nervous breakdown that could destroy you totally.' " But the idea of lying down on a couch stopped him in his tracks. "I said, 'Look, I am a conductor. I have a *superiority* complex.' " And today the gangling conductor with the French accent and Old World air says, "I'm still waiting for the nervous breakdown."

Like Phyllis Curtin, Abravanel wears the mantle of artist in residence. As with Curtin, the title is just a handy label. To see Abravanel on the Tanglewood grounds is to picture him as the sort of twinkly-eyed grandfather every kid ever hankered after. He stops to chat with students in the cafeteria, putting an arm around their shoulders and asking about their progress and problems. He sits in on student rehearsals, keeping in the background while others do the coaching, but is always available with suggestions based on his fifty-five years of conducting experience. He faithfully attends BSO and student concerts with his wife, and frets if they become separated. ("At my age where will I find another one?" he moans.) BSO officials call him a living link to a disappearing European tradition. The last thing he seems is a candidate for a nervous breakdown, or the owner of a superiority complex.

To the world at large Maurice Abravanel is not a household name. Musicians know better. In particular, his association with Kurt Weill, his premières of all of Weill's American productions, and his thirty-two years as director of the Utah Symphony — the orchestra Joseph Silverstein inherited in 1984 — have earned him a place in the pantheon.

Greek-born and Berlin-trained, Abravanel held the Utah podium from 1947 until 1979, when a series of heart attacks forced him into retirement. He taught conducting at Tanglewood for two weeks in 1981 and returned the following summer, at the age of seventy-nine, as acting director of the Music Center while Gunther Schuller was on a sabbatical. Schuller came back the next year, and so did Abravanel. In fact, the BSO kept bringing Abravanel back every summer after that, even though it no longer had a clearly defined job for him. As the kids would say, he was hanging out. He was a counselor, a role model.

From the start Abravanel was flabbergasted by what he heard and saw.

From 1956 to 1979 he had served as director of the Music Academy of the West, a summer program in Santa Barbara, California. That, he proudly said, was a "pretty good school," with a distinguished faculty of its own, but it had "nothing like this concentration of work." Nowhere but at Tanglewood, he said, has he found so high a level of students, and so many who have "the stamina, the health, the devotion and commitment to go through this 'torture course,' as Gunther Schuller once called it."

Just before the 1982 Festival of Contemporary Music, one of Curtin's student sopranos, Margaret Cusack, submitted to the torture chamber. Abravanel saw her go, without a break, from a grueling rehearsal of the solo part in a new chamber work, Bernard Rands's *Canti Lunatici*, into a rehearsal as the Marschallin in the finale scene of *Der Rosenkavalier* under Erich Leinsdorf.

Abravanel was incredulous.

> In Europe [he said] you would never find that. A young artist in Europe would be a devotee of Stravinsky or a devotee of Richard Strauss, but not both. Usually, you know, they get one thing they like and they feel they will be good in, and they go all-out for that one thing. I mean, this is an incredible concentration of commitment. So I am really, honestly overwhelmed.

He was also overwhelmed when the students, faculty, and administration benefited enough from his presence in his year as acting director for the BSO to invite him back as a permanent minister without portfolio.

> If you ask my personal impression, this is the craziest thing I have ever gone through. I have conducted for fifty-five years in my life — *fifty-five years* — and I never had a position where I worked without conducting. I am surprised every day when I hear the students get a lot from my presence, or the faculty, they feel great. How can that be? Because all I do, really, is conversations — you know, presence, a little nod, a little question, a little discussion. I mean, yes, a few decisions had to be made, of course.

But to be a big shot at a school without having the "natural line of contact" provided by conducting was "a very strange thing."

Even in his earliest days as a musician Abravanel was doing strange things and was attracted to strange places. His first conducting engagement, he recalls, was in the German town of Neustrelitz, in a pavilion in a deer park near a castle. As with Salt Lake City a quarter-century later, he was so bewitched that "I used to think if they gave me that to live in, I would have stayed for life." He made the westward migration to Salt Lake City exactly a century after another patriarch, Brigham Young. Founded in 1940 as a Works Progress Administration orchestra, the Utah Symphony had been limping along under private sponsorship for two years when Abravanel arrived in 1947 to try to make music grow in the Mormon desert.

Born into a Sephardic family, Maurice Abravanel moved with his parents from Greece to Switzerland at the age of six and, at their urging, began working toward a medical degree at the University of Lausanne. Although he said he was "born in the theater" and began playing the piano there at thirteen, he at first did not expect to make music a career. In time his interest grew, and a mutual friend brought him to the attention of the composer and pianist Ferruccio Busoni, who suggested study in Berlin with Weill. The work with Weill led to coaching and conducting in smaller German opera houses — still the traditional route for a conductor learning his trade in Europe. By the time Hitler took power, Abravanel had worked his way up the ladder to Berlin's theaters.

Germany, however, was no place to be, and he left to conduct ballet in Paris and later lead a British troupe on an opera tour of Australia. In 1936, on the recommendation of Wilhelm Furtwängler and Bruno Walter, he joined the Metropolitan Opera, where he conducted French, German, and Italian works. In an era of specialization the mixed repertoire aroused other conductors' jealousies, which forced him out in 1938. He then turned to Broadway, leading musicals, including his series of Weill premières.

It was again on Walter's recommendation that he was appointed director of the Utah. He turned down an offer to conduct the much stronger Houston Symphony to do it. (Not willing to give his life to Broadway, he had earlier refused a lucrative opportunity to become music director of the Radio City Music Hall.) He said Arthur Judson, the powerful artists' manager, counseled him against going to Utah. Walter, despite the recommendation, told him he was crazy. Why, then, did he do it?

> Because I loved it. In other words, I love people. I love places. And so when I went to Salt Lake City, first of all something had happened to me. All my life, whenever I was successful — let's say in Paris, at the Berlin State Opera — I always thought, "Oh, well, they are a first-rate ensemble, they played first-rate anyhow. But it is they and somebody else who built that orchestra, it's not me."

In Salt Lake City the question became: "Could I build it?"

Abravanel not only built it but gave the state its first performances of such standard works as the Beethoven Ninth and the Brahms Second and Third. He rode out the orchestra's bankruptcy in his second year, persuading the musicians' union to keep on playing

Maurice Abravanel discusses a student's work with her.

concerts until the organization could get back on its feet. He brought in twelve leading instrumentalists — friends of his — from New York to serve as a cadre and coach the other musicians. He went on to do a series of pioneering performances of avant-garde works. He did, as far as he knows, the first all-Vivaldi orchestral program in the United States. He made the first recording of a Handel oratorio other than *Messiah* — *Judas Maccabaeus*. He recorded the Mahler Sixth, Seventh, and Eighth symphonies before other conductors would touch them. He took the Utah on a triumphal tour of Europe in 1966 and made more than one hundred recordings.

"I had good friends in New York," he said, "composers who told me, 'Ah, marvelous, you're going to Salt Lake. Now I get a world première.' I said, 'No, thank you, because I have a Utah première of the Schubert C Major. That's more important right now.'"

Looking back, Abravanel said the other reason he stayed in Utah was that he was "just lucky, I guess." In the wilderness he could ignore fads and trends and concentrate on what he thought was important.

I don't know about you [he said], but if I had a child who had gone through measles and polio and God knows what, he's the child I would love most, right? And so Salt Lake got into my skin. I had other offers but they were fewer and fewer because people knew I stayed in Salt Lake. And I don't regret it because I was able to build something. I had an opportunity that I don't think anybody else ever had.

It was because Abravanel got under people's skin at Tanglewood that the BSO brought him back even though there was logically no place for him. His BSO employers speak of him as a "treasure" who adds a "spiritual dimension" to the hurly-burly of student life. More practically, they describe him as an ombudsman, ever available to talk to students — particularly over lunch tables at the cafeteria — about anything from new scores to orchestra life. Alone among harried Music Center faculty and staff members, he attends every student concert (and many a student rehearsal), consulting with the faculty afterward about weaknesses and strengths in programming and performance. Out of his conversations and observations, and his experience as director of the Santa Barbara academy, he gets to know students in a way that busy teachers often cannot. Richard Ortner, administrator of the Music Center, calls him "a living link to a European dedication to music that's not much in evidence in this country."

And his presence as an interim director had an effect on students that no one else's ever had. At the final Music Center Orchestra concert of the 1982 season, in one of his last acts as director, Abravanel announced to the audience that the students had asked to forgo the traditional end-of-season prizes and contribute the prize money to create two new fellowships for future students. The apparently unprecedented gesture meant that about twenty-five prizes, worth $100 to $500 each, would go into a $3,500 fund. With Seiji Ozawa standing beside him and the ten faculty department heads ranged behind him, Abravanel said he, Ozawa, and the faculty had concurred in the "beautiful sentiment." And so Abravanel completed his Tanglewood directorship with a flourish — something he never did in Utah, where, at his insistence, there was no announcement that his Verdi *Requiem* of March 1979 would be his farewell program.

At Tanglewood Abravanel finds both an excessive emphasis on contemporary music and excessive caution about it. On the one

hand, he said, American arts organizations — including, by infer-
ence, Tanglewood in its week-long Festival of Contemporary Music — support too many composers, too indiscriminately. On the
other hand, orchestras and conductors tend to be too insecure to
play much new music in the face of audience resistance. His philosophy, he said,

> may be very cruel, but I am afraid that what we have been doing in America
> is the wrong way. We try to help hundreds of composers by performing
> them. It's like having a small backyard and being so happy with one
> beautiful tree you decide to plant forty trees. Then you don't get a single
> tree because there's not enough earth, not enough water, not enough
> sun. The public cannot support or believe in two hundred or four hundred
> composers. And the cruel thing, but I am afraid the necessary thing, is
> for each man with the possibility to make decisions to decide on a few
> but then fight for those few.

Students, free from outside pressures, give most of the performances in Tanglewood's contemporary festival. In professional
orchestras, Abravanel said, performance of contemporary works
"depends on the degree of confidence the conductor has in being
able to retain his job." Only an entrenched figure like Koussevitzky
or Pierre Monteux, in other words, could play a new work, get
terrible reviews, then play it again a week later and still survive.
Audiences, meanwhile, entrench themselves against new music,
"even new music of an old master. You know, you play an unknown
or little-known Mozart symphony and they say, 'Why don't you
play the G Minor or *Jupiter*?' " Yet with strong support for the worthy
few, Abravanel maintains, audiences will come around in time, as
they did with Schoenberg's *Verklärte Nacht* and Stravinsky's *Sacre
du printemps*. The chicken-and-egg question, of course, is how to
discover the Schoenberg or Stravinsky masterpiece in your midst if
nobody plays it.

In May 1985 Abravanel's wife Lucy, whom he had married in
1947, a month before taking over in Utah, died. He spent the 1985
summer alone but outwardly cheerful at Tanglewood. With Gallic
gallantry he still greeted the parade of visitors who stopped to chat
at his box in the Shed before concerts or at intermissions, and he
still kissed the younger women among them. The next summer he
showed up with an old friend from Salt Lake City, Carolyn Firmage.
On the day of the first 1987 concert, a song recital by Elly Ameling,

they slipped off to the home of Justice of the Peace Rita Paysan in Lenox, thinking nobody knew. That night, in an announcement from the stage, Ameling dedicated her Schubert program to the surprised newlyweds in the audience. Tanglewood was off to another summer. And so, at the age of eighty-four, was Maurice Abravanel.

*   *   *

Unlike Abravanel, who came for one season and never left, guest conductors rise and fall over the years. In the late 1970s and early 1980s André Previn was the Tanglewood favorite, leading more concerts than any other conductor except Ozawa. Then players said Previn was bland, and with his appointment as director of the Los Angeles Philharmonic his engagements dwindled. Two East Germans, Klaus Tennstedt and Kurt Masur, followed similar trajectories during the same decades, becoming pets of players, audiences, and critics, and then sinking from sight. By the late 1980s Charles Dutoit was king, with Leonard Slatkin the heir apparent. Edo de Waart, though a regular, aroused little enthusiasm among players; Stanislaw Skrowaczewski, who has slipped from programs altogether, even less. Over the years only Leonard Bernstein has remained a constant, and even he has had his ups and downs (see chapter 4).

As Bernstein's (and Ozawa's) experience suggests, some bad blood between a conductor and an orchestra is inevitable, especially for a music director, with his power over players' lives. How else can it be when one musician tries to bend one hundred, each as well trained and well supplied with temperament as he, to his will? Admiration or respect is usually the most a conductor can expect from his musicians. (In Koussevitzky's case the respect was laced with a heavy dose of fear.) Among recent Tanglewood guests the exception to the rule is Colin Davis, the BSO's principal guest conductor from 1972 to 1984, whose mellow ways put a glow on music and somehow got hard-bitten musicians to accord him the aura of a saint. Of himself, Davis said on his last Tanglewood visit, in 1980, when he was fifty-two, "I've gotten older. One feels that either one is there now or is never going to be — on a plateau above the struggles of oneself, where one can be at ease with the repertory and stand up and there be no shame in it."

Few conductors can take such a laid-back attitude toward their

Charles Dutoit on the podium.

work. And one of those furthest — at least in the BSO's book — from the ideal Davis represents is Erich Leinsdorf, the former music director. To a sigh of relief on all sides, Leinsdorf departed the BSO at Tanglewood on August 24, 1969, after seven years of acrimony, accusations, and — in the midst of it all — accomplishment. He contended he had been overworked and the orchestra underworked. The players respected him as a musician but many said he had ice water in his veins. Like Byron kicking the dust of England from his heels, he vowed never to return.

But here it was, 1982, and Erich Leinsdorf, strolling musician, was back at Tanglewood, and relishing every minute of it. In front of a class of conducting students at Seranak, he was smoking a cigar, asking pointed questions about scores, and saying, "We are very democratic here. We vote. And those who don't vote go to the State Department." And in front of his old nemesis, the BSO, he was guest-conducting a pair of Schubert-Liszt-Stravinsky programs and calling the orchestra better than it had been in his time.

Erich Leinsdorf instructs the conducting seminar.

Surveying the sun-dappled vista of lake and hills from the front terrace at Seranak, Leinsdorf, now seventy, broke open a fresh cigar from his leather pouch and said in his Viennese accent: "I love it. I love it still and again. We are both delighted — my wife, too. We are having a very good time, and the last few days the weather has also been very nice. So there is nothing left unfulfilled."

Could this be the man who, in his 1976 memoir *Cadenza*, said that Tanglewood "is one place I shall not readily revisit lest one of my most cherished recollections dissolve into gray fog"? Could it be the man who, in his 1981 treatise *The Conductor's Advocate*, said that "I have always refused to teach conducting, supporting my refusal with the argument that the motions are of no consequence"?

Indeed, it was the same Leinsdorf, not mellowed but savoring the role of what he called "a strolling player" — a freelance who, since quitting Boston, had held no permanent position but had roamed the world as a guest conductor. The same hard, clear intelligence was there in his two BSO programs, and the same ice water. But now, without the tensions inherent in the relationship between an orchestra and its music director, he and the BSO could enjoy making music together. In his hands Stravinsky's *Sacre du printemps* emerged in all its vivid and even shocking colors — but also without the visceral excitement that other conductors, like Ozawa, find in it. BSO veterans of the Leinsdorf years spoke no better of him personally but found his economy of gesture and clarity of line refreshing when no longer enforced by the lash of his tongue and power to command their lives.

If hard feelings remained, so did the accomplishments. One of Leinsdorf's undisputed contributions was a reinvigoration of the Music Center after a period of decline under Munch, who took a casual attitude toward teaching. Leinsdorf was also responsible for initiating Tanglewood's Weekend Preludes and attempting program innovations, such as building seasons around anniversaries or themes — an idea that is still trundled out from time to time. It was also during his regime that the Boston Symphony Chamber Players was formed.

Now, back in the classroom, he saw no serious contradiction between his objections to teaching conducting and his role as a conducting teacher. He said one of the greatest problems facing young conductors, dating back at least as far as his own apprentice days in prewar Austria, is the temptation to ape other conductors' recordings. At Seranak he was out to make students look more closely at the scores and at each composer's place in history.

> I show them what enormous musical background — cultural background, because language comes into it, and poetry, and so on — what kind of a background they must have in order to have the right to stand up in front of a hundred people, or if there is a chorus or opera two hundred people, and tell them how the greatest works of these last three hundred years should be performed.

On the podium he found the BSO stronger in every section than it had been in his day, although in *Cadenza* he took great pride in the improvements he had made. "Through normal attrition," he now said, "every vacancy that occurred has obviously been filled with an improvement." Even a strolling musician could command better performances.

Leinsdorf's grievances in Symphony Hall, as recounted in *Cadenza*, were many, but they boiled down to a contention that the orchestra was flabby — it refused to perform on Sundays and it stuck to the rules on overtime — and that the officers and administration were patsies for those lazy musicians. The only part of the BSO that he spared from his indictment was Tanglewood, where, he wrote, he spent "the happiest times of my Boston years." His valedictory Beethoven Ninth on that last day of Tanglewood, 1969, was, by all accounts, a stirring event. But until late 1980, when he relented enough to conduct two sets of Symphony Hall concerts, he made good on his boast never to return. Finally, by 1982, he and management were ready to try again at Tanglewood.

The other prodigal son who returned to Tanglewood in 1982 was Klaus Tennstedt, the fiery East German émigré who created a sensation in his 1974 BSO debut, which was also his first appearance in the United States. Tennstedt's troubles were also, at one level, temperamental. More fundamentally, they involved qustions of musicianship and technique. He was an unknown when the BSO, having heard of his success a year before with the Toronto Symphony, took a chance on him in 1974. (The Toronto debut followed his defection to the West while on a tour of Sweden in the early 1970s. His wife joined him later. They settled in West Germany, where they still live in Kiel, on the Baltic Sea.) After his acclaimed Boston debut he first conducted at Tanglewood in 1975, again driving critics and the audience into ecstasies with his Bruckner and Beethoven. In the years after that he developed an almost fanatical following with his hot-tempered performances on both sides of the Atlantic. Indeed, he became the only conductor with an organized fan club, the International Klaus Tennstedt Society. The Klausketeers — a moniker the members happily accepted — issued a newsletter documenting their hero's exploits and followed him about from performance to performance, like a claque.

From the start, however, there were technical difficulties in the conducting that troubled some BSO players: a jittery, imprecise beat (which had critics reaching for phrases like "nervous scarecrow" and "demented stork" to describe him). Tempos and dynamics that ran roughshod over scores. Gaps in the repertoire, which was strong in Bruckner, Mahler, and Beethoven (though better in the odd-

Klaus Tennstedt in a fiery moment with the BSO.

numbered symphonies than the even) but thinned out elsewhere. Lapses in accompaniments, which led the orchestra, on at least one occasion, to go on automatic pilot. A growing tendency to talk too much during rehearsals as his English improved. Even those who admired his interpretations suffered disillusionment. After six years of increasingly troubled performances, the BSO decided to give him a rest in 1981.

The BSO is apparently the only orchestra with which Tennstedt has had such a prickly connection. Although reports of difficulties have filtered out of Cleveland, his career with other major orchestras, in terms of public and critical acceptance, has been a nearly unbroken string of successes. A 1982 return to Tanglewood, however, was a bad day at the music factory. Whatever point Tennstedt was trying to make about Stravinsky's *Petrushka,* it was so shakily led and played that the performance broke down at one point and came close to doing so in other spots. Reports from backstage afterward said Tennstedt had apologized to the players for his lapses.

In the years immediately following, Tennstedt made only two more Tanglewood appearances, both the following summer, when he led an incandescent Bruckner Fourth and a ponderous Brahms *Requiem.* By now bad chemistry had set in. Other forces also were at work. Acclaimed like a conquering hero in other musical capitals, Tennstedt was more and more in demand on the international scene and, in 1983, became director of the London Philharmonic Orchestra. Meanwhile, health problems, including throat cancer, were forcing him to cut back. He returned to Boston in 1987 in a pair of well-received programs, but the early passion seemed spent. Like Leinsdorf, who also did not return, Tennstedt had become a strolling visitor from the past.

Sitting on the terrace at Seranak, Leinsdorf had said that in eight days of meetings with the twenty or so student conductors he found only two or three with clear signs of talent. By contrast, the student orchestra, which he led in the last act of *Rosenkavalier* with Phyllis Curtin's students as soloists, was almost *too* good, he said. He gave the example of a cellist who knew an alternate bowing for the opening of Wagner's *Tristan.*

"Listen," he said, "this is already a degree of experience and awareness — that a young kid knows already how many possible bowings there are for the opening of *Tristan* — which outshines some of the conductors, you see. And this is where the problem of the conductor begins and ends." The conductor, in effect, knows less than the people playing for him. He is a *Wunderkind,* a wise guy.

Well, two years later at Tanglewood another BSO prodigal and *Wunderkind* returned. Michael Tilson Thomas, an older and wiser thirty-nine, was back. Missing for ten years, Thomas returned to conduct two BSO programs, one all-Russian (he was restudying the Russian orchestral literature), the other a mix of Beethoven, Ravel, and Barber. And he admitted that, yes, he had been a bit of a know-it-all when he was the BSO's assistant conductor in the late 1960s and early 1970s. But his youth and inexperience, he said, made him do it.

Anyone could have picked him out on the grounds. With his white sleeveless on over his white shirt and slacks, he was the only person wearing a sweater at Tanglewood on Parade on one of the hottest days of the year. He said the heat did not bother him; he had come from Los Angeles, where the weather was worse. Besides, he said, "It's just a question of what you've made up your mind to experience and do at that particular time."

What the BSO experienced until the time of Thomas's more or less mysterious disappearance from the podium was increasing irritation. After two spectacularly successful summers as a Tanglewood conducting fellow — he won the Koussevitzky Prize in 1968 and served as Leinsdorf's assistant the next year — Thomas became the BSO's assistant conductor in the fall of 1969 in Steinberg's first season as director. But Steinberg was a sick man, and in the middle of a Carnegie Hall concert that October he could not finish.

Enter Michael Tilson Thomas, born in Los Angeles only twenty-four years before. He not only completed the concert, gaining national attention for doing it, but went on to lead the BSO in thirty-seven more of Steinberg's programs during the rest of the season. Critics and the public were talking of a second Leonard Bernstein in the BSO's midst.

But something went wrong. After those thirty-seven concerts Thomas appeared less and less on the BSO podium. In 1971 he became director of the Buffalo Philharmonic, which Steinberg himself once had led. He officially remained associate conductor in Boston until 1974 but was clearly in disfavor. His BSO association ended with a pair of concerts during the 1975-76 season. There never was any official explanation of the rupture; who, after all, publicizes the details of a messy divorce? But neither was there much doubt that BSO veterans had had enough of the brash youngster who was constantly brushing the forelock out of his face.

Then in December 1983 the BSO brought Thomas back for a pair of programs in Boston, just as, three years earlier, it had brought back Leinsdorf. Orchestra members were impressed. They spoke of the former *Wunderkind*'s probing mind and concern with the music rather than his own image, although no one had doubted his talent right from the start. The kid's grown up, they said.

With a laugh, Thomas said he was glad to be, like Leinsdorf, a musician from a previous "geological era" who was returning to the fold. Only in looking back, he said, did he realize how much

Michael Tilson Thomas in the Green Room.

of a brat he might have seemed to others during his Boston years. But, he added,

> I don't know how I could have survived, how I could have managed to do the things that I did at that age as rapidly as I did them, and with as much midnight oil in preparing pieces the night before for very important performance opportunities, without a very strong sense of ego — you know, a feeling of "I am doing this and I am meant to do this and I am going to do it." That may have affected certain people as being cocky or arrogant, but wasn't consciously designed to be so. I was just trying to proceed and get a lot of things done.

Since that geological era Thomas had learned and performed opera and chamber and contemporary music in addition to the standard symphonic repertoire. He had embarked on a series of Gershwin performances and recordings, which culminated in Broadway productions, and worked the repertoire from the classical period with the English Chamber Orchestra. He quit the Buffalo in 1979, becoming, like Leinsdorf, a strolling conductor with no permanent position of his own. He served as director of the Los Angeles Philharmonic's institute for young conductors — a program, based on Tanglewood's, that he and Bernstein helped to launch in 1982. And in 1986 he spent the first of three summers as director of the Great Woods performing arts center near Boston, where the Pittsburgh Orchestra is in residence.

Thomas's Tanglewood return reflected his new ventures and re-thinking of the old. Tchaikovsky's Fourth and Beethoven's *Pastorale*, the centerpieces of the two programs, sounded fresh in the stripped-down conceptions but also, at times, choppy or reticent, as if he were afraid to let his feelings out. The BSO, however, thought enough of the concerts to bring Thomas back in succeeding years for more chamber-style performances by a big orchestra, along with an in-fusion of Gershwin. The *Wunderkind* had grown up. But he was also, in some ways, still the *Wunderkind*, fussing with the music as well as illuminating it.

Looking back on his early Tanglewood days, Thomas recalled a dinner with Bernstein and Aaron Copland, who was then chairman of the faculty, at one of the Berkshires' tonier restaurants. It seems Bernstein challenged his young colleague to show how much he knew about Gilbert and Sullivan. Thomas began singing some of the patter songs, and Bernstein soon joined in, much to Copland's embarrassment as diners began looking and listening. The discus-sion turned to Stravinsky's *Les Noces*, a work for voices with heavy percussion accompaniment. Warming up to their act, all three men proceeded to sing through the piece, using knives, forks, glasses, plates, and anything else available as the percussion battery. Every once in a while Copland complained, "Fellows, we can't do this — stop it!" But, Thomas said, the momentum was irresistible, and "I think the diners were amused."

Thomas said he looks at his scores from that period and finds them a "wonderful scribble" of red, blue, green, and purple crayon markings, penciled notations, strikeouts, revisions, pasteovers. But now he was moving into "a whole new generation of scores." Each "tends to be a much clearer road map of the interpretive priorities I've decided upon." His ideas would continue to change, he said, "but certain of the architectural foundations are set." The ideal was "to arrive at a performance that is personal, really personal . . . an organic, humanist, life-involved performance of the piece, in which your own experiences and your own personality are truly involved in the music, and vice versa." In the fall of 1988 Thomas became principal conductor of the London Symphony Orchestra. Like Bernstein, he was destined never to direct the fortunes of the BSO, which gave both their start. He was another of the strolling players.

*   *   *

And then there is Bernstein himself, the strolling player *par excellence*. What other guest conductor could turn the place upside down as he did with two soloists he picked — out of the air in one case — for his BSO concerts in 1985 and 1986? One crashed and one soared higher, but both departed with the cachet of a debut with the Boston Symphony Orchestra under Leonard Bernstein at Tanglewood.

"Incredible!" Marek Drewnowski murmured, over and over. He wandered around in a daze. For him, it was "total absolute destiny" to be making his American debut — his first appearance anywhere outside the Soviet bloc as a symphony orchestra soloist — with Leonard Bernstein at Tanglewood.

An international dragnet brought the thirty-nine-year-old Polish pianist to the Berkshires for that improbable Saturday night in 1985. A year and a half earlier Bernstein, an insomniac, had tuned in WNCN-FM, a New York classical music station, one night when he could not sleep. A recording of some Scarlatti keyboard sonatas came over the air. The pianist's name did not ring a bell but something in the playing caught Bernstein's ear. The next morning he dialed his assistants in New York and asked them to find the pianist. Before it was over, those assistants would ransack Europe to locate Marek Drewnowski. When he finally made it to Tanglewood, they told their BSO counterparts they thought Bernstein had "lost his mind" to go to the trouble over an unknown Pole with no career and no prospect of a career.

Drewnowski appeared more like the one unhinged by the experience. Drifting about Tanglewood between practice sessions and rehearsals, the slender, good-natured, slightly absent-minded pianist kept murmuring in his fractured English, "Incredible. Incredible. A dream." Or, switching to Italian, he would exclaim, "*Avventura!*"

Stymied in their careers at home, Drewnowski and his wife Anna, a violinist, had left Poland five years before with their three-year-old son to seek performing opportunities in the West. They wound up in Rome, where Anna Drewnowska found work as a member of the Academy of Santa Cecilia, a well-known orchestra. Marek played recitals in Rome, Milan, Paris, and a scattering of smaller European cities but could get no major engagements. He was "absolutely unknown" in the West, he said. Back in Poland as a student and young concert artist, he explained, switching to French and raising his eyes skyward, he had thought of Bernstein as *"un dieu dans le ciel."* But Bernstein was never a god who would track him down and ask him to perform, least of all at Tanglewood.

It had to be destiny that brought him here, Drewnowski said. He had not played a concerto in public since leaving Poland and desperately needed the break. He had "dreamed of coming to America" to rebuild his career. But what were a poor émigré's chances of its happening? "Incredible."

If it were anyone less than Bernstein, it might not have happened. WNCN denied it had aired any Scarlatti sonatas when Bernstein thought he had heard them. The station had never heard of the record or the pianist. Bernstein must have made a mistake. That, at any rate, was the report to Bernstein from his sleuths at Amberson, Inc., the corporation that manages his affairs. Bernstein, whose ears seldom make mistakes, refused to accept the answer. He said to try again.

Persistence paid. It turned out the WNCN engineer on duty during the mystery hour had not been able to find the record scheduled to be played during that time slot. To fill the space, he grabbed a record off the shelf. It was a disc of Scarlatti sonatas that had apparently come in unsolicited from the Polish company Polskie Nagrania.

Now the Amberson gumshoes were armed with the name of the pianist and his record label. The next step, since they were dealing with a European record company, was to put Bernstein's company, Deutsche Grammophon, on the trail. The Hamburg-based concern drew a blank when it sent a telegram to Pagart, the state agency that manages Polish musicians. Pagart said Marek Drewnowski was no longer under contract and it could provide no information about him.

There matters stood until, a few weeks later, Bernstein's phone rang. It was Drewnowski. As Amberson and Deutsche Grammophon pursued their habeas corpus, Pagart had finally sent a telegram to

Drewnowski in Rome, telling him to get in touch with Deutsche Grammophon because Leonard Bernstein wanted to speak to him.

Drewnowski thought it was a joke. He called Deutsche Grammophon only because he could not understand why anybody would play such a trick on him. Deutsche Grammophon told him it was no joke and he should call Harry Kraut, the former BSO staff member who was now at Amberson as Bernstein's manager. Drewnowski called and Kraut gave him Bernstein's number.

Bernstein, it turned out, was to be in Milan in June 1984, about three months later, to assist in the production of his operas *Trouble in Tahiti* and *A Quiet Place* (a sequel) at La Scala. Kraut made arrangements for Drewnowski to travel up from Rome to audition for Bernstein in Milan.

The audition was pretty much a waste, Drewnowski said. He played three or four short pieces, but Bernstein was absorbed in details of the operas and barely listened. He asked Drewnowski to come back the next week.

Again Drewnowski took the train up from Rome. This time Bernstein hardly let him say hello before making him sit down and play. As they conversed in Italian Bernstein said he liked the audition and wanted Drewnowski to appear as a soloist with him. But he was surprised to discover a man still in his late thirties. From the recording, Drewnowski said, laughing at the image of himself, "he thought I would be an old man with a long white beard — very conservative."

If Bernstein was surprised, William Bernell, then the BSO's artistic administrator, went into something like shock when Bernstein called early in 1985 to discuss details of his Tanglewood program. The conversation went something like this:

Bernstein: "I want to play an all-Brahms program."

Bernell: "Yes, of course, Lenny, that's fine with us."

"I want to do the First Piano Concerto."

"Yes, Lenny, we can do that."

"I want Marek Drewnowski as my soloist."

"Marek who!? Marek what!?"

Nevertheless, an all-Brahms program it became, with the D Minor Concerto and the First Symphony, and Drewnowski as the soloist.

Unable to bring his wife along on his BSO fee, Drewnowski traveled to the Berkshires alone. He flew from Rome to New York and took a bus from there to Lenox. (*"Boh-nahn-zah!"* he said, savoring the name of the bus line on his tongue.) Bernstein meanwhile arrived from a conducting engagement in Chicago. While the Maestro stayed in a private home in Great Barrington and drove about in his beige Mercedes convertible, Drewnowski moved out of the pricey Berkshire inn into which the BSO had booked him. He found the back room oppressive and the rate too steep. The BSO arranged for him to put up at Seranak, where he slept in Koussevitzky's old room.

Twilight faded into a perfect Tanglewood evening, starry, comfortable, and clear. It was the night of the annual Serge and Olga Koussevitzky Memorial Concert, Tanglewood's most prestigious event, traditionally led by its most prestigious alumnus, Leonard Bernstein. A king-sized audience of 15,000, attracted by Bernstein, the weather, and perhaps a whiff of mystery about the pianist, packed the lawn and Shed. The crush in the parking lots and at the gates delayed the start of the concert by fifteen minutes. But somewhere in the crowd were New York critics and managers who could help to make Drewnowski's dream come true if he made the right kind of impression.

The public dress rehearsal that morning had gone badly. Drewnowski, playing the long, gnarled concerto in public for the first time since a student performance in Poland fifteen years before, muffed notes and played with a shallow tone and little consistency. The audience of more than 6,000 seemed to throw him. Now, looking dazed, he walked onstage with the master to open the evening concert before an even larger crowd.

The Brahms D Minor Concerto occupies a curious niche in Bernstein history. In 1962, at a concert with the New York Philharmonic, he stood before the audience and read a speech disassociating himself from the performance he was about to conduct. Glenn Gould was the soloist. Bernstein said he would perform the concerto Gould's way out of respect for him as an artist, but the conception was too slow and grandiose for him to swallow.

It was as if Gould's ghost had now come to visit. Both the concerto and the First Symphony, which followed the intermission, moved at a broad, grandiose, magisterial — not to say glacial — pace, in keeping with Bernstein's latter-day style. Blazing detail stoked the fires of drama.

Marek Drewnowski is applauded by Leonard Bernstein and the BSO after his performance of Brahms's Piano Concerto no. 1 with Bernstein.

Whatever Marek Drewnowski thought or felt about the D Minor Concerto, he was not a Glenn Gould. After a few unsettled moments at the beginning he summoned muscle and tone enough to bring off Brahms's massive trills and octave passages. Yet at the heart of the playing lay a gentleness that colored the music differently. It must have been that dreamy, almost ingenuous quality that attracted Bernstein to Drewnowski's playing on the radio and in Rome. But there was also something malleable in the playing that allowed Bernstein to bend the soloist and performance to his wishes, putting his stamp on both. Perhaps, backstage, it was even necessary for him to shake Drewnowski out of his reveries. Unlike Gould a quarter-century before, Drewnowski was not going to quarrel with destiny or question a god in heaven.

At the end Bernstein and Drewnowski embraced onstage and the audience awarded them a generous ovation, though one lacking in the usual Bernstein lightning and thunder. (The noisy demonstration was reserved for Bernstein alone after the symphony.) During the intermission Bernstein sent word out to the critics via his press representative, Margaret Carson, that Drewnowski's playing had met his expectations. That and the BSO fee were all that Marek Drewnowski's breakthrough brought him. After a few days with American friends he flew back to Rome and disappeared again into the obscurity out of which he had briefly and spectacularly emerged.

Only Bernstein could top an act like that. To do it, he had to come up with drama as wildly improbable as a mystery pianist plucked out of the midnight ether. The star's name was Midori. She was fourteen years old.

Despite her years and lack of a last name, the young violinist was hardly a mystery. Just a year before, she and Bernstein had toured Europe and Japan together with the European Youth Orchestra, giving a concert in — among other places — Hiroshima on the fortieth anniversary of the first atomic bombing. As an eleven-year-old she had made a solo debut with the New York Philharmonic under Zubin Mehta. Since then, under the guidance of her teacher, the noted Dorothy DeLay of the Juilliard School of Music, she had gone on to a series of carefully selected engagements as a recitalist and soloist with many of the country's major orchestras, on television, and in performance with Isaac Stern and Pinchas Zukerman. Even without Tanglewood it was quite a record for little Midori Goto, who was born in Japan — she herself dropped her last name in 1983 — and lived there until the age of eight, when her mother brought her to the United States to study with DeLay.

Quite a record, but none of it preparation for what happened on the Saturday night of the 1986 Koussevitzky Memorial Concert, with Tanglewood's favorite son on the podium and a rainy-night crowd of nearly 9,000, many of them camping under tents or umbrellas on the lawn.

It was, as far as Tanglewood old-timers could recall (the BSO keeps no record of such things), the first time a child prodigy had appeared on the stage of the Shed. Bernstein towered over her like a gnarled giant as they walked onstage to open the program with his *Serenade* (after Plato's *Symposium*) for solo violin, string orchestra, harp, and percussion. (Tchaikovsky's *Pathétique*, in a performance much like the previous summer's Brahms First, would end the concert.) With her spindly arms protuding from her shiny green dress, Midori looked like a windup doll.

Appearances were misleading. The *Serenade* opens with a long, arching violin solo representing Phaedrus' lyrical oration in praise of Eros in the *Symposium*. From the first note Midori summoned up such command, poise, and sweetness and depth of tone that anyone not looking might have mistaken the violinist for a Perlman. The range of tone colors, effects, and moods that followed — now lyrical, now jesting, now dancing, now brooding — was just as extraordinary. The BSO flattered the solo part with playing of suppleness and transparency. Smiles passing between Midori and Bernstein testified to the totality of the rapport.

Then, five minutes before the end of the half-hour piece, the unexpected happened. The E string on Midori's violin snapped.

Midori was playing a child's violin, seven-eighths the size of an adult instrument. She would have to leave the stage for a new string or switch to someone else's full-sized instrument if the performance was to continue. Without a moment's doubt Midori did exactly what any experienced soloist knows to do in such an extremity. With the same poise she had shown in her opening solo she walked over and lifted concertmaster Malcolm Lowe's Stradivarius out of his hands, giving him her child's instrument in return. Lowe quickly swapped instruments with assistant concertmaster Max Hobart, his stand partner. There was a gap of about a second in the music while Bernstein waited for the two transactions to be completed. The performance resumed so seamlessly that no one hearing it on the broadcast could have guessed at the onstage drama.

A minute later, incredibly, the entire scene was reenacted as the E string on the second violin snapped. This time Midori was near the end of a phrase, and Bernstein, watching her out of the corner of an eye, kept the performance going while she unhesitatingly retraced the ten or so steps to the concertmaster's chair. Lowe again yielded his violin. But now, with Hobart trying to make do on Midori's crippled instrument, the leader of the string section suddenly had neither a usable violin nor anywhere immediate to turn for one. Second violinist Ronald Knudsen quickly passed his instru-

Midori performs Leonard Bernstein's *Serenade* on the fateful night that required three violins.

ment across the aisle. Lowe again rejoined the performance as Midori, missing only a handful of notes, coolly played to the end on Hobart's Guadagnini.

Various musicians advanced explanations for the double dose of bad luck. One blamed the humidity. Another had it that Midori was using extra pressure on her bow to project her sound out into the Shed. The truth was that nobody knew why it had happened. On a cooler night Hobart would have attempted replacement of Midori's string. But because it was warm the BSO men were playing in their shirtsleeves, not their jackets, where they carry spare strings in the pockets.

Near-bedlam broke out after the performance. The audience, transfixed up till then, leapt to its feet in a stamping, whooping, whistling ovation, to which Bernstein added his customary hugs and kisses for his soloist as he and she faced the crowd together. The orchestra, now also standing, joined in the applause, and curtain call followed curtain call. In the mob scene backstage violinist

Harry Ellis Dickson, a forty-eight-year BSO veteran, compared Midori to Yehudi Menuhin, whom he had heard when Menuhin was an eleven-year-old prodigy.

The press coverage — extensive whenever Bernstein is on the podium — was led by the *New York Times,* which put the story on page 1. Television and magazines picked up the beat. An ABC-TV camera crew, dodging thunderstorms, rushed up from New York by helicopter to get film of the concert and interviews about it. The wire services took the picture and story from Massachusetts sources and sent them across the world. Reporters from all points, preceded or followed by camera crews, scrambled for interviews when Midori got home in New York. Soon Midori, or anyone speaking for or about her, was in everybody's newspaper, on everybody's television screen. Even Tanglewood's fiftieth-anniversary celebration the next summer did not generate such a firestorm of publicity. Overnight Midori became not just a child prodigy but a star.

As the hoopla spread, the doll-like violinist, whose artlessness as a person matched her art as a musician, took the sanest attitude of anyone. "What could I do?" she said when the *Times* caught up with her for an interview. "My strings broke, and I didn't want to stop the music."

The success story raised troubling questions, especially in the light of Marek Drewnowski's experience. Two broken strings in a row are a freak occurrence, about as probable — and significant — as consecutive license plate numbers turning up side by side in a Tanglewood parking lot. Yet the story in the media was always, as the *Times*'s page 1 headline put it, "GIRL, 14, CONQUERS TANGLEWOOD WITH 3 VIOLINS." The point was that Midori was a rare and wonderful talent, and her bravery under fire was of a piece with — and incidental to — her poise and mastery as an artist. The interviewers got the point. They got it all too well. They knew that for an audience weaned on show-biz as usual, art was a foreign language. Midori became girl, fourteen, with three violins and Leonard Bernstein in front of several thousand people on a summer's night.

Midori returned to Tanglewood the following summer, performing Paganini's First Concerto with Charles Dutoit as her conductor. She demonstrated the same fire and aplomb, one year further advanced, that she had shown in the Bernstein *Serenade.* Over the two years following her Tanglewood debut she went on to debuts in London and Spain with the London Symphony Orchestra and a Berlin debut with the Berlin Philharmonic; she made a recital tour of Germany and played with — to name only the better-known orchestras — the Orchestre de Paris and the Chicago and Montreal symphonies.

Drewnowski was never heard from again. A handful of American supporters, including pianist Malcolm Frager, who lives a mile up the road from Tanglewood, performs regularly at the festival, speaks Polish, and befriended Drewnowski during his visit, interceded with the BSO and New York management agencies on his behalf. Neither Bernstein nor the BSO would reengage him, and the talent managers said he was not "exciting" enough to market elsewhere in the country. Was Drewnowski Bernstein's discovery or Bernstein's folly? American concertgoers will probably never know. The managers and interviewers were waiting for the next sensation.

* * *

What, then, does make a soloist "exciting"? Dazzling technical skill, musicianship, and a strong, preferably outgoing personality are basic. Household entree via television helps, as does an ethnic identity (consider Midori). And who does not recognize Itzhak Perlman's crutches or American Express card or Luciano Pavarotti's handkerchief? Even in music a trademark never hurts. Stardom such as these gifts and badges confer comes to be like a brand name, which the buying public sees as a guarantee of quality.

Among the stars who have crossed the stage of the Shed over the past decade — Perlman, Mstislav Rostropovich, James Galway, Alfred Brendel, Rudolf Serkin, Jessye Norman, Leontyne Price, and Marilyn Horne are of the legion — few have become as closely identified with Ozawa and the BSO as Yo-Yo Ma. The popular cellist made his BSO debut both in Boston and at Tanglewood in 1983 in the Dvořák concerto. The next year he returned to Tanglewood in Richard Strauss's *Don Quixote,* a performance the BSO took on tour in Europe and later recorded. He has been back regularly ever since, playing both concertos and chamber programs and then spending three weeks in residence in 1987. He is one of a handful of soloists who can be counted on to fill the Shed and — even more exceptional — to justify stage seating for recitals in the Theater–Concert Hall.

Yo-Yo Ma in his role as a soloist.

Ma possesses all the obvious star qualities, plus others that make him especially congenial to Ozawa. Born in Paris in 1955 to Chinese parents (his father was his first teacher), he shares with Ozawa an Oriental background and an instinctive approach to music. Unlike Ozawa, he was educated in the United States. But that very education, which brought him a Harvard degree, gives him a Boston identification other soloists lack. (A resident of Winchester, a Boston suburb, he is, in fact, the only hometown musician to appear regularly as a BSO soloist.) In place of crutches or a hankie, his trademarks are his name and his smile. His frequent recital and chamber music partner, pianist Emanuel Ax, tells how, as a fellow Juilliard student, he for half a year brushed off suggestions that he look up Ma as a possible performing partner, simply because of the improbability of the name.

Ax soon came around, and so did the public. Ma's gift has as much to do with warmth of personality as with style or technique, although his command of the instrument — at once dazzling and natural — makes him the envy of string players. With his boyish smile under the stage lights and with the obvious joy in music making that it radiates, Ma is the sunshine kid of music. For most listeners the combination of attractions is irresistible.

The 1987 residency, a product of Costa Pilavachi's negotiations to put a BSO guest to use at the Music Center, starred the thirty-one-year-old Ma in the new role of teacher. During the three-week period he gave six master classes covering the spectrum from Bach's unaccompanied cello suites to the concerto literature. He also prepared and performed in four Tanglewood programs, including three with Ax, who, finding the Berkshires to his liking, rented half a house in Stockbridge and moved up from New York with his family to spend the entire summer.

Apart from a one-week residency earlier that year at the Gregor Piatigorsky Seminar at the University of Southern California, Ma's only previous classroom experience was an occasional master class. Yet teaching, he said, is something he felt compelled to do. At Tanglewood he tried to do it "in a very intensive form" impossible during the winter, when touring and family life make too many other demands.

By coincidence, it was Matt Haimovitz, a seventeen-year-old cellist who made his BSO debut at Tanglewood that summer, who brought Ma to teaching. Both Ma and Haimovitz studied with Leonard Rose. Rose was "very proud" of Haimovitz, Ma said, and a few months before his death in 1984 the sixty-five-year-old cellist told Ma, "Look, I want you to take him as a student." Ma accepted the challenge. Around the same time he also began giving private lessons to an *au pair* girl helping him and his wife with their two children.

"So suddenly I had two students," Ma said. But because of his mixed liberal arts and conservatory studies at Harvard and Juilliard, he was "always interested in what is the thing that motivates people, that gets people to want to do things, to learn." He found he wanted to teach the cello, but in a way that was "really more music" — the sense of compositions — than manipulation of the instrument. The goal, of course, is precisely Tanglewood's in its student program.

Along came Tanglewood, offering a residency to supplement the teaching by the full-time faculty, which includes no less a cellist than Joel Krosnick of the Juilliard String Quartet, to say nothing of the BSO's principal cellist, Jules Eskin.

> At a certain age, when you're about thirty [Ma said], certain strange things happen. My teacher died, my manager died, a lot of people that you count on aren't there. But also younger people are coming up, who want to learn things. So you're not young any more, and you're not old, either, but you're kind of caught in between.

Ma laughed at the predicament — a happy but slightly nervous laugh. Then he finished: "Suddenly you realize there's a lot that you know you've gotten, and you want to transfer that, in a certain way that you believe in, to another generation that's coming up."

Dressed in jeans and sipping from a can of Coke, Ma listened at the side of the room while the young woman played the prelude to Bach's Suite no. 1 for the class. In the wood-paneled auditorium at Miss Hall's School in Pittsfield, the Tanglewood Music Center's dormitory and home away from home for students, forty students and adult auditors fanned out on plastic chairs, across tabletops, and up the staircase to the balcony. Applause from both class and teacher greeted the young woman's performance, according to master class etiquette. Ma advanced to the center of the room, still applauding.

"Beautiful. Gorgeous. Nice character," he told the student, the familiar smile playing across his boyish features. But in a master class praise is the carrot before the stick. Getting out his cello to illustrate his points, Ma went to work with suggestions for improving her bowing, her phrasing, her sense of Bach's harmonic movement. He made her try the piece his way. It was tough going. She could not, for instance, get the variety he wanted in a series of running sixteenth notes. Each time they came out sounding alike.

"The best thing that can happen from that is that you put people in a trance," he finally told her. He urged her to give certain notes — whichever ones struck her as most important — "an extra push."

Then the carrot: "You have such a nice pulse [rhythm] that you can afford to do it," he assured her.

After thirty-five minutes the student's trial by fire was over. Ma told her and the rest of the class that the goal should be the freedom to choose among possible ways to play a piece. When you can go seven different ways with it, he said, "it can be a source of unbelievable joy."

The young woman was one of four students to go before Ma during the 2¼-hour session on the Bach suites. The next two volunteers, both women again, also played preludes from the suites. Understanding of the music took precedence over dexterity. Trying to get at the essence — to teach music rather than cello — Ma told one player, "It's a very large piece. It's about the world. He's giving you this in a two-octave range, and you have to describe the world. It's like you have to describe the world in thirty words."

Ma's other master classes described the worlds of the cello-piano sonata, chamber music, and the concerto. In two concerto sessions — one each with the Music Center Orchestra and the high-school-aged Boston University Young Artists Orchestra — student cellists took turns as soloists in readings under student conductors. The sessions also provided lessons in the art of accompanying. Each cellist returned to his place in the orchestra to assist when others played solo parts. Maurice Abravanel, Leon Fleisher, and other faculty members joined Ma in giving pointers.

Ma found the concerto sessions especially productive. Musicians, he said, should feel "completely involved in whatever they do. No matter if they're sitting last stand inside in the orchestra or whether they're playing solo, it's the same music." If players "don't feel they're contributors, they're not going to be contributors." In the concerto readings the student cellists supported one another "like crazy," Ma said. "Whenever one guy came on and played, everybody was rooting for him. And, boy, that is the only way to study music. Unfortunately, it's not always the case."

The classes bore fruit in a performance of the Mendelssohn Octet that traveled to the Mostly Mozart Festival in New York. Ma and another long-time chamber music partner, violinist Young Uck Kim, coached and then performed the piece with the Shanghai String Quartet — one of two resident student ensembles that summer — and two other fellows, violinist Katie Lansdale and violist Judith Ablon. Tanglewood and Mostly Mozart occasionally share professional ensembles and performances. This performance, modeled on

Pianist Emanuel Ax and cellist Yo-Yo Ma require stage seating to accommodate the overflow audiences at their joint recitals.

the touring Music from Marlboro programs, was a rare instance of students joining professionals to take a Tanglewood offering on the road.

Ma's four concerts during his residency included a BSO program with Ozawa, in which he played concertos by Boccherini and Shostakovich, and a performance of the Beethoven Triple Concerto at Tanglewood on Parade. In the Beethoven Ax and Kim were his partners, and Ozawa conducted the Music Center Orchestra — another case of professionals performing with students, now before a large Tanglewood crowd. In the Theater–Concert Hall Ma and Ax played a recital together. A week later Kim joined them in an all-Dvořák trio program. Both concerts had been sold out almost as soon as they were announced in March. Concertgoers began queuing up before noon for the ninety stage seats put on sale on the day of the programs.

Although Ma and Ax had been playing together for seven years by then, there were (and are) differences in style between them.

Some cellists, like Rostropovich, soar like eagles; Ma's litheness suggests a gazelle. Ax's playing, on the other hand, has a more probing, inward quality. Differences like these can cause musicians to fly apart rather than pull together. Yet when Ma and Ax perform, communication is complete. In a Tanglewood talk that summer Ax said that the partnership "is just as exciting as it ever was, and maybe more so."

Ax, who has a wry, self-deprecating sense of humor, described the Ax-Ma-Kim trio as probably the shortest-named trio in the history of music. He said Ma, Kim, and he were "very good and old friends" who had been playing together for five years. On tours, he said, Kim is the "absolute arbiter" with hotels and restaurants, handling all hassles at the desk while his partners politely fade into the background. As for the others' duties, Ax said, "Yo-Yo generally makes sure that I dress decently, and I'm the one that carries all the music."

At Miss Hall's the last of the evening's four students was neither a woman nor a Bach exponent. Instead, a young man played the second movement of Prokofiev's bristling Symphony-Concerto, with a student as his accompanist in a piano reduction of the orchestral part. The cellist declared himself "scared to death" to play for Ma, but the fifteen-minute performance sent sparks flying.

At the end Ma staggered out of the back of the room, where he had gone to listen. "Whew!" he said, mopping his brow. "I have nothing to say! That was absolutely unbelievable!"

The young man had something to say. He was not satisfied with the sound he was producing. He did not think it was "getting down to the core of the note."

Ma observed that he had played the piece only once himself and was not sure he could help. Upon reflection he agreed that there was something unfocused about the student's sound. And so the last fifteen minutes of the class became a seminar on sound production, Ma offering suggestions on how to both tighten up and loosen up through bowings and fingerings. In one place, he said, Prokofiev's music actually requires an ugly sound, "like lemon juice and sand." Summing up the evening's lessons, he told the class that the performer must, above all, find the character of the music. "And anything you can do, increase the whole character. Go for the whole beanbag."

The young man, Ma said later, not only played well but recognized his own weakness. He had deliberately chosen the difficult Prokofiev work, he told Ma, because he wanted to challenge himself. That kind of dedication, the weary but exhilarated Ma said as his three-week visit was ending, is what makes the school the "pulse" of Tanglewood — "a place that will make people have individual voices" as musicians. And it is voice, he said, that gives a musician his character and identity, for better or for worse.

The residency, Ma said, was a thrill: because of the teaching and beauty of the surroundings "you wake up in the morning and say, 'I'm really lucky to be here!'" Tanglewood, which sees honored guests come and go for reasons both honorable and equivocal, thought it was lucky to have him. It brought him back for another residency the following year.

* * *

Like the hero in an opera, Thomas D. Perry, Jr., was a long time in saying farewell.

Perry was counting the days until September 1, 1978, when he could retire as the BSO's chief operating officer. December came and he was still counting. Thomas W. Morris, the man he had groomed as his successor, had come down with mononucleosis during the Tanglewood season and had not yet recovered. Instead of sitting and working around his house on the Berkshire mountainside as he had dreamed of doing, Perry was traveling back and forth to his old desk in Boston.

Perry insisted the BSO staff was doing all the work. All he was doing was "sort of helping to hold things together." But that kind of talk fooled no one who knew how Perry had held things together in his low-keyed way at Symphony Hall and Tanglewood for twenty-four years.

Perry is the man some concertgoers know through the tuxedos he wore to Tanglewood concerts — probably the only person so turned out in the entire audience — until he yielded to the times and switched to a business suit the summer before his retirement.

Others know him through the 1936 Ford convertible in which he chugged around the Berkshires, occasionally with guests who had bought their rides in the BSO's fund-raising marathon.

Others remember his memorabilia-stuffed office under the trees

Thomas D. Perry, Jr., in his memorabilia-filled cabin when he was the
BSO's executive director.

at Tanglewood, which he called Uncle Tom's Cabin and which Morris (though also a Tom) disdained in favor of a cubbyhole nearer
the orchestra in the Shed.

Others recall, with a feeling of happy satiety, the banquet-like
picnics the Perrys spread in the Tanglewood Tent and at parties and
receptions at their home.

Others, with long memories of Tanglewood, may recall Perry as
the man who in the late 1940s tried to make women in shorts cover
up. The offenders promptly pilfered the wraparound skirts, with the
name Tanglewood prominently displayed on them, that they received at the gates. The scheme was one of what Perry remembers
as "a number of plans I had that were no damn good." (Another
such scheme was a movie about Koussevitzky to be shown after
Tanglewood concerts to keep listeners around longer and thus thin
out traffic jams. Koussey vetoed the plan.)

Still other habitués, especially BSO members, will recall Perry as
the infamous author of memos. There was the classic, for example,
limiting cars on the Tanglewood grounds to those bearing "burdens." It cautioned that "with the exception of certain world-

famous conductors and other performing luminaries, 'PERSONS' are not construed as 'BURDENS.' ''

This is the man who said of his tenure that ''the major achievement is that I survived and the orchestra survived.'' Then, on reconsideration, he modestly allowed that ''the orchestra is in terrific condition, and that's the major achievement.''

The Perry–BSO love affair began in the summer of 1940, when Tod — the name everyone calls him — and his newlywed wife, Helen, arrived at Tanglewood to take part in the inaugural session of the Music Center. Perry, out of Yale in 1935 and then running the concert program at the Curtis Institute of Music in Philadelphia, came ''just to be in a musical setting'' rather than for any particular studies. The final report for the season shows that in a student production of Handel's opera *Acis and Galatea* the costumes were by Helen Perry and the properties by Tod Perry. One Tod Perry also danced in the show.

From Tanglewood Perry graduated into managerial duties at two concert halls in Boston, with two years out in the middle for service as a pharmacist's mate in the navy. Then in 1946 George Judd, the BSO's manager, took Perry on as an assistant. When Judd retired in 1954 after forty years with the orchestra, Perry succeeded him.

Just as Judd had spent eight years grooming Perry, Perry spent five years grooming Morris. In 1973, to begin the transition, Perry moved up from manager to the newly created position of executive director — the job from which he finally retired early in 1979 — and Morris became manager. The division of duties put Perry in charge of long-range planning (scheduling of major musical events, fund drives, and the like) and relations with the trustees, while Morris took over operational responsibilities for the orchestra. When Morris moved into the big office one story above noisy Massachusetts Avenue in Boston, the two jobs became one again.

Looking to both past and future, Perry said:

I am an immense admirer of Seiji Ozawa, among other things, and I would like to keep in touch with him. I have a sort of sappy but happy attitude toward music, and I am very grateful to many, many musicians for all the pleasure they have given me. Of the four main operating elements of the orchestra, I think they're in very good condition. The music director is terrific. The orchestra's ability to play music and its spirits are very high. The present board of trustees is absolutely great. The management team I see around me is very good, indeed. . . . With those four elements in excellent condition, I feel perfectly justified in putting my hat on and going off to read a book.

The place that Perry, then sixty-four, and Helen went off to was the country home they had built fifteen years before three miles west of Tanglewood. On a mountainside with rolling views of the valley, and the Ozawas just up the road, the house had served until then as a summer and weekend retreat. (On winter weekends the couple would put on snowshoes and trek in over the long, winding driveway from the road.) But that spring, just before the Tanglewood season began, the Perrys gave up their Boston apartment and landed in the Berkshires in what he called "a great big heap."

Perry's goal for the first year of retirement was simple:

I want to watch the year come and the year go, the birds come and the birds go, the colors come and the colors go. I want to read a book. I want to play the piano. I want to listen to some music that is not symphonic. I want to listen to chamber music. I have rediscovered the human voice. One thing I want to do is finish my house.

There was no danger Perry would become a recluse. At a farewell party at Tanglewood the trustees gave him and Helen plane tickets to Greece for a vacation with their son Thomas III and his wife. (There is another son, Rodney.) Their presence at Tanglewood was also assured. The BSO staff gave them a bronzed lifetime pass to their box, no. 27, and a permanent plaque for their old parking space near the Main Gate. In the final Tanglewood program book for the year, the staff paid tribute to Perry's "stylishness and charm, grace and humor, warmth and common sense." And to draw on his experience the BSO trustees that fall elected him to the board.

Unlike Perry, a music lover but no musician, Thomas W. Morris is a percussionist who, when an extra body was needed onstage, would go out and whack a drum or cymbal. He also brought a different management style to the big office. Perry, as the staff's tribute suggested, is a gentleman of the old school, still trim in his seventies. (It was that gentlemanliness that apparently drove Leinsdorf up a tree. The conductor called Perry a pushover for both the players under him and the trustees over him.) Morris, a graduate of the Wharton School of Finance, took a harder-nosed approach to running the business. But he was also a practical joker, and one of the high points of his Tanglewood summers was the treasure hunt he laid out for staff members, leading them across the lower half of Berkshire County in the middle of the night. His masterpiece was the night when, by arrangement with the State Police, everyone who finished the course was thrown into jail as a prize. In Boston the staff retaliated for such stunts one April Fool's Day by planting a vine in the manager's private toilet.

Morris resigned in 1985, worn down by the administrative pressures, which he said distracted him from the primary task of organizing concerts. His seven years were marked by controversy, most conspicuously litigation and a public uproar when Vanessa Redgrave's pro-Palestinian activities led to cancellation of a BSO production of Stravinsky's *Oedipus Rex*, in which she was to have been the narrator. (Sam Wanamaker eventually became both director and narrator for the 1982 Tanglewood performance.) After a vacation Morris set himself up as an orchestral consultant, operating partly out of London.

After a year-long search, during which assistant manager Daniel Gustin filled in as acting manager, the BSO named a surprise successor to Morris, Kenneth Haas, the Cleveland Orchestra's general manager. The surprise was not Haas's record; insiders and outsiders agreed he was one of the best in the business. It was that, after sixteen years of success in Cleveland, he would make the lateral move to the less stable position in Boston. But it was precisely the challenge of a new situation, in a somewhat larger organization, that appealed to him, he said.

A few months later a bigger surprise burst. As Haas's successor the Cleveland hired Morris. The two orchestras, in effect, swapped top managers — the equivalent, more or less, of the Red Sox swapping with the Indians.

Under Haas, a bearded six-foot-seven giant and long-distance bicyclist, the BSO entered a new period of orderly change such as it had enjoyed during Perry's reign. But something was lost even as something was gained. And what was lost was personified by the man in the blue suit, with the wildflower as a boutonniere, sitting in box 27.

Perry is one of the last veterans to have known and worked with Koussevitzky. The chief bearer of the tradition, Koussevitzky's widow Olga, died in 1978 at the age of seventy-six. Through her final summer she had been a constant presence at Tanglewood, living at Seranak, attending concerts and rehearsals, taking a personal interest in students, greeting visitors, and giving her reminiscence of Koussevitzky each year at the Music Center's opening exercises. One by one over the years Koussevitzky's old players retired or died. When Perry went off to read his book, the connection in the executive offices was broken. In a new time new men would do things (including hiring a woman, Anne H. Parsons, as orchestra manager) in new ways.

Perry remained, by his own description, a "compulsive concertgoer" — nowhere more so than at Tanglewood, where he now could listen and greet friends in box 27 without worry about backstage emergencies. He also remained a trustee for eight years. But with his seventy-third birthday coming up on December 31, 1986 — he passed the milestone "without a tremor," he said — he faced the mandatory retirement age for board members. At the end of Tanglewood 1986 he again passed through the Main Gate into retirement, becoming a trustee emeritus.

Tod and Helen skipped town that August. For the first time in forty years of Tanglewood-going they missed an entire month of concerts. (The most before had been a week.) They flew off to a vacation in a borrowed house in a village on the Seine about fifty miles below Paris. The village is so small they could not even find it on the map.

Preparing to depart, Perry said he still loves the BSO, "one of the great institutions." He still loves Tanglewood, where, "just walking across the lawn on a pleasant day, you see all sorts of people you'd like to know better." And he still loves "everything about the Berkshires, including the climate." That is more than many a winter-weary resident will say.

No longer a BSO insider, Perry took his place, along with Phyllis Curtin, Maurice Abravanel, and assorted conductors and soloists — many of whom he had once hired — among Tanglewood's honored guests.

Chapter IV

MUSIC CENTER

E VERYONE WHO GETS
to know Tanglewood well comes to the same conclusion: the Music
Center is the heart of the place.

Getting into Koussevitzky's school is not easy. There are ten applicants for each of the hundred and forty to hundred and fifty full-
tuition fellowships awarded each summer. The auditioning process
for applicants can be grueling, as conducting students find when
they go before a professional orchestra and a jury of faculty conductors on the Symphony Hall stage. Once admitted, a student faces
a demanding routine of classes, rehearsal, and performance in both
orchestral work and smaller ensembles. Occasional parties provide relief, and who should show up once a year to party till dawn
with students but Tanglewood's most famous alumnus, Leonard
Bernstein?

In its inner workings, too, the Music Center can be less than a
summer idyll. The current director is Leon Fleisher, a brilliant pianist who had to give up a performing career in the 1960s because
of a hand injury. He succeeded Gunther Schuller, a composer, conductor, writer, and teacher who resigned in an angry protest against
the BSO and Seiji Ozawa. He accused them of compromising the
school's artistic integrity by catering to commercial interests.

Only a year before, Schuller himself had been the target of a
protest resignation. In that controversy Paul Fromm, the chief patron of Tanglewood's Festival of Contemporary Music and a leading
supporter of new music in the United States, withdrew his support,
accusing Schuller of giving the programming a narrow, academic
emphasis. The irony took a further twist when Oliver Knussen, an
English composer and former protégé of Schuller's, succeeded him

as director of contemporary music activities and put some of Fromm's favored composers on the program.

Tanglewood's most celebrated teacher, of course, is Bernstein, who returns to the Music Center for one to two weeks nearly every year — even in years when he has been in seclusion or boycotting the BSO — to lead the conducting seminar and student orchestra. The full-time faculty is built around a nucleus of first-chair BSO players but also includes such distinguished string players as Louis Krasner and Eugene Lehner, who knew Bartók, Schoenberg, and Berg in prewar Vienna, and pianists Gilbert Kalish and Peter Serkin. Other teachers range from soprano Elly Ameling, who gives an occasional master class, to cellist Joel Krosnick, who is present for the entire summer and lends a special intensity. Krosnick has taught both individually and as a member of the Juilliard Quartet, which spent a summer at Tanglewood while regrouping with a new violinist. During that summer there were two quartets from the Juilliard School of Music in residence, the professional group teaching and performing, a younger group studying as the first ensemble admitted in a new Tanglewood residency program.

While attending that student quartet's final concert, Leon Fleisher spoke a truth that sooner or later impresses habitués: although summer is normally a time of rest for musicians, the intensity of the work and friendships at Tanglewood makes it a place where summer is the main musical season and winter is only preparation.

*　　*　　*　　*　　*

It comes down to this: You have spent most of your young life studying and working to become a conductor. Now you are in Boston, on the stage of Symphony Hall, about to have the audition that determines whether you will go to Tanglewood to study.

You're nervous. You have twelve minutes with a pick-up orchestra and you must impress a jury made up of Seiji Ozawa, Gunther Schuller, Maurice Abravanel, and Gustav Meier, veteran conductors all. The opportunity to work with some of the masters — Ozawa, Kurt Masur, and Erich Leinsdorf this summer, Leonard Bernstein, Klaus Tennstedt, and André Previn among those in other years — hangs in the balance. Being seen and heard in such company, and maybe winning the Koussevitzky Prize, can mean recognition, job offers, invitations to other podiums. You know that Tanglewood has launched the careers of Bernstein, Zubin

Mehta, Claudio Abbado, Lorin Maazel, and Ozawa himself. The orchestra of twenty-three Boston professionals — strangers to you — will play the assigned excerpts from Mozart, Stravinsky, and Debussy-Schoenberg exactly as you direct, mistakes and all. Two to six conductors will win fellowships. You think you're good enough. But have you ever been up against competition and judges like these before?

Twelve men in their twenties and early thirties submitted to this special brand of torture on a spring day in 1982 — a typical Tanglewood audition year — when others their age were running a few blocks away in the Boston Marathon. The competitors in both events were an elite from Europe, Asia, and the Americas, the competitions themselves world events. Trial heats in both had weeded out the less fit. Tanglewood's twelve finalists were the survivors from preliminary auditions held the previous day, in which twenty-six men and two women had gone before the same orchestra in a Symphony Hall rehearsal room.

Those twenty-eight candidates were, in turn, part of a still larger body of thirteen hundred musicians who auditioned for Tanglewood at thirteen locations across the United States, from Boston to Los Angeles, from Chicago to the University of Texas. To the best would go the 140 to 150 fellowships that the BSO awards each summer to conductors, composers, singers, pianists, and other instrumentalists. Each would receive eight tuition-free weeks of study, with free room and board for those who needed it, at the Tanglewood Music Center. Whether still in conservatories or universities or already out earning a living, these students planned to make their lives in music. Tanglewood expects them to have mastered their instruments. There is, in fact, no instruction on instruments as such. Music Center activities concentrate instead on ensemble work — preparing and playing music in groups.

Failure to get into Tanglewood does not necessarily spell the end of a career. But again and again applicants — both winners and losers — have said that the Tanglewood audition is the most important one, and therefore the most nerve-racking, up to that point in their lives. That is how coveted Tanglewood study is.

In the half-century since Serge Koussevitzky realized his dream of an academy where the best young musicians of the day would work side by side with the best professionals, other institutions like it have sprung up across the country. But the Tanglewood Music

Center remains not only the most venerable of these summer academies but also the one where expense-paid study and performing opportunities — and experience with master performers — cover the widest territory. What Ozawa, Bernstein, and others are for the conducting fellows, first-chair BSO players and leading soloists, chamber players, and composers are for other students. With those opportunities come the enriching lessons of BSO rehearsals and concerts and visiting artists' concerts and master classes. Schuller, the former artistic director of the Music Center, once described it as a "last haven" where young musicians could "dedicate themselves more or less freely to their art," unencumbered by financial worries, degree requirements, or "the jobbing and gigging scene" they would encounter when, soon enough, they scrabbled for work.

You mount the podium, perhaps remembering to shake the concertmistress's hand. The judges are sitting at two tables at the back of the cello section. Schuller, who clearly is running the show, tells you, "Start with the Mozart, please." You raise your baton and bring the orchestra in. The overture to The Magic Flute *wells out through the hall, whose rich acoustics make your small band take on some of the sheen of the BSO itself. You realize —* miraculous! *— that you are working on the stage of one of the acoustically great concert halls of the world, one of the three greatest, as a matter of fact, along with Amsterdam's Concertgebouw and Vienna's Musikverein.*

As you conduct, Schuller confers with Abravanel, who will be the acting director of the Center this summer while Schuller goes on a sabbatical. Ozawa quietly beats time with his fingertips on the table, checking your tempo and rhythm. You go through the slow introduction and bring the orchestra in, forte, at the allegro. *Then, just as you're really getting into the piece, Schuller taps his pen loudly on the table. That's all of* The Magic Flute *that the judges want to hear.*

The auditioning process begins in February each year. Although some details differ under Schuller's successor, Leon Fleisher, the system remains unchanged. So does the objective: to make sure that the most promising of those thirteen hundred applicants get to Tanglewood.

For two months before the conducting auditions Schuller and three colleagues from the Music Center faculty — Louis Krasner, the noted violinist and teacher; Roger Voisin, the BSO's retired principal trumpeter; and Sol Schoenbach, the former principal bassoonist of the Philadelphia Orchestra — criss-crossed the country to hear the instrumental applicants. Schuller, in fact, heard all the auditions except those of the singers and pianists, whom the directors and coaches of those programs hear separately. Krasner sat with him for the string auditions, Voisin for the brass, and Schoenbach for the woodwinds. They taped each instrumentalist and filled out a report evaluating each for tone quality, stage of advancement, sight-reading ability, musical intelligence, and physical aptitude for performance.

Later, back in Boston, Schuller and the first-chair BSO players, who serve as the nucleus of the summer faculty, studied and compared reports — and listened to tapes where necessary — to decide who among the instrumentalists would get good news and who would get regrets.

Richard Ortner, the administrator of the Music Center, who travels around the country as a member of the auditioning team, said:

> We get lots of people who come in and play the Tchaikovsky concerto or the Sibelius concerto for their auditions, but you put a first-violin part from a Mozart symphony or a Brahms symphony in front of them and it's as if they were from another planet. They can't even make sense of it. They are not all going to become soloists. In fact, hardly any of them are going to become soloists. If they're lucky they'll get good orchestra jobs. And yet they come out of school totally unprepared for that work. It's one of the areas in which Tanglewood feels it fills a real educational gap.

The audition process is not perfect. Schuller remembers a strange case from the mid-1970s. A jury that included Ozawa, Schuller, and the celebrated European conducting teacher Franco Ferrara unanimously turned down an unknown English conductor. When Simon Rattle began to establish himself shortly afterward as one of Europe's brightest young conducting lights, the jurors realized their mistake. Years later Schuller and his colleagues could only conclude that Rattle had a bad day "and we didn't know enough about him to know that he had a bad day."

"The Royal March, *please," Schuller says. You know why they chose this one. The* Royal March *from Stravinsky's* Soldier's Story *is a test of a conductor's ability to dovetail irregular rhythms and meters. You think*

you've got the piece under your belt but when you dig your score out of the pile and get the ensemble marching, it isn't long before you stumble.

Ozawa has been jotting notes in Japanese. Meier, the head of the Tanglewood conducting program, has been leafing through your dossier. Both look up. It is Ozawa who, politely but firmly, taps on the table and makes you stop. He tells you to back up and try the passage again. You stammer an apology — or, if you're like one auditioner, you try to explain to the orchestra what you want. "Don't talk! Don't talk!" Ozawa interrupts. "If you can't start the Royal March, something is wrong."

In general, Schuller looked for three qualities when he heard those thousand or so young instrumentalists trot out their sonatas, quartets, and concertos for something like ten minutes apiece.

First came "a high level of technical command of the instrument." That enables a performer to move on to the second level, which is "to express the music's essence." Schuller wanted "a certain kind of flexibility, musically, to adapt to the requirements of a conductor or coach or to the stylistic demands of a piece." This is a particularly critical area for young musicians, who might have "lots of digital skill but not the knowledge or experience how to use it."

Finally, Schuller sought a "certain total dedication to the art of music," as opposed to the ego trips and technical exhibitionism to which classical musicians, no less than athletes and rock stars, are prey. The candidate, in other words, had to show promise of an ability to work with others in molding a performance, even when "the going gets tough at Tanglewood, as it does around the sixth week" — the week of the Festival of Contemporary Music. Whiz kids who thought they had arrived, they knew it all, were in for a shock when acceptances went out.

Music Center standards have changed little under Fleisher, although he does not sit in on each instrumental audition. The tone of the auditions is fatherly, the jurors sometimes giving encouragement or advice even to unqualified applicants. To one violinist who clearly was not Tanglewood material, for instance, Krasner offered not only tips on how to play the music but also counsel on where to find a better teacher. All this took the audition over the allotted ten minutes, keeping qualified candidates waiting even longer.

The auditions remain an ordeal nonetheless, but never tougher than on young conductors. Every instrumentalist aged eighteen to thirty who applies will get a hearing at one of the thirteen locations from coast to coast, or on tape if necessary. Singers get the same consideration, and scores speak for the composer. The age range for conductors is higher than for instrumentalists — up to thirty-eight. But since a conductor's instrument is an orchestra, only one set of auditions is held. It is in Boston, and participation is by invitation only.

Out of 130 conductor applicants in 1982, 32 from the United States and abroad were invited. The 28 who came, all at their own expense, had to survive not only the preliminary round with the orchestra but also a fifteen-minute interview afterward. For seven hours, straight through until midnight, Schuller and Abravanel tested each comer on his ear training and knowledge of three scores which he claimed to have mastered. None, it is safe to say, felt he knew his scores nearly so well on leaving the room as he had on entering.

The process was hard on the judges as well as the judged. Between interviews, after eliminating two conductors from consideration, Schuller slumped in his chair and sighed a Yiddish proverb: "It's sure a tough way of making a living."

Schuller now calls for the Debussy. What he means is the Prelude to the Afternoon of a Faun *in the arrangement for chamber orchestra by Arnold Schoenberg. Besides that, Schuller throws you a curve: instead of beginning at the beginning and establishing your conception of the piece, you must start in the middle.*

The problem in this hybrid music is the balance of timbres. The small ensemble must somehow suggest the shimmer of Debussy's full orchestra amid the astringency of the Schoenberg transcription. You don't even get to show your — and the flutist's — skill in shaping the famous flute solo. Just as you get to the point where it reenters, Schuller taps his pen again and says, "Thank you very much. That's all." You pick up your scores and march offstage with as much dignity as you can muster, while the orchestra shuffles music in preparation for the next candidate, and the judges scribble notes. If you're lucky, one of them shakes your hand as you pass their tables on your way out.

An ordeal? Only once during the three-hour session was there any indication that a conductor had scored a hit. When Paul Hess, a twenty-nine-year-old American living in France, finished his Stravinsky excerpt, Schuller and Ozawa simultaneously exclaimed, "Very good!" After his Debussy, which was faster and more impassioned than that of his fellow auditioners, Schuller inquired, "Did you really mean to take it so fast at the beginning?"

"Absolutely!" shot back Hess, who then delivered a short lecture on how he was only going back to the original performing tradition. Suddenly Abravanel, who had said little up till that point, interrupted to agree. He knew the original conductor of the piece back in France, and that was the tempo he had used. As Hess left the stage several orchestra members stamped their feet — the orchestra player's sign of approval. Ozawa, impressed, recalled during a break that Hess had auditioned once before and not made it; he seemed more experienced and mature now.

Backstage afterward Hess recalled that, since that earlier attempt in 1975, he had spent two years in Europe on a Fulbright scholarship and won a prize in the conducting competition in Besançon, France, where Ozawa himself once won first prize.

> Tanglewood for me [said Hess] is the best opportunity in the world for this kind of program. I've been all over the world in workshops, in the States and Europe, and this is by far the most professional available. And, of course, with the environment — the Boston Symphony and chamber music — it's the most desirable. However, that means it is also very difficult to get in.

Hess did not get in. Instead, the judges chose Christopher Wilkins of Concord, Massachusetts, a 1975 Tanglewood fellow on the oboe; Charles Peebles of England; Yakov Kreizberg, formerly of Leningrad but then a student at the University of Michigan; and Grzegorz Nowak, a Pole studying at the Eastman School of Music. At Tanglewood they would be joined by Derrick Inouye, a Canadian who was in the separate conducting seminar the previous summer and won direct entry into the higher-level fellowship program on that basis.

Clearly, the something special that Tanglewood covets is more than the ability to play the Tchaikovsky concerto or conduct the *Royal March*, even if it means losing another Simon Rattle.

*   *   *

After twenty–two years at Tanglewood, the last twelve of them as head of the Music Center, Gunther Schuller in 1984 fired a shot heard round the American music world. He resigned.

Not only did he resign: he departed with a blast at the BSO and Ozawa, accusing both of having caved in to commercial pressures. At the Music Center, Schuller said, his "goal was to maintain the purity of the Koussevitzky vision"; the BSO sought merely "to give concerts for dollars." Management's attempts to impose artistic standards on him, as in the choice of guest conductors for the student orchestra, made it impossible for him to go on. He said that, rather than leave gracefully, he would go public with his resignation as "an artistic and philosophic statement against the heavy hand of Fifty-seventh Street on management decisions." If this Sodom and Gomorrah — the center of artist management in the American music industry and a target of other critics — heard the eruption, the seismometers failed to register a reaction.

The resignation, which came at the end of the 1984 Tanglewood season, took nearly everyone by surprise. But as early as 1979 there had been rumblings from the Music Center. That year Schuller departed from his customary welcoming remarks to incoming students to deliver an attack on American symphony orchestras for mediocrity, cynicism, and a "corporate mentality," and on "absentee" music directors at their head.

> There are those that will try to tell you that the ills of the modern symphony orchestra are entirely financial [Schuller said, rising to evangelical fervor]. If only the board could raise more money or people would support symphony orchestras more or if that NEA [National Endowment for the Arts] grant could only be tripled, all our problems would disappear. Not so, my friends. The problems of the symphony orchestra are by now mostly *within*. In fact, orchestras have become in some ways too much successful businesses; their techniques of survival are now those of the American corporation, including the full panoply of managerial and public relations accoutrements, as well as absentee musical directors, and orchestras run not by artists, but by committees.

Schuller mentioned neither the BSO nor Ozawa by name. The speech, however, came at a time of mounting complaints, both in the press and among players, about glossiness in the BSO's programming, performances, and promotion. After the talk Schuller said he had meant to include both Ozawa and the BSO in his indictment insofar as they were guilty of the abuses he cited among American orchestras in general. Qualify the criticism as he might, the meaning that BSO members and other Tanglewood regulars in the audience

Gunther Schuller doubles as conductor and master of ceremonies at a
July Fourth concert, one of his rare appearances with the BSO.

took from the remarks was a slap in the face — an assault on colleagues, employers, and friends in their own house. A virtual shock
wave rolled through the Theater–Concert Hall as he spoke.

True to his faith, Schuller repeated and elaborated on his indictment in a series of addresses to orchestra officials, music educators,
and other groups across the country. Freed by his resignation from
the Tanglewood administrative and auditioning straitjacket, he
plunged deeper into his other musical interests, including composing (three commissions), writing (a two-volume history of jazz),
conducting, publishing music and records, and — a trump card —
running a music festival with its own school. The Festival at Sandpoint, an up-and-coming summer program in Idaho, caught him

on the rebound from Tanglewood. He became its chief conductor and artistic director.

There always was something of the saint or ascetic about Schuller at Tanglewood. His own compositions can be eclectic, weaving jazz, folk, or popular elements into symphonic or chamber styles with the abandon of a latter-day Charles Ives. He can also be as severe a critic as anyone of the skull-cracking complexities of much atonal music. Yet, as his care in student auditions and his remarks about the Grail of "the Koussevitzky vision" suggest, he refused to compromise with public taste or admit impurities in the Music Center program. The conductors the BSO had engaged for the student orchestra in the summer of his resignation were, in addition to Schuller himself, Ozawa, Kurt Masur, Joseph Silverstein, Gustav Meier, and André Previn. (Previn had to cancel because of illness.) Ozawa and Previn are, unmistakably, the kind of conductor that bears the Fifty-seventh Street odor. Ozawa, in fact, is managed by Ronald Wilford, his Berkshire neighbor and tennis partner and the president of Columbia Artists Management, Inc., the most powerful — and criticized — of the Fifty-seventh Street firms. But, whatever the criticisms of Ozawa and Previn, are they no more than commercial products?

Neither Ozawa nor the BSO ever responded publicly to the Schuller indictment. But BSO officials suspected a certain amount of jealousy and pique in it. Schuller has conducting ideas and aspirations of his own, but his podium appearances across the country usually cast him in the role of defender of American music. At Tanglewood, for instance, he rarely conducted the BSO except in patriotic or tubthumping galas of the July Fourth and Tanglewood on Parade variety. He *did not* play by Fifty-seventh Street's rules. The same qualities of mind and temperament that made him a teacher in the academy made him a teacher on the podium, but a teacher without the Bernstein flair.

Schuller's criticisms of orchestras and their players, managers, and conductors stung because of the truth in the charges. On bad nights at Tanglewood, as he said, an attentive listener can see boredom on players' faces and hear it in their work. Despite a sometimes prickly exterior, moreover, Schuller himself is a warm, humane person as well as a fine musician and an idealist. But, in the wooing and winning of large audiences as in other forms of politics, idealism must be tempered by a sense of how far the crowd can be led. Schuller's departure was a loss to Tanglewood, and probably to Schuller as well. As in a divorce, however, the gulf between partners had become too wide for a reconciliation.

If Schuller's resignation was a surprise, the choice of his successor was hardly less of a bombshell. As the fifth in a line of Music Center directors going back to Koussevitzky, Munch, and Leinsdorf, the BSO picked Leon Fleisher, fifty-six, a pianist and teacher with no previous experience in running a school.

Up to the day of his appointment in early 1985, Fleisher was best known as a brilliant pianist who, in the 1960s, wrecked his right hand through overexertion at the keyboard. Even before that setback, however, he had pursued a second musical career as a piano and chamber music teacher at the Peabody Conservatory in Baltimore, where he joined the faculty in 1959. It was largely on the basis of that experience, and a quarter-century association with the BSO as a pianist and conductor, that a BSO search committee unanimously chose him from among fifty candidates. The committee had another concern: it wanted a leader who would not be bound by Schuller's policies, philosophy, methods, or achievements.

But what was in it for Fleisher? Why did he give up his usual summer of teaching, chamber music, and occasional left-hand piano performances (he is the ranking performer of the limited body of solo pieces for one-handed pianists) to take on Tanglewood's headaches?

"Well, it's certainly a good way of keeping me off the streets," he said with an easy laugh, lighting a cigarette.

Fleisher, who wears a stiletto-like beard trimmed to the shape of his jaw, is surprisingly soft-spoken for someone who is so dark, muscular, and intense. He pointed out that he had learned the administrative ropes as director of the Annapolis (Maryland) Symphony and the Theater Chamber Players at the John F. Kennedy Center for the Performing Arts in Washington. (He had, in fact, headed the chamber group since he helped found it in 1968.) And he had been approached from time to time over the years by conservatories shopping for a leader.

"Those times I just didn't feel ready for it," he said. When the BSO made inquiries in 1984, a few weeks after his Tanglewood appearance with Ozawa in Ravel's Concerto for Left Hand, the idea had "matured subconsciously." To Tanglewood he said yes.

Fleisher walked into a troubled paradise, and he knew it. But in characteristic Fleisher fashion he both walked and talked softly as he established his presence. He made no comments or commitments — in public, at any rate — about the Schuller critique. Partly because of previous engagements he spent only four weeks in residence during his first summer and listened as much as he talked. By 1986 he was a full-time artistic director. He became more deeply involved in the school's contemporary music program and conducted the Music Center Orchestra in the first of a series of annual appearances. He was an intent listener at concerts and rehearsals. He initiated classes in Feldenkreis therapy, a form of muscle stretching and body awareness akin to yoga. Most of all, he took charge and made music happen, just as Schuller had. There were noticeable differences — a few new faces on the faculty, new composers on contemporary music programs, a more relaxed management style. But they were simply differences, not a revolution. Life went on much as it had before.

Fleisher was one of his generation's most gifted pianists when his right hand began failing him in 1962. He admitted that he had damaged the muscles and tendons by practicing too hard in a quest for the keyboard perfection attained by the brilliant, slightly older William Kapell. The damaged hand would turn numb at critical moments; the fourth and fifth fingers curled up in a soft fist (a problem that persists to this day). In 1965, after three years of alternately fighting and ignoring the malady, he canceled a tour of Russia with the Cleveland Orchestra under George Szell, a mentor, and gave up a full-time concert career. A year passed in what he later described as desperation. Needing at last to play, he began to learn the left-hand repertoire.

For seventeen years Fleisher tried every kind of therapy that came to his attention: psychiatry, injections, traction, acupuncture, shock treatment, biofeedback, rehabilitative exercises, myotherapy (a kind of gouging of tight muscles by the therapist's thumb or elbow). He tried to work out the problem at his instrument. Nothing helped.

Finally in 1980, at the suggestion of Gary Graffman, a fellow pianist and victim of a failing right hand, Fleisher found his way to Massachusetts General Hospital in Boston. For ten months a team of three specialists checked him over. The decision was to operate. In January 1981 the team's surgeon severed a ligament in Fleisher's right wrist and removed the irritated tissue around it, in the hope that reduced pressure on the nerve would allow the muscles to regain their power.

In September 1982 a miracle seemed to have occurred. On national television Fleisher made his comeback as a two-handed pianist, playing César Franck's *Symphonic Variations* with the Baltimore Symphony Orchestra to help inaugurate its new $23 million hall. On page 1 of the *New York Times,* its senior music critic, Donal Henahan, wrote: "Leon Fleisher, the two-handed pianist, is back, doing again what he once did as well as any pianist in the world." Other newspapers, magazines, and television also hailed the triumphal return. Overnight Fleisher was a national hero and a full-fledged pianist again.

Four years later Fleisher had not played any of the two-handed repertoire since that second debut, and he had no idea when he would. He said the Baltimore appearance was a mistake. He had originally intended to play the greater — but also longer and more demanding — Beethoven Fourth Concerto, but even the fifteen-minute Franck work was too much for his damaged muscles. To get through the performance, he used them "in a way that I shouldn't have," weakening them again.

But out of darkness came light. To keep busy musically when his afflictions began, Fleisher had taken up conducting and redoubled his efforts as a teacher. Besides leading the Annapolis orchestra, he served as associate conductor of the Baltimore Symphony for five years, guest-conducted many of the major American orchestras, including the BSO at Tanglewood in 1971, and led performances by his Kennedy Center chamber group.

Fleisher makes no secret of his desire to return as a whole pianist someday; he has "every hope and expectation" that he will. But until that day, conducting and teaching have been "more than a compensation."

It sounds almost Pollyanna-ish to say that with this personal tragedy there's a silver lining [he said. But the handicap] fostered my first look into conducting in a focused and acute way. And teaching is an extraordinary kind of activity in which I think the teacher probably learns more

Leon Fleisher coaches a student ensemble.

than the student. It's very difficult to balance that out, but it's really quite incredible that you learn new ways of passing on this information, which just sharpens it for you, the teacher.

Another compensation has been a heightened awareness of the interdependence of mind and body, and Tanglewood students soon began hearing about that. The eight weeks at Tanglewood, Fleisher said, "can be really quite pressurized for these young people." Yet students think that, because they're young, "they're very flexible, they can bounce back from the physical abuse that they impose on themselves." It is not that easy, he declared from experience. To teach and relieve the dangers of practicing as much as twelve or fourteen hours a day, he instituted the Feldenkreis program with a therapist from Israel, where the treatment was born.

At Peabody Fleisher urges his students to take up body movement or dance to break up the tensions. It is advice that he himself took. "In order to convince them that it was the thing to do, I started to take ballet at Peabody," he said. "And though I look like a stranded manatee, it's been great fun and given me a totally different perception of movement, of myself."

Among pianists in Fleisher's predicament in the past, probably the best-known is Robert Schumann, who also damaged his hand by too much zeal in practice. Unlike Schumann, a one-handed pianist today has at his disposal a small but respectable body of orchestral and chamber pieces commissioned by Paul Wittgenstein, a wealthy Austrian pianist who lost his right arm in World War I. The orchestral works include the Ravel concerto, two pieces by Richard Strauss, Britten's *Diversions* for piano and orchestra, and the Prokofiev Fourth Concerto. All told, Fleisher has tracked down four hundred one-hand works composed at the behest of Wittgenstein and lefties like him.

To no one's surprise more than his own, Fleisher has not wearied of playing the best five or so of these pieces again and again.

I'm amazed [he said]. I must've played the Ravel upwards of four hundred times. [This was in 1985. More performances have followed, including a 1988 Tanglewood performance in which he doubled as pianist and conductor as part of a BSO program in honor of his sixtieth birthday.] But I hear it still with new ears, and it's an extraordinary piece. I think doing it with Seiji at Tanglewood last summer opened up a new awareness of various elements in it, and it continues to remain fresh for me.

I think it's a function of how one approaches art, basically. If it gets to be rote, that's unfortunate. I think the things you have to pass on to the next generation are: What are the myriad elements, the various levels, upon which the piece is built or that it contains? Why is a Beethoven symphony, a Mozart symphony — why has this music lasted so long? Because in a sense it is so all-inclusive, and no matter how large a percentage you achieve, in a single performance, of what your desires are, it's always the carrot in front of the donkey. There's always more, something else, to go for.

Because of his winter teaching at Peabody, Fleisher cannot audition each of Tanglewood's instrumental applicants as Schuller did. Nor do his speeches strike the oracular note that Schuller's did. But, he says, he can offer a deep involvement in contemporary music from his earliest playing and his work with his Kennedy Center ensemble. He can teach — he believes that is where his greatest usefulness lies — and he can conduct. He has the support of a group of musicians and administrators for whom he has the highest respect. He can lead and inspire. All in all, not a bad prospect, he cheerfully says.

Twice divorced, Fleisher married Katherine Jacobson, a 1975 Tanglewood graduate who became one of his Peabody students, six weeks after his Baltimore comeback. He was then fifty-four, she twenty-eight. The concert might have been a mistake, but this Mrs.

Fleisher, he said, echoing conductor Pierre Monteux's description of his third wife, is "my *Eroica*." Perhaps if the Beethoven symbolism holds, Tanglewood will be Fleisher's Ninth Symphony, if not his Fourth Concerto.

*   *   *

Oliver Knussen, according to a newspaper back home in England, is a six-foot-four bearded Viking who looks "like someone who would be happiest grappling with a pint of beer in a pub." The *Daily Telegraph*, which committed this libel, also described Knussen's suburban London studio as "a composer's paradise but a cleaner's nightmare."

"It's a picture of my split mind — part of it chronic confusion, and the rest manic order," Knussen concluded gloomily in the article.

Knussen, as it happens, is a Viking descendant, and if he were the seafaring kind his cargo would have been more order and disorder as Tanglewood's 1986 Festival of Contemporary Music loomed on the horizon. That summer's composer in residence, he was responsible for putting together the week-long orgy of seven concerts and three "electro-acoustic preludes."

"You can't help but make a festival like this a reflection of one's own personality," Knussen said over a large Coke at the Tanglewood cafeteria, amid interruptions by composers, performers, and staffers seeking guidance on everything from conflicting rehearsals to missing scores. "But if your prejudices are fairly widespread, then it shouldn't be too bad."

Knussen's prejudices are conditioned, first of all, by his activity in England, where he is regarded by many critics as the brightest composer of the new generation, and one of the brightest conductors of new music. His other prejudices include a fondness for — and long association with — Tanglewood, where much of his best music was born. Above all, he wanted to bring to the contemporary festival an "unpartisan approach" in which many kinds of music could exist happily together. This, he says, is what music "should do, and what it does do in the mind of anybody who actually likes music. Regardless of what the style is or regardless of what it represents, if it's a good piece you like it, and if it isn't you don't."

Oliver Knussen.

Knussen, who was thirty-four that year, was a protégé of Gunther Schuller, the driving force behind contemporary music activities at the Music Center for twenty years until his 1984 battle with the BSO. Partly in hopes of mending that rift, Knussen put Schuller's *Concertino da Camera* on the program for the opening festival concert. But Schuller, still miffed, and busy conducting and teaching at his Sandpoint festival, did not come. Seiji Ozawa had made a similar gesture the summer before, programming Schuller's *Seven Studies on a Theme of Paul Klee* with the BSO. The results were the same.

Schuller's departure had been preceded by another family squabble. A year earlier, at the end of the 1983 season, Paul Fromm had severed his twenty-year connection with the contemporary festival in a dispute over programming and direction. This time the target was Schuller.

Tanglewood without Paul Fromm was like a birthday party without a favorite uncle. Since the establishment of the contemporary festival in 1963 the Fromm Music Foundation at Harvard had sponsored the annual event jointly with the Music Center. Although the amount of Fromm money was relatively small — between $25,000 and $30,000 a year — Paul Fromm, who died in 1987, was one of the leading patrons of contemporary music in the United States. His support helped to pay for about three commissions to composers each year (and thus three world premières for the festival) and gave an important seal of approval.

Born in Germany in 1906, Fromm left school at sixteen to go to work in Frankfurt-am-Main. In 1938 he emigrated to the United States, where, he has written, "I became particularly concerned about the anomalous position of composers in a society which was not only musically conservative, but also insistent that music make its own way in the marketplace as if it were a commodity of some kind." He became well-off through a wine-importing business in Chicago. In 1952 he established his foundation to help composers through commissions and performances.

By 1983, however, Fromm concluded that he could no longer support "the very narrow view of contemporary music" taken at Tanglewood. He complained of an academic emphasis in the programming under Schuller. Some of the programs, he said, "sounded like summer concerts of the New England Conservatory" — an allusion to the composers Schuller had befriended during ten years as the conservatory's president, and had programmed at Tanglewood. The missing composers, Fromm suggested, included the so-called minimalists, such as John Adams and Philip Glass, and those working in electronic media. To provide a voice for such outsiders, Fromm asked for an advisory role in the selection of the works to be played, with the final decisions still left to Schuller.

Schuller refused. He said he had to retain control of what was not only an artistic but also an educational endeavor. The BSO stood behind him and refused to compromise his direction. A year later Fromm threw his support to the Aspen Festival in Colorado, which launched a "Fromm Week" like Tanglewood's, but with a different spectrum of composers and with problems of its own: the performances soon came under heavy criticism for poor preparation. Tanglewood soldiered on without Fromm or the Fromm commissions.

A year after that Schuller left and Leon Fleisher replaced him. Busy with his winter teaching and performing, however, Fleisher did not want full responsibility for the contemporary programming, and a new leadership for the festival evolved. Fleisher remained chairman of the board, so to speak, but the composer in residence (Harvard's Leon Kirchner in 1985, Knussen in 1986) became the chief operating officer. Each laid out the year's programs with the help of an advisory committee, matched compositions to performers, and conducted the orchestral concert. New composers, including minimalists from the United States and Europe, began to appear on the programs. Fromm left one year too early to see his objections at least partly sustained.

"Ol-ly! Ol-ly! Ol-ly!" the players shouted as they stamped their feet in rhythm to the name.

The chant from the Music Center Orchestra recalled Knussen from the wings at the end of the 1986 festival's climactic student concert. Earlier four composers from four countries had come out of the audience to take bows with him after performances of their works. But it was the shambling, shaggy conductor in the baggy black suit whom the students had taken to their hearts.

The orchestral concert carries the highest musical charge of any program in the week-long contemporary series. It is not only the final student concert in the festival but also the only one in which all the school's instrumental fellows take part. Because of the new repertoire and the challenge of a conductor skilled in its ways, the involvement is intense. It can be intense in front of the proscenium, too. While the chamber concerts attract mostly aficionados, the orchestral program usually fills the Theater–Concert Hall with listeners of many stripes. Throughout the festival, but especially at the orchestral concert, other composers, performers, record company producers, publishers' agents, and some of the Northeast's most high-powered critics will be in the audience. For the composer whose work is played, the stakes can be high.

The orchestral programs under Schuller had mixed twentieth-century classics — sometimes neglected ones, like symphonies by William Schuman and Roger Sessions, Edgard Varèse's 1920s sound collages, and Jean Barraqué's monumentally complex *Le temps restitué* — with more recent works. Knussen chose four works composed within the previous four years. Three were American premières. All four composers were close to Knussen, and all were present to advise, listen, and receive the crowd's cheers.

From Japan came the première of *Dream/Window,* a 1985 work by Toru Takemitsu, at fifty-five the only composer over forty on the program. Takemitsu's music, Knussen said, is a good model for students because it "is drawn from an immense knowledge of both traditional Japanese and Western" styles, including Hollywood music. *Dream/Window,* typical of Takemitsu's impressionistic pieces, painted sound pictures of Japanese gardens, particularly of the Kyoto region.

From the United States came *Ecstatic Orange,* composed in 1985 by Michael Torke, a Tanglewood graduate. Knussen described it as "a very heady and bouncy explosion of energy." It splashed reds and yellows as well as Dayglo shades of orange through the busy orchestra.

England was represented by Robert Saxton, who took over some of Knussen's composition classes while Knussen was busy with the festival. Saxton's 1984 *Concerto for Orchestra* was another première. The thickly scored work mixed rushing figures in the strings and woodwinds with solemn chords in the brass. To Knussen the concerto, like all Saxton's music, had a "visionary level."

The program culminated in *Manhattan Abstraction,* a 1982 composition by Poul Ruders, also in its American première. A Dane's counterpart to Gershwin's *An American in Paris, Manhattan Abstraction* peppered New York with violent collisions. Knussen likened the piece to "watching that huge machine in the Charlie Chaplin *Modern Times* film, with all those cogs going in and out." It was the first of Ruders's major orchestral works to receive an American performance, according to Knussen.

As always in these programs, whether under Schuller or under a successor, the orchestra played brilliantly. Takemitsu, who spent part of the summer in residence and worked with Knussen's students, received the noisiest ovation, along with "*Ol-ly!*"

As composer in residence, Knussen followed in a distinguished line of composer-teachers going back to Aaron Copland's twenty-five-year reign. From the United States in recent years have come figures such as Jacob Druckman, Ralph Shapey, and John Harbison. Europe has sent Olivier Messiaen, Hans Werner Henze (in 1983 and again in 1988), and Luciano Berio. The youngest person ever to run the contemporary festival, Knussen wanted the programs to reflect his age. Thus, most of the selections — even those by senior composers like Henze and Britten — were less than a decade old. (There were also more works from Europe than in the past, and a total of four works by Takemitsu — the most by any one composer.) Knussen also wanted to recall the Tanglewood he had known during his three years as a student. Some of the programming thus became "a little photograph" of composers, including fellow students, he had worked with in the Berkshires.

The Tanglewood family supplied works by Schuller and Yehudi Wyner, a current teacher, and by such Knussen contemporaries as Simon Bainbridge and Jonathan Lloyd of England and Deborah Drattell, Marc Neikrug, Nicholas Thorne, and Torke of the United States. From an older generation Knussen chose the 1986 Pulitzer Prize–winning work, the Woodwind Quintet no. 4 by George Perle, a former composer in residence, who was seventy-one that year. Another septuagenarian, Elliott Carter, was represented by this 1985 *Penthode*. (Both composers attended their performances.) Two sixtieth birthdays were celebrated — Henze's, with his *Fandango sopra un basso del Padré Soler* (an American première), and Morton Feldman's, with his *Piece for Four Pianos*. Britten's String Quartet no. 3 provided what Knussen described as a "testament piece" by a composer who knew he was dying.

There were five student concerts, four chamber (including vocal works) and one orchestral. Others were given by the Juilliard String Quartet, which was in residence, and by the violin-piano duo of Joseph Silverstein and Peter Serkin. Both these programs reached back to an earlier generation of composers, such as Irving Fine, Henri Dutilleux, Bartók, Stravinsky, and Messiaen.

The advisory committee that helped Knussen plan the festival consisted of four previous composers in residence — Kirchner, Henze, Harbison, and Druckman. Each suggested works to be played and evaluated other selections. The three "electro-acoustic preludes" were Knussen's idea, intended to remedy a lack of synthesizer-generated music. Each program lasted a half-hour and offered three taped works, chosen from tapes solicited from centers of electronic music in the United States and France.

Knussen flew to Boston twice during the winter and spring to plan the festival and go over applications from student composers. One of those trips involved looking at six hundred scores in two days. It was "just terrifying," he said, but he was "rewarded with the nicest bunch of composers you can imagine."

Modestly Knussen limited his own works in the festival to the short *Fanfares for Tanglewood* and *Coursing,* which, as a pair, opened the week's programs. (*Fanfares* was so new that Knussen, whose disorderly ways extend to his own composing methods, was still writing parts of it the day before the first concert.) A week earlier, however, the BSO played his *Music for a Puppet Court,* a witty pastiche of Renaissance and twentieth-century ideas, to give the composer recognition before a Shed audience. Knussen conducted.

Though he admitted a certain amount of serendipity in assembling a festival of about fifty compositions, Knussen was happy with both the diversity that resulted and the level of performance. Each work, he said, was carefully rehearsed by the student performers over several weeks, "not just crammed into a couple of days." Under such conditions, "the kids can actually get to know the stuff. To somebody coming from London, where sight reading is the name of the game, actually that is very refreshing."

Born in Glasgow, Oliver Knussen comes from a musical family. His father, Stewart, was principal bass in the London Symphony Orchestra. His grandfather played cello in the Hallé Orchestra of Manchester, England, and his great-grandfather was a violinist in Buffalo Bill's Circus Band.

The scion's association with Tanglewood goes back to composition fellowships in 1970, 1971, and 1973. Returning without official status in 1975 and 1980, Knussen "hung around" — his term — and composed. During one of these summers he was supposed to be in residence at Vermont's Marlboro Festival. He came back again in 1981 to teach and help with the première of his Third Symphony, which Schuller conducted during Fromm Week. In one way or another, Knussen said, he has written "most of my music — most of my best music, at any rate — within a hundred miles of this spot."

Among that music is a large part of the opera that won him attention in the early 1980s on both sides of the Atlantic, *Where the Wild Things Are,* a collaboration with the children's author and artist Maurice Sendak. He and Sendak followed that success with a second opera, *Higglety, Pigglety, Pop!* The two works make a twin bill, with the later work performed first. (They were planned that way from the start, Knussen said.)

Fond of *Higglety, Pigglety* now, Knussen thought it was "dreadful" while composing it. "It's one of Sendak's most dark and strange and turned-in books, and it's one of my strangest pieces," he grimaced and said. "It refers to God knows what. It's an opera about an opera and it's an opera about . . ." For once words failed this composer.

There is, Knussen confessed, a connection between his operas on childhood themes and the American composer (and Tanglewood graduate) David Del Tredici's obsession with *Alice in Wonderland* in his series of *Alice* pieces. Knussen heard Aaron Copland conduct the world première of Del Tredici's first *Alice* piece, *The Lobster Quadrille,* in London in 1969, and the next year he wrote his own *Winnie the Pooh* songs, "my first piece along this tack." Although there was no conscious connection, "I think that something must have clicked and I realized that it was possible to use those levels of imagery." Those childhood images, he said, "remain the things to which you return again and again." From the two operas "I discovered an enormous amount about not just what makes my music tick, but why I was writing it at all."

Knussen's wife, Sue, is a former horn student and librarian whom he met during his student years at Tanglewood. On their return in 1986 they and their nine-year-old daughter Sonya lived in a composer's cottage at Seranak, where he worked on a piece entitled *Chiara.* For soprano soloist, two harps, twenty-four women's voices, and small orchestra, *Chiara* is about "angels flying around, and the strange things that angels do," according to Knussen. It was another piece that he began during his student years at Tanglewood. In 1987, as the composer settled in for what appeared to be a long Tanglewood career, he returned as chief of contemporary music activities, and finished portions of *Chiara* had their American première by Phyllis Curtin's students in the contemporary festival. Knussen conducted the orchestral concert again that year, and the stamping of feet and cry for *"Ol-ly!"* went up again at the end. Schuller and Fromm were gone, but the traditions lived on.

*   *   *

The heat was already rising off Tanglewood's driveway at 9:30 on a July morning in 1982 when Eric Ruske rolled in aboard a yellow school bus. He walked through the Main Gate, its flags drooping in the heavy air, and went to the back of the Theater–Concert Hall, where he took his French horn out of its case and began to warm up under the trees among his fellow students.

A little before ten he and about eighty-five of those other musicians drifted onstage for a rehearsal of the Tanglewood Music Center Orchestra. Two conducting fellows took them through a pair of contemporary pieces that would open the concert program, Boris Blacher's *Variations on a Theme of Paganini* and Gunther Schuller's *Klee Studies*. After a break in the rehearsal the East German conductor Otmar Suitner, who a few days earlier had led the BSO in a Shed concert, took over for Schubert's "Great" C Major Symphony, the major work on the program.

At 12:30 the rehearsal ended, and the musicians headed off to lunch in the cafeteria. During the afternoon there would be other rehearsals, chamber music coaching, master classes, and meetings with teachers, depending on this student's program. Ruske attended a chamber music session and then a cello master class. What's that, a brass player consorting with cellists? Yes, a hornist can learn about tone and phrasing from cellists — other instrumentalists sit in on vocal classes for the same reason — and Tanglewood scheduled a cello class as part of his day.

Around 5:30 Ruske hopped another yellow shuttle bus, which took him back to Miss Hall's School, the girls' prep school six miles to the north where most of Tanglewood's fellowship students board. He went for a swim in the pond, had dinner, and, with hardly a minute to glance at a paper or his mail, caught a bus back to Tanglewood to hear a voice students' recital. Back at Miss Hall's the 125 conductors, instrumentalists, and singers unwound at a post-concert party with beer, wine, and dancing. Then it was off to bed for Ruske and the others. Another day of rehearsals and concerts would begin at 8:45 in the morning.

That, as nearly as anyone can summarize it, is a day in the life of a Tanglewood student. But there really is no typical student or typical day in this setting. There is simply an assembly of gifted young musicians living and working together — 135 of them in the fellowship program that summer, the ten student composers residing apart in the splendid semi-seclusion of Seranak, the former Kous-sevitzky mansion.

In any Tanglewood year the hundred instrumental fellows, who make up the orchestra and play in chamber ensembles, will be joined by two to six conductors, seven to ten pianists, eight to ten composers, twelve singers, two vocal coaches, and two piano technicians, who tune and maintain instruments. These are the winners of the nationwide auditions. Another ten to twelve students will take part in the conducting seminar and about twenty-four in the vocal seminar, both lower-level programs that offer classroom work but no public performance opportunities. The Boston University Tanglewood Institute, which offers a similar spectrum of activities for mostly high school age students, also is housed under the Music Center roof. It attracts about 350 students over the course of two four-week sessions.

Some fellowship students, like Ruske, are still in college or at conservatories. Others are graduate students or have already embarked on careers, typically in a minor league orchestra, and are at Tanglewood for a final polishing under professional guidance. Ruske, who was nineteen that summer, came from LaGrange, Illinois, a suburb of Chicago. Out of the thirteen hundred candidates who had auditioned, he was one of two admitted on the spot. Richard Ortner, who attended the Chicago auditions, recalled that the auditioners, Schuller and Roger Voisin, were so taken by Ruske that they said, in effect, "That's the kind of student we want. Grab him."

Blond and athletic — he runs, lifts weights, and once worked as a lifeguard — Ruske comes from a non-musical family. His father is a sales engineer for an electrical supply company, his mother a second grade teacher. Eric, who is given to easy, frequent bursts of laughter, might have been like any other sophomore-to-be at Northwestern University if it had not been for one thing: his commitment to music.

Where do they come from, these young devotees of music scorned by their rock-addicted contemporaries, these votaries who shout and stamp their feet for "Ol-ly"?

With his parents' encouragement Eric Ruske began to play the guitar at the age of five. The horn arrived when he was in the fourth grade and wanted to play trumpet in the school band. He ran into the classic dilemma: there were already enough trumpeters and "the

band director said I had to play horn or I couldn't play anything."
By the time he reached Tanglewood Ruske was studying with Dale
Clevenger, principal horn of the Chicago Symphony Orchestra. He
had played in the Chicago Symphony's training orchestra, the Civic
Orchestra of Chicago, and by winning a competition had got to
play a solo with the Chicago Symphony itself in a youth concert.

"Boy," he recalled, "was that fun! I played part of a Mozart concerto. Just to stand up there and have the Chicago Symphony playing behind you — that was awesome."

Enthusiasm like that sprinkled Ruske's conversation at Tanglewood. He liked his room at Miss Hall's. He liked the food. ("A real
health nut," he had only orange juice for lunch and did his serious
eating back at Miss Hall's.) He liked his fellow students, including
the conducting fellows under whom he played. "Sometimes it's
hard to go from someone like Seiji Ozawa or Otmar Suitner to them,
but you've got to respect them," he said. "They know an awful lot
about the music they conduct." He liked the Blacher piece the orchestra was rehearsing, which gave him a chance to play first horn.
He did not even mind the heat that engulfed the Berkshires during
that suffocating spell in July; he was used to it in Chicago. It was
the mosquitoes, not the heat, that kept him from sleeping.

The format of a student orchestra concert remains as it was under
Koussevitzky. Conducting fellows take the first half of the program,
which they have prepared under the supervision of the week's senior
conductor. Two or three fellows lead shorter works — an overture,
a tone poem, a short symphony, or perhaps suites like those by
Blacher and Schuller. After intermission the senior conductor takes
over to do a longer symphony or other major work. It was in this
format that Leonard Bernstein in 1940 came to the world's attention
as Koussevitzky's protégé. Ozawa, Mehta, Maazel, Abbado — all the
well-known conducting graduates came out of the same regimen.

The players in the orchestra, like orchestra players everywhere,
are more anonymous, even though each is named in the program.
But the players enjoy more varied performance opportunities than
their baton-wielding comrades.

Besides playing in the orchestra, each instrumentalist performs
chamber music in programs open to the public. Although fellows
get occasional solo parts in chamber and orchestral works, the clos-

est Tanglewood comes to a solo recital for students is in Phyllis Curtin's vocal program. There, four to six students will perform songs or arias, with faculty accompanists, once a week in group recitals. But most classes, rehearsals, and concerts are devoted to ensemble rather than solo work. As the summer home of a symphony orchestra, Tanglewood sees its primary educational mission as the grounding of future professionals in the essentials of teamwork, whether in orchestral playing, chamber music, or opera. As Schuller said, the whiz kid, the star who is expecting to make a name and wow the crowds, had better look elsewhere.

Attendance at Music Center concerts is another tradition going back to Tanglewood's beginnings. The programs are open without further charge to Tanglewood Friends, who sign on for an entire season for a modest sum — $50 the minimum for individuals, $75 for families. Others are welcome for a nominal fee ($5 or $6 per concert), which, like the Friends' memberships, benefits the Music Center. The orchestral concerts are particular favorites with the audience. Even under student conductors the playing is tightly disciplined and often brilliant. Besides that, there are not the crowds at the gates or on the lawn that there are at bso concerts. The word is getting around, though. In recent years it has been necessary to arrive fifteen minutes to half an hour early to get a seat for most programs.

The chamber programs, though seldom played to capacity houses, are also popular, and for the same reason — the absence of crowds, the thrill of discovery. The young players' first encounters with masterpieces of the past or music of today can be as exhilarating for listeners as for the students themselves. That, too, is part of the tradition. It is not just famous conductors who have come out of the Music Center. The bso likes to say that 20 percent of the musicians in the major American symphony orchestras are Tanglewood graduates. In the bso itself the figure approaches 50 percent.

The next day at Tanglewood was a July scorcher. Ruske had another orchestra rehearsal in the morning; Suitner and the two student conductors put the finishing touches on the program they and the orchestra would give the next afternoon. Ruske had his glass of orange juice for lunch, hit the bso beach at Stockbridge Bowl for a swim, and set off on his afternoon rounds. They began at 1:30 with a reading of some contemporary music for winds. The session took place on the stage of the Theater–Concert Hall under the supervision of Roger Voisin — the same Roger Voisin who had admitted Ruske to Tanglewood.

The first piece was Vincent Persichetti's *Serenade for Ten Wind Instruments,* two of them horns. As in the orchestra, Ruske played first horn — a coincidence, since the Music Center rotates parts within sections. Next came Ingolf Dahl's *Allegro and Arioso for Five Wind Instruments,* in which Ruske was the only brass player. Because of their superior firepower brass players are supposed to drown out woodwinds. But when Ruske got the lead the woodwinds overpowered him. Voisin, who was conducting, stopped the performance.

"Don't be too violent," the former trumpeter corrected the all-male quintet. "You guys are too aggressive. You're good but you're covering the horn."

They tried it again. This time the balance was right.

"That's lovely," Voisin said. "I like that. It's fun, eh?"

For Ruske the session ended at 2:30. He popped over to the Main House, the rambling, Gothic hub of Music Center activities, to reserve a practice room for a reading of the Mozart Quintet for horn and strings. He was in luck. He obtained a corner room on the third floor, with a view of the lake and a breeze through the windows.

Ruske had arranged the reading, somehow inveigling four women string players into joining him amid their own crowded schedules. Although he would participate later in the season in a public performance of a Mozart serenade for winds, this outing was mostly for pleasure. He and the string players wanted to try out the Mozart quintet, one of the staples of the chamber repertoire.

The women were not due until 3:30, so Ruske sat down to practice by himself. At 3:30 they arrived in a group, talking excitedly. In honor of the heat wave one of the violinists warmed up with a snatch of *Jingle Bells.* The five players sat down in a semicircle to begin. They first closed the door to spare others in the building the pleasure of the third-floor Mozart. The room quickly turned stifling. One of the women reopened the door.

"If someone doesn't like it, they'll come up and shut it," the cellist said.

"How could they not like it?" Ruske joked.

There was much laughter and joking all through the reading, which stopped often for corrections, adjustments, and groans at clinkers. At the end the group cheered its performance. Ruske thanked the women for having come and they thanked him for having asked. It was 4:30 and time for the next reading, rehearsal, or bus.

The orchestral concert the next afternoon went well despite the unrelenting heat. The following week, however, Eric and his fellow students were in for rough weather of a different kind. Rehearsals began for the Festival of Contemporary Music.

Serious involvement in music of their time is a novel experience for most Tanglewood fellows, and often daunting because of the new harmonies, sonorities, and ways of counting, coordinating, and listening. To get the students past the jitters and obtain polished performances (the high quality of the performances is usually the only thing on which critics agree), the Music Center allows two to four weeks of rehearsal for each piece, often with the composer present as a coach. As Oliver Knussen observed, it is an extravagance the players will not often meet in the world outside.

Like most other instrumentalists, Ruske would perform in the climactic orchestral concert. His other major assignment was to play one of the two horn parts in *Points on a Curve to Find*, a 1974 work for piano and twenty-two other instruments by Luciano Berio, that summer's composer in residence. The piece was so complex that in early rehearsals it tripped even the student conductor, who was supposed to have learned it. Finally, on a rainy afternoon Berio himself, along with Ursula Oppens, the professional pianist who would play the solo part, came to a rehearsal in the Theater–Concert Hall. Also on hand to help out — or lend moral support — were Maurice Abravanel, the Music Center's acting director, Theodore Antoniou, Schuller's lieutenant for contemporary music activities, and Voisin.

Under the student conductor's sometimes halting guidance, the ensemble went through the piece once while Berio listened from a chair in the audience section of the nearly empty hall. It was hard, grinding work, with many rough edges. At the end of the reading Berio, an Italian, then in his fifties, who is built like a wrestler, went up to the stage. He made a number of seating changes, spreading the players farther apart and bringing the piano closer to the front.

He also suggested changes in the performance, among them more "brilliance" from the pianist. The group tried again. Berio pronounced the performance "much better" and after fifty minutes the session ended. More hard work lay ahead, however.

Ruske said the piece was hard to play and understand but growing on him. But he was sleepy. There had been another party at Miss Hall's the night before in celebration of the student orchestra's concert under Erich Leinsdorf. The blast had gone on until 4:15 A.M.

"It's so intense here you've got to have some of that," said Ruske. "It is summer, after all. You've got to have some time for the kids to enjoy themselves." Luckily, he had no classes scheduled that day until 12:30. The less fortunate had 8:45 A.M. dates with their teachers.

In spite of the grueling schedule Ruske considered himself lucky to have come to Tanglewood. He thought Chicago a great city for woodwinds and brass but found Tanglewood's strings and overall student performance level better. As for how his lip held up through the battering by as much as twelve hours of practice a day, Ruske said not to worry. His lip was "going to be like iron" when he got home.

A year later, while still a student at Northwestern, Eric Ruske applied for a vacancy in the horn section of the Cleveland Orchestra. The orchestra told him, politely, to get lost: it needed an experienced musician, not a college kid. Persistence got him into the audition, with an implied warning that it would be a waste of time. At the end of the day he was offered a contract as associate principal horn of the Cleveland Orchestra. After completing a European tour with the Chicago Symphony as an extra hornist, he began work in Cleveland in February 1985.

There might be no such thing as a typical Tanglewood student. But for those like the iron-lipped Ruske the road that leads to Tanglewood usually leads to even bigger things beyond.

*   *   *

If big things often lie beyond Tanglewood, the most colossal of all was the career that came to Koussevitzky's protégé Leonard Bernstein. From his arrival in 1940 as a twenty-one-year-old son of Russian immigrant parents and a Harvard graduate, he has grown to be the symbol of Tanglewood as well as America's — and very likely the world's — most deified conductor, composer, teacher, and culture hero. His 1986 concert with the Tanglewood Music Center Orchestra showed him in all his larger-than-life flamboyance. No one who was there — neither performer nor listener — will soon forget it.

It was a warm night in July. Senior citizen clubbers, T-shirted kids from the summer camps, business groups on cultural safaris, autograph hounds, groupies, students, faculty, unvarnished music lovers, certified patrons and Friends of Tanglewood, anyone and everyone who could not pay BSO prices or could not get into Bernstein's sold-out BSO concert — all joined in the rush for Shed seats, unreserved for his annual appearance with the Music Center Orchestra.

To applause the evening's first student conductor, Richard Westerfield of Pound Ridge, New York, preceded the Maestro to the podium. He opened the program with Debussy's *La Mer*. Romely Pfund, a woman from Dessau, East Germany, followed with Haydn's Symphony no. 102. Both were "Koussey" works, chosen by Bernstein to honor his mentor. Both performances had been prepared under Bernstein's supervision, and both bore the Bernstein stamp: high-strung, brilliant, firmly sculpted — the manic wrestling the depressive.

It was nearly ten when the audience returned from the break. (Anyone who attends Bernstein concerts learns not to expect speed or punctuality; he gives full measure, but it is usually more than full measure, and at his own pace.) "L.B.," as Tanglewood insiders refer to him, chose to end the program with a longer Koussevitzky specialty, Sibelius's Symphony no. 2. The crowd quieted and the house lights went out; only the orchestra was illuminated as it finished tuning. At last Bernstein entered from the right. He grinned at the crowd as he made his way across the stage, and flourished his stick at his musicians. Applause rose, swelled, and faded as he bowed and hopped onto the podium, and turned quickly to his work. The baton went up. Silence.

Sibelius's music is often called old-fashioned. The only old-fashioned thing about the D Major Symphony in this performance was its statement of the eternal human truths of loneliness, pain, and triumph. Beautiful as the playing was — and it was very beautiful, each section blended with the others until the ensemble resonated like a great organ — Bernstein did not stop at pure sound or even musical expressivity. The performance became an affirmation of human dignity.

The deep, rich tone that he wrung from the strings, the etching of the woodwinds, the burnished brass — Bernstein was Merlin in his command of his medium and musicians. For a dramatic entrance by the brass he did one of his patented levitations. The leap, coinciding with the shock of sound from the brass section, drew a gasp from the audience.

The man conducted with his fingertips, elbows, shoulders, knees, and eyes. In this Finnish epic he made a pause in the *andante* so wide that a steamship could have sailed into a fjord through it. No one in the audience stirred, mistakenly thinking the movement was over.

Tempos were on the slow side, but they could dare to be so because he and the orchestra put so much shading and detail into the fluctuations — the telling rise and fall of the narrative. Phrase built upon phrase, movement upon movement. The arrival of the main theme in the finale ached with poignant lyricism. The summation, where that theme returns in brazen splendor, rose level by level, grade by grade, until the final affirmation burst upon the audience like the sun-struck view from a summit, glimpsed after a heroic climb.

During the thunderous ovation there were the familiar Bernstein hugs and kisses for his players. Because of the crowd he attracts, the program was moved from the Theater–Concert Hall, the orchestra's home, which seats one thousand, to the Shed, which holds five times the number. It is one of the many privileges, both large and small, that only Bernstein enjoys at Tanglewood.

There was another student party that night at Miss Hall's (there always is after Bernstein's concert). The talking and dancing went on until dawn. After the lines of well-wishers and autograph seekers at the Shed's Green Room had melted into the night, Bernstein drove to Miss Hall's to join the party (he always does). He stayed till the end, talking, smoking, drinking, and dancing. Here and there in the crowd, a dancer shot into the air, legs slightly tucked. It was

"Lenny's leap," as it became known from Bernstein's Sibelius choreography, now part of the dance-floor rhythms.

Bernstein's visit is an annual highlight and headache of the Music Center schedule. A member of Koussevitzky's original Class of 1940 and the two succeeding classes, he remains Tanglewood's most illustrious graduate and the inheritor of the Koussevitzky mantle — literally; from time to time he appears in a Koussevitzky cape, along with Koussey cufflinks, left at Seranak when the master died. Even Ozawa, who studied under Munch, does not command such veneration. But by the time Ozawa became the BSO's music director in 1974, Boston was ready for someone with a whiff of youth and the exotic in his lineage. When Koussevitzky, who retired in 1949, proposed Bernstein as his successor, it was not yet time for a brilliant but brash young American Jew out of Harvard and the Curtis Institute of Music, with one foot in Broadway musical theater.

Let others guard their privacy. Bernstein — "Lenny" to fellow musicians and friends, "Mr. Bernstein" to students, "L.B." to BSO management (but not to his face) — is an advertisement for himself. He arrives with a retinue of up to a dozen, including some or all of his three children (all adults now, working in music or theater), a housekeeper, and his manager, Harry Kraut, a former BSO assistant manager. He drives onto the grounds and up to the Shed — until a recent switch in cars — in a beige Mercedes convertible with the roof open and a New York plate modestly imprinted "MAESTRO I." Waving like a president in a motorcade, he exchanges greetings with students and astonished tourists.

He stays for ten days to two weeks, usually taking over a country house that the BSO rents for him from a patron or a patron's friend. Besides the student orchestra program he conducts the BSO's Serge and Olga Koussevitzky Memorial Concert, a premium-priced season highlight. Invariably demanding and getting extra rehearsal time with both orchestras — three rehearsals plus overtime with the BSO, when most conductors are lucky to get two — he works everyone to a state of exhaustion or frenzy. At BSO concerts that he is not conducting, he sits, visible to all (and sometimes providing a running commentary on the performance), in a box on the main aisle at the center of the Shed. Once a box-section usher, enforcing the rules, had to threaten him, very gently, with ejection if he did not put out his cigarette. He did.

Between rehearsals, concerts, reunions with old BSO friends, and conferences with BSO officialdom, Bernstein meets with student conductors and composers, to whom he offers analytical and hands-on advice. He chain-smokes and chain-signs autographs. The BSO staff is at his service. When he departs with a final wave from his convertible, the sigh of relief that goes up from the back of the Shed, where management has its offices, can be heard all the way to Boston. Yet he returns most or all of his fee — the conducting engagement by itself brings him something in the neighborhood of $50,000 — as a gift to the Music Center, which now has an endowment in his name. One thing no one has accused Leonard Bernstein of is forgetting his origins.

Bernstein's classes and rehearsals are as heavily attended by Tanglewood music makers as his concerts are by consumers. By all odds the best show is his conducting seminar. Although four or five other BSO conductors each summer (including Ozawa) meet with the conducting students in similar classes, Bernstein's larger-than-life name, presence, and career make him a star attraction here, too. Not only apprentice conductors but also other students, staff members, Tanglewood patrons, outsiders with musical pretensions, and any writers who happen to be in the vicinity show up at the extravaganza. Theoretically, the classes are closed to the public. In reality, hardly anyone is turned away. It is no accident that Bernstein is as comfortable on television as on the podium. He does love an audience.

The class is gathered in the living room at Seranak. Under a life-size portrait of a pleasantly scowling Koussey clutching his double bass, two baby grand pianos and a conductor's stand are set up in a clearing at one end of the room. At the other end, beyond the hearth and squeezed in among the dark, bottom-heavy 1930s furniture, most of which has been pushed to the walls, about seventy-five metal folding chairs accommodate the rows of eager acolytes. Others, too late for a seat, stand along the walls or wedge themselves against sofas and chairs.

Bernstein holds forth in the clearing, gesticulating with his cigarette as another teacher might with a piece of chalk. Ozawa is often

---

Leonard Bernstein draws an audience at a rehearsal with the Boston University Young Artists Orchestra.

Seiji Ozawa and Leonard Bernstein observe a student conductor at work during Bernstein's conducting class at Seranak.

there; Gustav Meier almost always is, watching over his charges. Two young Japanese women, whose sole vocation is to read orchestral scores at the keyboard, sit at the pianos, acting as the afternoon's orchestra. The student conductors — the two to six conducting fellows, in all the glory of the senior class, and the ten or twelve members of the conducting seminar, like freshmen and sophomores — occupy the first row or two of folding chairs. Each student is equipped with a baton, carefully transported in a cylinder resembling a mailing tube, and a set of scores. Each is nervous. The opportunity to impress Bernstein — or the possibility of failure — weighs on young shoulders like the globe.

What happens next can depend on the score to be learned, Bernstein's mood, the weather (there is no heating or air conditioning at Seranak), or a dozen other imponderables. Bernstein once showed up with his new recording of Mozart's *Haffner* Symphony with the Vienna Philharmonic. But as soon as two assistants in his train hooked up the compact disk player, it jammed. The class, which had nothing to do with the *Haffner*, went on as if under a sentence. At the end, Bernstein had not forgotten. He held the students until they heard the record on the hastily replaced machine. He cocked his head and conducted the disk as it played, and commended the performance for its spontaneity.

A typical scene was described in the *New York Times* by Helen Epstein, one of the legion of visiting writers. Bernstein and Ozawa were taking the students through Bartók's *Concerto for Orchestra* when Ken Takaseki, a conducting fellow, got hung up on the Hungarian accents — or what Bernstein insisted were Hungarian accents. Bernstein posed as a trumpeter in the duo-pianists' orchestra and asked Takaseki to sing to him how the trumpets' line should go.

Mr. Takaseki gulps, then tries to sing, and it comes out a squeak.

"Are you afraid? Are you embarrassed? Are you nervous?" [Bernstein asks.]

Mr. Takaseki nods. The class bursts out laughing.

"I just think you're so gifted that it's worth spending all this time," says Mr. Bernstein, moving forward, scattering ash like baptismal water over the heads of the students. "I'd like you to sing that trumpet line because I think I feel what you hear but I don't *hear* what you hear or *see* what you hear. Do you understand? Whatever is inside of you has to be communicated to the orchestra but *first* you have to express it to yourself."

Mr. Takaseki listens, squeaks again.

"Again."

Mr. Bernstein works with the students the way he does with orchestras, exploring one telling detail of the music until it is perfect. His memory of details, musical or literary, is impressive. "What is a novel but details?" he says later, after reciting, verbatim, a passage of Thomas Mann.

"Let's make up a word in Hungarian to go along with those trumpets," he says now. "Anyone have a word? I have a word. *Budapestü.* Let's say it means: I am a citizen of Budapest. Can you repeat it?"

The class repeats: *"Bu-da-pes-tü"* several times.
"Now sing it the way Bartók wrote it!"
Mr. Takaseki sings, *"Bu-da-pes-tü, Bu-da-pes-tü . . ."*
"Sing it!"
"Bu-da-pes-tü, Bu-da-pes-tü . . ."
"Now do it again but *mysteriously.* Just between us. It's something that appears in the night. Bartók's always writing this night music. Translate that to the beat and sing it with your *hands*!"
Mr. Takaseki's face is now grim with determination. He gestures.
"Now we're getting something," says Mr. Bernstein.

Bernstein's rehearsals with the student orchestra are no less painful or painstaking. Typically, he shows up in boots, jeans, and a sweatshirt (sometimes with "Harvard" emblazoned across the front), looking like one of the gang, only a bit graying, paunchy, and gaunt. He works with a score, putting glasses on to consult it during a pause, ripping them off again to conduct. The students are "great," "terrific," or "beautiful" as they play; he only wants them to be more great, terrific, or beautiful when he asks for a correction or adjustment, louder or softer, smoother or gruffer, one part more prominent, another more discreet — whatever it is, always more. Another *Times* writer, John Rockwell, caught him exhorting the orchestra with this line of patter while rehearsing the Sibelius Second:

> "Think dark, even when you're playing high," he cried, trying to elicit a Nordic feeling. "You can make a diminuendo on an upbeat — *you* don't think you can do it, but *I* tell you you can do it. . . . Thank you for that fortepiano; *Sibelius* thanks you. . . . Doesn't he say *tenuto* or something? Well, *I* say it; he *told* me to say it; we talk." To the first oboe: "This tiny entrance is like fifty trumpets." Then: "A great orchestra is a flexible orchestra: 'Lenny and his flexible cats.' . . . Pelvic pulse. Excuse the expression, but that's what it is. *Passion* . . . now it's really throbbing; the whole orchestra is alive with this throb. . . . You gotta cry and suffer, and that upbeat is part of it. . . . I love you; what can I say? You're just terrific."

Bernstein told the students the first rule of orchestral playing is that "it's all chamber music," and, indeed, in performances like his Sibelius Second that is how it comes out: every strand in place, every instrument carrying its burden, each blending yet each clear — transparency that at once focuses and magnifies the music. Because the students love playing for him, they gladly put in the hours and labor he asks. It is a sacrifice that professionals often make grudg-

ingly, especially when "Maestro 1" begins to lecture them about
what one or another composer means. The mark of a good conductor, to an orchestra player, is that he can make his baton speak
for him. And he finishes his rehearsals on time.

In a letter to his parents on the day before his 1940 debut with the
student orchestra, Bernstein wrote:

> ... I have never seen such a beautiful setup in my life. I've been con-
> ducting the orchestra every morning, & I'm playing my first concert
> tomorrow night. Kouss gave me the hardest & longest number of all —
> the Second Symphony of Randall Thompson, thirty minutes long — a
> modern American work — as my first performance. And Kouss is so
> pleased with my work. He likes me & works very hard with me in our
> private sessions. He is the most marvelous man — a beautiful spirit that
> never lags or fails — that inspires me terrifically. And he told me he is
> convinced that I have a wonderful gift, & he is already making me a *great*
> conductor. (I actually rode in his car with him today!) ... We've been
> working very hard — you're always going like mad here — no time to
> think of how tired you are or how little you slept last night — the inspi-
> ration of this Center is terrific enough to keep you going with no sleep
> at all. I'm so excited about tomorrow night — I wish you could all be
> here — it's so important to me — & Kouss is banking on it to convince
> him that he's right — if it goes well there's no telling what may hap-
> pen. ... [Burton Bernstein, *Family Matters*]

Yet relations between the BSO and its most famous son have never
been easy. Though the early tensions with the trustees have faded,
hidden resentments occasionally break into the open.

The problems arise partly from temperament. All that hugging
and kissing, not just for the women but for the male soloists and
first-chair players, too; all those hours of overtime in rehearsal,
which cost the orchestra money and the players hours with their
families or on the golf course; all those tricks with tempos, which
get slower and slower as the years go by; all the talking and swinging
and jiving — it is too much for 105 professionals who hear and
react to music in their own ways. But in the end complaints come
to nothing. Bernstein's concerts, with both the BSO and the student
orchestra, are among the best played and most electric of the summer. When, from too much smoking or brooding or partying, he
falls from the pinnacle, the orchestra does its best to pull him back
up (as, indeed, it will for any conductor it respects).

Lauren Bacall at the Bernstein birthday
celebration.

During three summers in a recent five-year stretch, Bernstein withdrew from his Tanglewood appearances. In 1978 it was because of
the death of his wife, the Chilean-born actress Felicia Montealegre,
from cancer. In 1980 he took a sabbatical from all conducting to
devote himself to composing.

In 1982 came the severest test: he and the BSO were not speaking.
The summer before, Bernstein had come to Tanglewood expecting
to double as the soloist and conductor in Gershwin's *Rhapsody in
Blue* in a July Fourth gala with the BSO, a performance he would
then record. Management, which had apparently encouraged the
recording project, had second thoughts a week or two before the
concert. Then because of the disagreement the *Rhapsody* also was
scratched from the concert program. Tempers flared; the players
became unruly at rehearsals. There was an argument over money.
In the aftermath Bernstein canceled all his 1981-82 BSO dates, including three in Symphony Hall that were part of the BSO's centennial celebration. That summer Tanglewood's most distinguished
alumnus shifted his allegiance to the Los Angeles Philharmonic,
serving as co-director of its new institute for young conductors, a

Beverly Sills hosts the Bernstein birthday gala.

project modeled on the Tanglewood Music Center's conducting program.

The boycott lasted just one year. Bernstein returned to Tanglewood the next summer and turned over the reins of the Los Angeles project to his co-director, Michael Tilson Thomas. Never during the travails, in fact, did his loyalty to the Music Center falter. In 1978, after he had told the BSO he would not be available, he arranged to spend twelve days with the students. He taught, coached parts of his *Songfest*, and conducted the Music Center Orchestra in a hastily scheduled concert. In 1980 he again emerged from seclusion to help the school celebrate its fortieth anniversary. Aaron Copland, who had served as the first chairman of the faculty, also showed up for the festivities and to conduct the BSO in a program of his own works for his eightieth birthday. At Seranak the two men palavered for the inescapable television cameras. Bernstein recalled that "it was forty-three years ago that I first stood on this lawn." Copland replied, "Everything has remained amazingly the same."

The reconciliation blossomed into an outright love fest in 1988, the year of Bernstein's seventieth birthday. As luck had it, the birth date, August 25, fell on the Thursday that began Tanglewood's final weekend. The BSO turned the weekend into a monster birthday party as part of Tanglewood's own fiftieth anniversary celebration.

The centerpiece was a four-hour BSO gala on the night of August 25. Before the lights and cameras of an international press corps — everybody from *People* magazine to *The Times* of London, from Tiffany's to Japanese and European television, was there — thirty celebrities from the worlds of music and entertainment conducted, played, sang, acted, danced, told jokes, strutted, or spoke in honor of Lenny. (For one night the name Bernstein was forgotten.) Beverly Sills was the mistress of ceremonies and Mstislav Rostropovich, Yo-Yo Ma, Midori, Christa Ludwig, Victor Borge, and Lauren Bacall were among the performers. Each star and each piece of music — many, of course, by Bernstein himself — was in some way associated with the guest of honor, who sat in his center box, smoking his cigarette. (No usher stopped him now.)

On Friday night the Music Center Orchestra gave a special program featuring more music and performers from the Bernstein legacy. (With three student conductors preceding him to the podium as he and his classmates had once preceded Koussevitzky, Bernstein had led his *Songfest* five nights earlier in his annual student orchestra concert.) On Saturday night 250 singers, actors, and dancers from the Indiana University Opera Theater gave a staged performance of *Mass,* Bernstein's 1971 theater piece celebrating the values of religion in the pop-rock language of youth. Bernstein himself closed the celebration and the season by making his annual BSO appearance Sunday afternoon in the Koussevitzky Memorial Concert. For the program he paired two more Koussevitzky specialties, Haydn's Symphony no. 88 and Tchaikovsky's Fifth. In between came a birthday garland of eight variations, each by a different composer, on the hit tune "New York, New York" from Bernstein's first Broadway musical, *On the Town.* Seiji Ozawa conducted the nostalgic, laughter-filled première. Neither Governor and presidential candidate Michael S. Dukakis, followed by a swarm of reporters, cameramen, and Secret Service guards and cheered repeatedly by the crowd of

---

Bernstein conducting at his concert concluding the seventieth birthday celebration.

14,000, nor Secretary of State George P. Shultz, who was also in the audience, received the adulation that Tanglewood heaped on its favorite son.

On reaching the biblical age of three score and ten, Bernstein still had the Music Center in his heart. At his request the celebration was a benefit for the school, with a goal of $1 million to be added to the Bernstein endowment. (Ticket prices for the birthday gala, which attracted arts patrons and socialites from the United States and abroad, were $20 on the lawn and $50 to $5,000 in the Shed.) Nothing Bernstein does, or nothing done for him, is modest; it took a fleet of forty cars, with forty volunteer drivers, just to ferry the stars and nabobs to and from airports, hotels, rehearsals, concerts, and a round robin of parties.

In the program book Bernstein quoted the closing line from *East Coker*, the second of T. S. Eliot's *Four Quartets — In my end is my beginning —* as his reason for returning to Tanglewood for the birthday. At the end of *Mass,* as the cheers from a standing audience engulfed him, he made his way out of the crowd to the stage. He was in tears. Addressing the hushed throng over the public address system, he described the student performance as "a miracle — a miracle of youth, first of all; a miracle of faith, a ceaseless miracle of America, and I hope a ceaseless miracle of Tanglewood."

In his end was his summation. The frequent references to Michelangelo during the birthday gala did not seem out of place. Bernstein cannot fix cars, as one of the performers noted, and he cannot sing — thank God, Sills said, because then there would be *nothing* left for other musicians to do. But the prodigality of talent onstage — the guest stars, three of whom had flown in from Europe on the Concorde that morning, had only a walk-on number apiece — matched the gifts with which Bernstein has been showered, and which he in turn has showered on the world.

You gotta cry and suffer. Everything about Bernstein is extravagant, if not excessive. Yet genius in all times and places makes its own rules. No one (except perhaps Gunther Schuller) has ever questioned whether that flaming ego — that mixture of the genius and the showman all in one breath — is a constructive force in the lives of young musicians. Perhaps no one has to. Bernstein can claim to have talked to Sibelius and, on that basis, can tinker with Sibelius's rhythms and tempos, simply because Bernstein can make the tricks work. For young conductors who cannot speak when the master calls on them to perform, the problem is to come to terms with the music and themselves first, and only then to do Lenny's metaphysical leap, if anyone can.

Lenny has mellowed, BSO members say. He has learned to live with himself. He is more in touch with the music. And no other conductor at Tanglewood parties till dawn with his students. No other conductor is Bernstein.

* * *

Fifteen minutes late, Elly Ameling swept into the Chamber Music Hall with her pianist, Rudolf Jansen. Petite, brunette, and clad in a loose-fitting pink dress on a sultry afternoon, the Dutch soprano apologized to the gathering of about 125 students, auditors, and visitors. There had been a mixup over drivers; hers arrived late to bring her to Tanglewood.

She and Jansen, who is also Dutch, got quickly down to business. They sat, facing the piano, at a small table set up for them on one side of the rustic, wooden stage. Ameling called her first student, William Hite, a tenor, out of the audience.

Like the four others who were to follow him during the next 2½ hours, Hite brought a student accompanist to the stage with him. Taking a recitalist's stance in front of the piano, he announced that he would sing a selection from Hugo Wolf's *Italienisches Liederbuch*. Ameling, Jansen, and the audience listened intently as he went through the song to the end. But there was competition. In the gardens near the open-sided, barnlike hall a set of chimes tinkled softly. They sounded a bit like Mozart's Papageno with his magic bells, only discordant with the music from the stage.

"I hear that strange noise outside when that beautiful voice comes," Ameling said, pleasantly yet with a note of pique, when Hite finished. She declared the bells "very interesting — almost as interesting as a song by Hugo Wolf." But they would have to go.

A Tanglewood functionary, ever alert to a star's comforts, had already hastened from the hall into the gardens. In little more time than it takes a famous singer to charm a roomful of people, the chimes were replaced by the distant sound of instrumental groups practicing. The master class could continue.

Ameling came to Tanglewood in 1984 to sing in a BSO program of eighteenth-century music under Kurt Masur and give a Schubert recital four nights later. It turned out that she was staying on a few more days to prepare for a recording session in Europe. On learning of her plans, the Music Center staff persuaded her to meet with Phyllis Curtin's vocal students. Master classes, including Curtin's own, are almost as common as mosquitoes at Tanglewood. But as a teacher Elly Ameling was different. She belongs to the rare breed of singer who prefers the intimate duchy of the art song to the world of opera. She is, in fact, to lieder, oratorio, and orchestral singing what Leonard Bernstein is to conducting or Oliver Knussen is to contemporary music. And at Tanglewood, of course, the song literature has been a mainstay of the vocal program since Erich Leinsdorf's 1962 abolition of the opera department.

Enthusiasm for the class ran high. Thirty students signed up to sing for Ameling and suffer her criticisms. John Oliver, head of the vocal department, and his assistants chose five of the group on the basis of their repertoire and experience. The class was scheduled to run ninety minutes. In the end, because of the care Ameling took with each singer, it ran an hour overtime.

Ameling and Jansen, who wore a yellow paisley shirt, looked like the coolest people in the room on the stifling afternoon. The soprano proved a gracious but stern taskmaster. She smiled and bestowed compliments freely but showed her five subjects little mercy. She and Jansen, both of whom speak almost flawless English, corrected the students on their pronunciation, dynamics, and phrasing — corrected them not just once but again and again. But mistakes also produced sympathetic laughter from the audience: from experience in Curtin's and other classes, each student knew how it felt to be up there making a fool of yourself in front of your peers.

A compliment was Ameling's first response to Hite after the silencing of the bells. "You sing that very beautifully," she told him. But hard work lay ahead. She said the Wolf song about his sweetheart's hair required him to portray the girl and his feelings about her with more character and expression.

"Let us see where is the imagination that shows us what you feel," she said.

Hite and his pianist began the song again. Ameling and Jansen interrupted them, reworked phrases, chided or encouraged, sang or played along with the music. Hovering close by, Ameling conducted now and then to keep the tempo going.

Hite struggled like a man who fell deeper into a pit each time he tried to clamber out.

"I would like more of a smile, much more of a smile, in spite of the fact that you are working and trying," Ameling said with a smile. The girl's hair, she said, is "like gold, also like silk," and the singer's voice must show the different colors in its tones.

After half an hour Hite still had not extricated himself. He and his pianist thanked their teachers and, in a fluster, prepared to leave the stage. With a tinkling laugh Ameling told him, "You must have a beautiful blonde girl to hold in your arms to learn this song." Amid applause he melted into the audience.

Marjorie McDermott, a mezzo-soprano, was next. She had chosen Mozart's *Abendempfindung,* a song about thoughts of love and death as evening falls. Like Hite, she sang through it once without interruption to show how she had prepared it.

Ameling worked first on McDermott's enunciation, breath control, and vocal production. Next she addressed the meaning of the song. She pointed out that the singer goes to heaven and, from there, speaks to friends below about peace. Stretching her arms wide, Ameling said the voice should expand to encompass the breadth of heaven.

That, she quickly added, "is my opinion"; she had "no experience" of the place.

McDermott sat down, and Elizabeth Gintz, a soprano, went up. Fauré's *La rose* was her offering. Ameling worked on the French pronunciation. She urged a slight break between words. Then, unsure of herself after all, she cautioned, "This is a thing you can never quite be sure of. One Frenchman might do it and another might not."

During the second time through Gintz suddenly got a better sense of the song and her voice blossomed. Ameling also brightened. "I hear another gear suddenly," she said. "You can use that gear."

"Overdrive," Jansen suggested. Ameling happily assented; laughter spread through the hall.

Karen Richards, another soprano, sang Schubert's *Nur wer die Sehnsucht kennt,* a song about longing for a distant beloved. "We should strive in this song to be like a violin," Ameling said. Demonstrating, she whistled the melody and bowed an invisible fiddle.

Richards tried again but still had not discovered the magic violin. As she appeared to grow disheartened, Ameling reassured her: "It is hard. It is hard. It needs a lot of vocal discipline, this song." A singer can, she said, "study it for months and years" and only then be able to give it the dark coloring it requires. She suggested that Richards try it in different styles and moods at home.

Probably the hottest person in the room was the baritone who sang last, David Taft. He walked to the stage in a three-piece suit, the vest and jacket blue, slacks gray.

He, too, sang Schubert — *Ganymed,* an ode to spring and God's embrace. His problem was meter. He sang in four beats to the measure. Ameling wanted two.

"Nobody can soar to the heavens in fours," she corrected him. He tried to soar in twos for her but remained firmly on the ground. Exhorting him, Ameling said, "All the love that's in you, you speak to the gods." But perspiration seemed his principal offering to the gods when his half-hour was up.

At the end John Oliver thanked the visitors for being so generous with their time. Standing and picking up her purse to leave, Ameling explained, "It takes a long time, but it takes a long time to say." She cheerfully added: "What you can use, use it. What you can't, leave it alone."

Applause ended another Ameling performance, and a swarm of students surrounded her on the stage. The 2½-hour class was not long enough for her admirers from the Music Center's eight-week regimen of concerts, rehearsals, and classes.

*   *   *

If Elly Ameling embodies the yin of Tanglewood teaching, Joel Krosnick embodies the yang. In a sweaty sport shirt, jeans, and running shoes on another hot afternoon, Krosnick sat facing a string quintet in an upstairs practice room in the Main House. A feeling of frayed nerves and spent air pervaded the room as he led the all-male group through a reading of the *adagio* of Schubert's great C Major Quintet. Holding a score in one hand, he conducted with the other hand, nodded to the instruments to cue them in, and swayed with the rhythm and the mood.

The student group was still feeling its way into the music when the second cellist fell behind the beat. Krosnick leapt up, snapping his fingers at the player to bring him up to tempo.

"Can't you guys play any softer?" he barked a few moments later as the music droned on. Then, as the instruments began a series of entrances, he demanded decisiveness: "Now *you* make your move!" he said to one player. "Move by move. Next move. Next. Come on, keep going!" His fingers snapped for emphasis.

After the second time through Krosnick told the exhausted group, "All right. It's not too bad. It's basically a very long line and it takes all night. It's very hard because nobody's got the melody."

Before the season ended, the group would perform the work in a Music Center concert.

"Those fellowship students work their butts off," Krosnick said later. "I mean, they barely have time to breathe. But there's a kind of all-the-way-out quality — that you either make music or you don't — and there's nobody sitting back. They're really trying."

It was 1983. Krosnick, who was forty-two that summer, is the cellist of the Juilliard String Quartet. Chunky and intense, with coiling dark hair, he has an all-the-way-out quality himself. He did not plan it that he would spend his summers at Tanglewood as a teacher. Pianist Gilbert Kalish, the head of the Music Center's chamber program and Krosnick's frequent partner on the recital circuit, enticed him with promises of a good program and good students.

When Kalish called in the summer of 1981 Krosnick already had his next summer booked with performances and rehearsals.

"That was it as far as I was concerned," Krosnick said. "I was starting to just quickly return phone calls and say, 'Well, look, please think of me next summer.' Gil called and said, 'What would you think of teaching . . . ?' "

Krosnick threw his head back and laughed. "I told him, 'There isn't anything else I could consider — *oh, my God!*' So he told me what it was and what I could expect to find, and said, was I interested? I said of course. There is an atmosphere here that's sort of permanently seductive."

Krosnick came in 1982. Kalish and the others in command let him steal time the first summer to meet previous commitments. By 1983, newly wed to Dinah Straight, a schoolteacher, and making a home with her in a rented summer place just across the state line in Austerlitz, New York, he had little incentive to roam. On top of everything else, he and Kalish were preparing a series of ten recitals

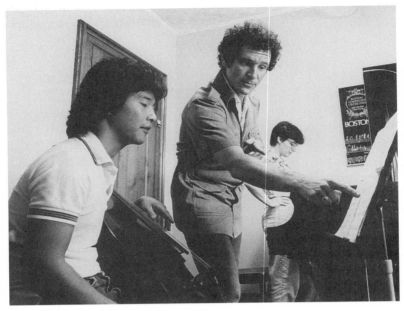

Joel Krosnick coaches a student cellist.

of American music they would give in New York and Washington during the coming season.

Krosnick is proud to be a member of the Juilliard, which he joined in 1974. He is particularly proud of its record of championing American music, which means mostly twentieth-century music — tough, unpopular music. He recalled that the violinist and quartet leader Felix Galimir — "a man we all [in the quartet] love very much" — once said that "a lot of quartets start playing American repertoire to get ahead, and then as soon as they get famous, they spend the rest of their lives on Beethoven." The Juilliard was an exception. "They played this American stuff and they keep playing this American stuff and they keep playing it."

The "American stuff" in the Juilliard's repertoire includes the quartets of Arthur Foote, Charles Ives, Elliott Carter, Roger Sessions, Milton Babbitt, Ralph Shapey, and Gunther Schuller. Krosnick likens such music to Twain's *Huckleberry Finn* in its "massive importance" as "part of our relevant past." Yet he knows that when the Juilliard tours "it's very hard to get people to listen." Concert presenters also have it tough: "There's an economic difficulty. You want to sell your concert series, right?" Who wants a session with Sessions?

A vicious circle is at work. Shapey's Seventh Quartet, for instance, is a work the Juilliard believes in. Wildly dissonant, it is as easy to grip as a porcupine for both audiences and players. Because of its lack of crowd appeal, the players may get six performances of it, at most, in a season.

"And that's hard," Krosnick said. "It's very hard for us to do it that way. So it's not something that people accept as part of their listening experience. But, perhaps first of all, it's not something that we performers accept as part of ours."

The Juilliard, of course, also plays the Beethoven cycle, and that, to Krosnick, "is wonderful, marvelous. That's a major emotional experience." But he is concerned that "one go on listening — as a performer that I lead the audience in going on listening in a fresh, new way; not that they're allowed to sort of listen to the few things they really like, and listen to them without really listening."

Krosnick returned to the middle of the *adagio*, where Schubert's impassioned writing calls for extreme agitation and dynamic stress by the five strings.

"I want a storm," he told the students as he stalked the room, hovering over them like a hawk. "I mean a *storm* — an apocalypse, like the end of the world!"

The students tried again. It was still on the timid side. Again and again, Krosnick called for "courage!" Still unable to conjure up his storm, he explained to the second violinist: "You've got to have more courage in running the inside. It's like you were about to fall off the waves because you were scared. You're *supposed* to fall down and drown."

Later Krosnick said that after three sessions the second cellist, who had been overwhelmed at the beginning, finally understood about getting a wider range of tone colors in his playing.

By the end of the lesson he wrung my hand out and said, "I promise you *I'll think about sound, I'll think about sound.*" Great — it's fantastic. But he has to feel okay about the program somehow. He has to have been made comfortable to go into a studio and just open up. If he feels it is competitive and that he better keep his game together, otherwise somebody's going to be down his shirt front, he's not going to feel comfortable like that. He's obviously feeling that he can learn — he can just open up and learn, let it go, you know.

To open up and learn, without a sense of competition: it is the ideal Krosnick and Tanglewood seek. It is not a quick or easy trip with guarantees of success, as Gunther Schuller warned. It is more like the long line of Schubert's *adagio* as Krosnick explained it to his students.

"It never stops," he said, describing a large, revolving arc with his hand. "It just never, never stops, you know. It's like a wheel slowly turning. You just reach inside and grab on."

In any given summer the Music Center faculty numbers about forty. (The Boston University Tanglewood Institute faculty is largely separate.) About half of these musicians come from the BSO, with first-chair players as the core. Some of the others, like Phyllis Curtin and Maurice Abravanel, are familiar to the public from performing careers. But most are distinguished by experience in ensemble work and, often, in new music. Kalish and his fellow pianist Peter Serkin, for example, have deliberately avoided the virtuoso-celebrity route to concentrate on chamber and contemporary music, including works they have commissioned. Or if they appear in a traditional soloist's role it is in unhackneyed repertoire or in a fresh approach to the familiar. Kalish, for instance, is noted for his performances of the sonatas and other solo keyboard works by Haydn and Schubert; Serkin likes to bring his clear, unsentimental style to Brahms. Kalish, a Tanglewood student in 1951, 1952, and 1953, joined the faculty in 1968 and succeeded Joseph Silverstein as chairman in 1985. Serkin was added to the faculty as Kalish took on more and more administrative duties in the 1980s.

Other faculty members, like Louis Krasner and Eugene Lehner, are even less known by the public but are legends in the music world. Both now in their eighties, these two string players — Krasner a violinist, Lehner a violist — knew and worked with Schoenberg, Berg, Webern, and Bartók in prewar Vienna. Krasner holds an even rarer distinction. He commissioned and gave the première of Berg's Violin Concerto, one of the few twentieth-century violin concertos that seem certain to endure into the twenty-first century. He also gave the first performances of the important concertos by Schoenberg and Sessions. Lehner, now retired from the BSO, performed in

Gilbert Kalish doubles as chairman of the faculty and a chamber music coach.

Schoenberg's Society for Private Musical Performances and was a member of the celebrated Kolisch Quartet, which championed works by Schoenberg's Viennese school but also was a leader in playing the standard repertoire. In the United States Lehner worked closely with the Juilliard Quartet in its early days, teaching it the Bartók quartets, which the Juilliard introduced into American musical life. The Juilliard still reveres him as a musical godfather.

In the summer of 1986 there were two Juilliard quartets at Tanglewood, both in new ventures, both working with Lehner. There was the Juilliard String Quartet, all-male, forty years old, and Tanglewood's first professional quartet in residence. There was also the Cassatt String Quartet, all-female and one year old, which studied at the Juilliard School of Music in the winter and became Tanglewood's first resident student ensemble.

There was a connection, of course. The Cassatt did study with the Juilliard Quartet in New York. Yet the Cassatt was at Tanglewood on its own merits, seeking new vistas with new teachers.

Louis Krasner works with a student ensemble.

Some quartets emerge full-blown when four players who have worked together unite to pursue a career. The Cassatt's birth was more difficult. Violinist Laurajean Goldberg and cellist Anna Lucia Cholakian had been friends since they were students together in 1977 at Charles Castleman's summer quartet program in Troy, New York, where they "just clicked" in their playing. Though only in high school then, they decided that someday they would be in a quartet together. They dreamed of traveling from town to town and rehearsing on trains — the kind of dreams starry-eyed young musicians have.

In 1983 Cholakian graduated from the Eastman School of Music and entered Juilliard to work toward a master's degree. Goldberg was already there, also studying for a master's. Reunited, they decided to organize the quartet they had talked about as high school students. For a year and a half they read music with both men and women in a search for suitable partners. It seemed hopeless. With each candidate, said Cholakian, "we'd read together and we'd close the book and say goodbye."

Destiny, however, was up to its usual tricks. The summer before, violinist Adela Peña, a former Music Center fellow, and violist Eufrosina Raileanu had met as students at the Yale summer music school in Norfolk, Connecticut. They, too, went on to Juilliard as graduate students. By coincidence they turned up at the same reading to try out with Goldberg and Cholakian. Just as with Goldberg and Cholakian themselves six years before, something clicked in the playing.

"This group with Adela and Zina just had a certain chemistry," recalled Goldberg. "It's hard to find that combination. So then we decided to work together."

The Cassatt was born in January 1985. Soon afterward the group approached Joel Krosnick, with whom Goldberg and Cholakian had coached the year before. They told him other music schools, like Yale and Eastman, had formal quartet programs, with student ensembles studying on scholarships: why not Juilliard? They volunteered to be Juilliard's first student quartet.

Krosnick sold the school on the idea, and the Cassatt, scholarships in hand, spent a year studying with Krosnick and two of his partners in the Juilliard Quartet, first violinist Robert Mann and violist Samuel Rhodes. (It was Mann who cast the decisive vote in the choice of the group's name. After the women had narrowed the possibilities to three — Piet Mondrian, the male painter; Mary Cassatt, the woman painter, and Ariel, the spirit — they asked Mann which name he liked best. He liked Cassatt.) The quartet played its first concert later in 1985 and won two first prizes and a second in competitions during the following year. Meanwhile the school formalized and broadened the residency program, and the Cassatt returned in the fall of 1986 for a second year of study.

It happened that 1985 was also a watershed year for the Juilliard Quartet: Earl Carlyss decided to retire as the second violinist. After readings with a handful of invited players, the remaining members chose a BSO violinist, Joel Smirnoff, as the replacement. Two of the four members now had Tanglewood connections. The BSO, knowing that the reconstituted quartet would need time and a place — preferably quiet — to regroup with its new violinist, invited it to spend the summer of 1986 at Tanglewood. Although the Juilliard normally takes the summer off, it seized the opportunity to get away from the city for intensive rehearsals, a reunion with Lehner, and a pair of trial concerts.

Tanglewood meanwhile decided to go ahead with its separate Ensemble Residency Program, in which, for the first time, a student ensemble could study under fellowships like those awarded to other instrumentalists. The program had been under consideration for three years but the Juilliard was the catalyst. With a professional quartet on hand to coach and advise, "it seemed the ideal time to do it," said Richard Ortner, the Music Center administrator.

For the Cassatt Tanglewood with the Juilliard in residence "seemed too good to pass up," according to Cholakian. The women could be near their mentors and study with senior Tanglewood faculty members like Krasner and Lehner, with their connections to the Central European tradition.

For the first year, because of the Juilliard's central role, Tanglewood limited candidates for the student residency to string ensembles. The Cassatt was one of the nine ensembles that auditioned. The seven judges included Krosnick, Krasner, Kalish, and Leon Fleisher. The Cassatt, said Ortner, was the unanimous — and "fervent" — choice of all seven.

The Cassatt spent most of the summer out of sight, practicing and coaching with its old and new mentors. It did, however, give two public performances. In the Festival of Contemporary Music it played Britten's valedictory Third Quartet, a performance arranged and coached by Oliver Knussen. On the final Saturday of the season, as the culmination of its studies and a showcase for the residency program, the group gave a full-length concert in the Theater–Concert Hall. The program consisted of Mozart's K. 465 (the *Dissonant*), Bartók's no. 5, and Beethoven's third *Rasoumovsky*, from opus 59.

Indian summer came to Tanglewood on the last Saturday in August 1986. It had been a dismal two months: rainy, dank, chill. Suddenly, after ten weeks of gloom, the sun appeared on a sparkling afternoon. The rest of the students had played their last concert at Tanglewood on Parade on Tuesday night and decamped. The throngs would return for that night's concert by the Israel Philharmonic, visiting under its music director Zubin Mehta, and the last day's *War Requiem* under Seiji Ozawa. But except for a few strolling tourists the grounds now were deserted. The Cassatt's audience numbered no more than three hundred — a shadow of the crowd that hears most chamber programs in the Theater–Concert Hall.

The players walked onstage in identical dresses in complementary shades of aqua, blue, pink, and white. They presented a strikingly feminine sight, like debutantes at a ball. But from the first note it was evident that the summer with Krosnick, Mann, Krasner, Lehner, and others on the Tanglewood faculty had bred Mozart, Beethoven, and Bartók into their hearts and bones — that neither femininity nor masculinity, only devotion to music, had anything to do with it. The playing was balanced, fierce, and scrupulous, demonstrating a faith in the power of music to move audiences.

Leon Fleisher was at that concert, as he is at nearly every student concert. Looking back on his first full year as head of the Music Center, he said he at last understood why, for those who become a part of Tanglewood, winter is the prelude to summer, rather than the other way around. The intensity of the Tanglewood experience turns the vacation period into the main musical season, while winter becomes a time of waiting and preparation.

There is something about the end of a Tanglewood season that suggests autumn and the snows beyond. Around 4:30 on a Sunday afternoon in late August, two months of the most intense activity — rehearsing, performing, teaching, studying, listening, discussing, making and renewing friendships — cease on a single chord. Hundreds of musicians who have been like a family scatter as the leaves already reddening on the New England maples will soon scatter.

But there, on a brilliant day at the end of the season of rains, a rebirth occurred: the Cassatt played a concert when there should have been no student concerts left — not only played, but played with the surging, "all-the-way-out quality" that teachers like Krosnick, Bernstein, and Knussen instill. Behind music like this a larger transaction takes place. The Cassatt learns from the Juilliard, and the Juilliard goes back to its work recharged by its experience with youth. Other students and teachers take similar nourishment. Generation follows generation, each replenishing the other and the art of music. As habitués like Fleisher discover, the Music Center, where these exchanges take place, is the heart of Tanglewood.

Chapter V

HISTORY AND SENTIMENT

O VER A HALF-CENTURY
any institution develops a history and traditions. One of Tanglewood's grandest traditions is the singing of Randall Thompson's
Alleluia, written for the opening of the Music Center in 1940 and
sung by incoming students during opening exercises every year
since. Nothing so raises the ghost of Koussevitzky as this a cappella
work and its echoes of summers and students past.

Twice in recent years outside events, both involving communist
superpowers, brought world history to the Tanglewood stage. In
1975, a year after their flight from the Soviet Union, cellist-
conductor Mstislav Rostropovich and his wife, soprano Galina
Vishnevskaya, came to give four concerts. On the date when Rostropovich was to conduct Shostakovich's Fifth Symphony, the composer, who was the couple's intimate friend in Russia, died in
Moscow. That night's performance became an unforgettable memorial to one of the twentieth century's major composers.

In 1979 the BSO traveled to China in the first U.S.–Chinese cultural
exchange since the two countries' resumption of diplomatic relations after a thirty-year lapse. The next year four Chinese musicians
repaid the visit by performing both Western and Chinese works at
Tanglewood. The exchange proved a triumph for music and international understanding. It also provided a glimpse of cultural
differences.

History occurs within the institution, too. Until 1979 no orchestra
except the BSO had ever played the big weekend concerts in the
Shed. But that year the New York Philharmonic, under Zubin Mehta,
Tanglewood '58, moved in to play the final weekend's concerts
while the BSO embarked on a tour of European music festivals. The

precedent having been set, the BSO departed a week early again in 1984 on another European tour. This time it left Tanglewood in the hands of the Cleveland Orchestra under its newly appointed music director, Christoph von Dohnányi, Tanglewood '52. The run of three concerts, marking the German Dohnányi's accession to the American podium, proved an extraordinary occasion.

Opera has played a major part in Tanglewood's history almost since the beginning. For the first twenty-two years performances took place in a student program. In 1980 Seiji Ozawa reinstated opera in a new format — semi-staged productions with star singers and the BSO as the orchestra. Troubled though the annual productions were by the Shed's stage limitations and Ozawa's lack of operatic experience, he pressed on because he considered opera essential to Tanglewood's standing as an international festival and his growth as a conductor. An enlarged program, perhaps modeled on the original student program, loomed in the future.

Just as the summer begins with the tradition of the *Alleluia,* it ends with another tradition — recognition of BSO members who are leaving the orchestra as the season ends. The ceremony takes place at the conclusion of the final BSO concert.

In 1987 six musicians with a total service of 218 years received a tumultuous farewell that was rich in both history and sentiment. One of the six, bassist John Barwicki, was the last active BSO member to have played in the initial Tanglewood season fifty years before. Another, the seventy-eight-year-old violinist and associate Pops director Harry Ellis Dickson, took up a new career as a guest conductor of pops orchestras across the United States and Canada. Between pops appearances Dickson joined the presidential campaign of his son-in-law, Governor Michael S. Dukakis, who was on hand to wish the departing players Godspeed.

*   *   *   *   *

There is a certain Tanglewood functionary — he shall remain nameless — who cannot get through the Music Center's opening exercises without dissolving into tears. Relief is part of his reflexes. He has worked hard to get another season out of the garage and onto the road. But something bigger is speaking in him: call it nostalgia, dedication, or love for Tanglewood's traditions.

Veterans will probably never be able to make the words "Tangle-wood Music Center" roll off their tongues. They will always want to say "Berkshire Music Center." That was the name Koussevitzky's school bore from its opening in 1940 until corporate image makers worked it over in 1984 to pinpoint the Tanglewood connection for recruiters, fund raisers, and their targets.

Veterans feel that special rush of affection when the students — about four hundred of them — gather early each July in the Theater–Concert Hall for the speeches and music that launch them on eight weeks of study. Veterans remember year upon year of opening exercises, session upon session of students, a legion stretch-ing back into the mists when Koussevitzky and followers like Aaron Copland exhorted them to pursue their art.

On that opening afternoon veterans think of the famous — Bern-stein, Ozawa, Mehta, Caldwell, Milnes, Price, Curtin — whom Tanglewood brought to light. They think of the lesser lights who went on to become orchestra players or teachers but also contributed their labors to music. They remember Mme. Koussevitzky, frail but aglow, speaking of her husband and early grandeur; tea and cookies in the gardens; renewals of friendships lasting through the years.

To those who were not actually there on July 8, 1940, however, nothing so much recalls the first Music Center opening, with Kous-sevitzky speaking of the place of music in the New World, as Randall Thompson's *Alleluia*. Composed at Koussevitzy's request and rushed to the festival with the ink barely dry for the 1940 opening, this unaccompanied choral piece was sung by the student body at the first exercises and has been sung by the student body at every open-ing since. It was the work Koussevitzky chose to open the Shed concerts in 1940 — from the start he wanted to integrate the stu-dents into the BSO season — and it was the work the chorus sang at the opening BSO concert in 1987 to signal Tanglewood's fiftieth anniversary.

The *Alleluia* disguises its art in simplicity. About five minutes long, it consists of the single word "alleluia" sung in a gently rising and then falling series of harmonizations, with the lower voices some-times enriching the melody, sometimes providing a mildly dis son-ant counterpoint. Performed at the end of the program, the piece never fails to produce a reverential effect, like the benediction after a sermon.

This is the scene: The students are seated in the center section of the rustic hall, faculty and guests in the two outer sections. Various speakers, such as Leon Fleisher, Seiji Ozawa, Kenneth Haas, and Phyllis Curtin, have offered reflections on the Koussevitzky heritage and good wishes for the summer. Ozawa has been both serious and comic in his remembrance of himself as a mixed-up kid who did not know anybody or anything — not even English — on his arrival by bus from Boston for his 1960 student year. Faculty members have provided a musical entr'acte. Applause has been generous. But by now the program has gone on for an hour or more. The students, BSO members, other teachers, parents, guests, and friends — a crowd of about one thousand in all — are getting restless. Some want to go swimming or to get back to families; others want to practice the music that has brought them here.

Now John Oliver, director of vocal music, comes to the stage. He asks the students to rise. Those in the back come forward, crowding into the center and side aisles, where they surround the seated spectators.

These students, most of whom have never seen one another before, will have rehearsed the *Alleluia* for about a half-hour before the exercises — as much as the very first class did, the parts having arrived a scant fifty minutes before the ceremonies. (Most students, indeed, will have come to the Berkshires, whether from the fifty states, Europe, or Asia, only a few hours before their rehearsal.) They will not have known the *Alleluia* before their arrival, and will hardly be aware of its significance.

But at that first harmonized "alleluia" under Oliver's direction, something magical happens. The piece is so ingeniously written, especially for young voices, that its sonorities seem to grow from, to magnify, and to illuminate one another. The minority of trained voices stands out, but gradually the raw ones blend in. Each "alleluia" rises out of the one before it, bolder and stronger. The piece swells to a climax. Then it subsides into a gentle affirmation, at peace. Oliver gives the final release, and the ceremonies end.

The traditional tea in the garden (unless rain forces it under shelter) now follows. But those four hundred students straggling out to refreshments are not the same four hundred students who straggled in. A transformation has taken place. They have been melded into a unit that will study, perform, work, play, and live together for eight weeks; they have been infused with the spirit of Koussevitzky, which seems to awaken in each of those swelling "alleluias." That spirit will grow as the summer progresses. (It will also dampen as the occasional setback or disappointment takes place.) But this has been the beginning, the initiation.

Tanglewood has many traditions. It even has a tradition of making a tradition of anything it says is a tradition. Just as Leonard Bernstein is a tradition, the *Alleluia* is a tradition. When it says Tanglewood is in session, the traditional functionary weeps the traditional tears. And, if tradition holds, others in the crowd, remembering the *Alleluias* and legions of students past, quietly weep with him.

*   *   *

In the *Alleluia* music and history combine as a cleansing force. On Saturday night, August 9, 1975, they combined on the Tanglewood stage with the force of a collision. Thomas D. Perry, Jr., then the BSO's executive director, could recall only one shock like it in BSO history — the Friday afternoon in 1963 when news of John F. Kennedy's death by an assassin's bullet interrupted a Symphony Hall concert.

This Tanglewood drama began in the Soviet Union a year earlier, when cellist-conductor Mstislav Rostropovich and soprano Galina Vishnevskaya, hounded and blacklisted by the government and in danger of arrest, went into exile. The full story goes back, however, to Rostropovich's student years in the 1940s at the Moscow Conservatory, where Dmitri Shostakovich taught him composition. The two men became lifelong friends, Vishnevskaya joining their circle when Rostropovich married her in 1955. He was already a leading cellist, though not yet a conductor; she was a young prima donna from the Bolshoi, whom the ebullient Rostropovich had dizzied with attentions even though she was married to another man.

Over the years Shostakovich wrote many works for the couple — two cello concertos for Rostropovich, song cycles and the Fourteenth Symphony for Vishnevskaya. (Among other composers who wrote for them, Britten was especially close.) The three friends talked late into the night and shared a profound unhappiness with the limits placed on their freedoms by the communist system, but a gulf in their responses to the restrictions separated them. Shostakovich, painfully shy and withdrawn, and forever in fear of arrest and execution, retreated into himself and his music. Rostropovich and Vishnevskaya wrangled with party bureaucrats and fought against the shackles.

In the end the fight cost them heavily. When Alexander Solzhenitsyn fell into official disfavor in the late 1960s for writing his exposés of the gulags and for winning the Nobel Prize, Rostropovich and Vishnevskaya took him in at their dacha near Moscow. As the attacks on Solzhenitsyn mounted, Rostropovich circulated an open letter in defense of his friend. By then a leading conductor as well as cellist, Rostropovich soon found himself barred from Moscow's concert halls and opera houses, and from going abroad. He could practice his art only in the provinces, where he sometimes performed before empty houses. Vishnevskaya still sang at the Bolshoi, but her name no longer appeared in reviews or in announcements on the air when her recordings were played.

The harassment had gone on for three years when, in 1973, the San Francisco Symphony went to the Soviet Union on tour. Seiji Ozawa, just named to the BSO podium, was still the San Francisco's music director and conductor for the tour. A concert in Moscow, booked far in advance, was to include Rostropovich as the soloist in the Dvořák concerto. Party officials tried to get him taken off the program. The Americans stuck by their contract and insisted that he appear. An impasse arose. Faced with the possibility of an international scandal, the Soviets gave in.

The concert was given in the Great Hall of the Moscow Conservatory. In her memoir, *Galina* (1984), Vishnevskaya tells what she saw:

> Of course, "all Moscow" attended the concert. Slava played splendidly, but I was shaken by the way he came on stage, the way he sat, the way he bowed to the audience. With what gratitude he looked at Ozawa, who was just beginning his career; how grateful he was to each member of the orchestra since it was because of them that he was playing in that magnificent hall. And suddenly I realized with horror that deep within Rostropovich a fatal fissure was beginning to open up, and that he could very soon be torn asunder.

Late that night, after the celebrations were over, Vishnevskaya was alone with her husband in ther home. Seeing him "so radiant and happy," she hesitated to speak. But finally she told him:

> . . . You must be able to travel abroad, otherwise it's all over for you. Playing in the boondocks all these years has left its mark on your soul.

You're losing the special quality of a great artist, who must be above the crowd, not with it. You're losing the loftiness of the spirit. . . .

In February 1974 Solzhenitsyn was arrested, stripped of his citizenship, and ordered out of the country. With the noose tightening, Rostropovich and Vishnevskaya knew they had to get out or face almost certain arrest. They applied for permission to travel abroad. Out of years of experience with the system, they played off party officials against one another in pressing their case. Appeals by Leonard Bernstein and Senator Edward Kennedy of Massachusetts helped. Leonid Brezhnev himself finally gave the approval. The couple received permission to live abroad for two years.

Rostropovich left first, going to England in May 1974. Vishnevskaya stayed behind for two more months to allow their older daughter, Olga, to take her entrance examinations for the conservatory, in case the family returned and she wanted to go on with her studies. "The last and most difficult thing" Vishnevskaya had to do in the Soviet Union, she says, was going to see the sixty-seven-year-old Shostakovich, already weakened by heart trouble, and taking leave of him. She put it off until the day before she and her two teen-aged daughters flew off to join Rostropovich.

> Shostakovich was the dearest of all I was leaving behind and the only one who could make us reverse our decision [Vishnevskaya writes]. I was afraid that before him I would lose all self-control and succumb to his unquestionable authority. But he knew that was the case, and didn't press me. He understood very well what was in store for us, and that our only way out was to disappear for a few years.

He and Vishnevskaya talked for a while, touching upon the Orthodox custom of giving a dead person a last kiss in the coffin. Now Shostakovich asked Vishnevskaya if she would kiss him before leaving — an unprecedented gesture for a man who shrank from human touch. She answered him, "Of course." Then:

> He tried to smile wryly, but the result was a pathetic grimace. "And it wouldn't disgust you?"
> "No."
> Now I was looking at that face, each line of which was familiar to me, and my heart was rent in two. How would I avoid showing him my despair? Where would I find the strength to get up and leave?
> "I'm going, Dmitri Dmitriyevich. . . . Good-bye."

We embraced, and I suddenly realized he was sobbing.

On the verge of crying out, feeling that I could bear that torture no longer, I frenziedly kissed him on the face, the neck, the shoulder. And with difficulty, I tore myself from him — from the living as though from the dead — knowing I would never see him again.

Exactly a year later Rostropovich and Vishnevskaya arrived at Tanglewood for a reunion with Ozawa and a joint appearance — her debut — with the BSO. It was a signal occasion. The couple were international celebrities, lionized for their independence of spirit and resistance to tyrants. The series of four programs — three with the BSO — featured Rostropovich as a pianist, conductor, and cellist. On the first night he accompanied his wife in a recital of Mussorgsky and Rachmaninoff songs as a Weekend Prelude. The next night, in his BSO conducting debut, he led the Verdi *Requiem,* with Vishnevskaya as a soloist. The following Saturday he returned to the podium in a Tchaikovsky-Shostakovich program, Vishnevskaya singing one of her most famous roles, Tatiana, in the letter scene from Tchaikovsky's *Eugene Onegin.* Sunday afternoon in the finale, Ozawa was the conductor and Rostropovich the soloist in Shostakovich's Second Cello Concerto, one of those works written for him.

Whether conducting, or greeting visitors in the Green Room afterward, Rostropovich embraces everything before him in a bear hug. That was how he seized the Verdi *Requiem.* The performance was both eccentric and electric, going to extremes in dynamics as it tried to move heaven and earth by sheer will. There was no reason to expect the following Saturday's concert to be anything less — or more. But when the couple were dressed and preparing to leave for the Shed from the house in Lenox where they were staying, the phone rang. It was Rostropovich's sister in Moscow. Shostakovich, she told them, was dead.

Vishnevskaya's premonition had been true. Still, the first half of the concert went on with no clue to the audience of the strain the guest artists were under. Perhaps Vishnevskaya sounded a bit tired when, as the young, impetuous Tatiana, she poured out her love for Onegin. But she was no longer a singer in her youth. And in any case Rostropovich stoked the fires of hell in the portrait of the damned lovers in Tchaikovsky's *Francesca da Rimini.*

The Shostakovich Fifth was to follow the intermission. When the orchestra and audience were seated and the house lights went out,

After conducting Shostakovich's Symphony no. 5, Mstislav Rostropovich kisses the score in memory of the composer.

Ozawa, dressed in everyday clothes, walked onstage with Rostropovich. The audience tensed, aware that something was wrong. With his arm around Rostropovich's shoulder, Ozawa announced the news that the Russian could not bring himself to utter. Ozawa asked the audience and orchestra, on Rostropovich's behalf, to stand with him in a moment of silent prayer.

It later turned out that the announcement was the world's first knowledge of the composer's death of a heart attack. The official

Soviet news agency Tass did not confirm the event until twenty-four hours later. At Tanglewood the audience of nearly ten thousand reacted with a shocked groan. After the moment of silence Rostropovich, openly weeping, picked up the baton to begin.

The Fifth Symphony was the work Shostakovich composed in 1937 to redeem his career — and perhaps his existence — from the death to which Stalin had condemned it for its refusal to glorify the state. The triumph at the end is hollow, because for Shostakovich there could be no triumph until his release from terror by death. Who better than Rostropovich could understand this? So the performance became a memorial to the composer — electric, like the Verdi *Requiem,* but also tender and searing by turns, informed by both love and history. At the end the audience could only sit in stunned silence, watching, while Rostropovich laid down his baton, picked up the score, kissed it, and gently replaced it on his music stand. Only then did he walk offstage and the noisy ovations begin.

As Rostropovich returned for his bows with the orchestra, a young man in the audience came up to the stage and threw a bouquet of red roses to him. Stooping down, Rostropovich gathered up the bouquet, which had broken apart on hitting the floor. On his next trip out from the wings he brought the roses back and placed them on the closed score. There they remained until, blowing a kiss to the crowd, he brought the house lights up and the ovations to an end.

Returning to their house, Rostropovich and Vishnevskaya stayed up much of the night, holding a wake, which Ozawa and a few other friends attended. From seclusion the next day the couple issued a statement through the Tanglewood press office:

> Shostakovich belonged to the entire world, and today the whole world is mourning this great loss. In his music he gave not only the sense of great beauty but also the feelings of the great contradictions of the epoch in which he lived. He lived a saturated and difficult life and until the last minute continued to create. His creative genius overcame everything which stood in his path. Death carried him away at the very pinnacle of his creativeness and fame. For a human being who left so much to the world, one cannot say he is really dead. But for close friends the knowledge is terribly hard to live through.

In one of the songs that make up the Fourteenth Symphony, Shostakovich sets a poem by the nineteenth-century German-Russian writer and revolutionary Wilhelm Karlovich Küchelbecker, who died in Siberia after twenty years in prison and exile. The song begins:

> O Delvig, Delvig! What the profit
> Of lofty deeds and poetry?
> Of talent, what and where comfort
> Among scoundrels and fools?

Answering his own question, the singer concludes that, for the artist, the reward is immortality:

> Firm in fortune and misfortune is
> The union of eternal lovers of the Muses.

> ["The Poets," 1820, tr. Robert A. Maguire]

The poem reads like an epitaph for Shostakovich and a memento for his friends.

In the West Rostropovich and Vishnevskaya resumed the international careers they had enjoyed before bureaucrats silenced them. Rostropovich went on to become the director of the National Symphony Orchestra in Washington. Solzhenitsyn also entered exile in the United States, secluding himself on a farm in Vermont. In 1978 the Soviet government stripped Rostropovich and Vishnevskaya of their citizenship, just as it had Solzhenitsyn, for activities hostile to the state. And still the flow of Soviet thinkers and artists to the West continued. The drama played out in the Shed became a part of both Tanglewood and twentieth-century history.

*　　*　　*

On their first morning at Tanglewood the four Chinese musicians showed up wearing "Mostly Mozart" T-shirts from the summer festival in New York. Assistant BSO manager Peter Gelb, who was overseeing their visit, took one look and ordered: "Off!" Soon the visitors were properly attired in T-shirts bearing the Tanglewood logo. Liu Dehai, China's premier performer on the pipa, the Chinese lute, embraced his new loyalty so wholeheartedly that he ground his Mozart T-shirt underfoot, Gelb reported.

Two major international events in 1979 affected the shape of the 1980 Tanglewood season. First the United States reopened diplomatic relations with the People's Republic of China after a thirty-year breach. That led to the Chinese musicians' visit. Then the Soviet

Union invaded Afghanistan. In the diplomatic fallout over that affair the United States boycotted the 1980 Moscow Olympics, and the Soviet Union retaliated by canceling cultural exchanges with the United States. Two Soviet musicians who were to have come to Tanglewood — conductor Gennady Rozhdestvensky, who had made his debut the summer before, and pianist Lazar Berman, who would have been making his first appearance — never arrived. Politically speaking, 1980 was the year of the Chinese, just as 1975 had been the year of the Soviet dissidents.

Tanglewood was enmeshed in history again. This time, however, the BSO had taken the musical and political initiative. In March 1979 the orchestra had traveled to Shanghai and Beijing as the first American performing arts organization to visit China under the treaties signed by President Carter earlier that year. The eight-day BSO trip achieved what three years of negotiations to bring a Chinese delegation to Tanglewood had not achieved. Repaying the visit now, the four musicians came for three weeks of performing, teaching, and — like other tourists — just looking around.

From the 1979 trip the BSO already knew the two senior members of the delegation. Han Zhongjie, who was fifty-nine when he came to Tanglewood, was the conductor of the Beijing Central Philharmonic, the BSO's host orchestra in the Chinese capital. Liu Dehai, forty-three, the shirt-stomping pipa player, had been the soloist in *Little Sisters of the Grassland,* a pipa concerto the BSO played in Beijing. To round out the delegation, the Chinese sent Jiang Jianhua, a nineteen-year-old woman who played the erhu (a two-stringed violin that stands in the lap), and Huang He, twenty-four, a male performer on the Chinese dulcimer. Each instrumentalist was a virtuoso, as BSO audiences were soon to discover.

Only Liu had been in the United States before. He was one of two Chinese soloists who had accompanied the touring BSO back to Boston, where he repeated *Little Sisters of the Grassland* in Symphony Hall and then recorded it with the BSO. At Tanglewood all four communist visitors made themselves at home in the guest cottage the BSO rented for them on an estate a mile and a half away. They rose at six in the morning to go running along the country road. They played tennis at the estate and swam in its pool. They also became addicted to chocolate chip cookies, Häagen-Dazs ice cream, and other Western goodies supplied by Laurie Robertson-Lorant, a

Lenox resident whom the BSO signed up to be their housemother. They had dinner at Seranak, at the fashionable Red Lion Inn in Stockbridge, and at the Ozawas' house, and back at the cottage they burned their mouths on Liu's Szechuan cooking. And they packed away their "Mostly Mozart" T-shirts and sat in on Tanglewood concerts and classes — all of the troupe, that is, except Han, who tended to keep to himself at his capitalist retreat.

It all began with Seiji Ozawa, of course. Born in Manchuria (though to Japanese parents), he had spent part of his boyhood in Beijing and retained an interest in China and its music. After the People's Republic reopened its doors to Western businessmen, scientists, and artists as part of a modernization program under Deng Xiaoping in 1977, Ozawa accepted an invitation to coach and conduct Han's Beijing Central Philharmonic. Out of that 1978 visit grew the invitation to the full BSO to tour the following year.

In China the BSO party discovered the country has a tradition of Western symphonic music going back to its introduction by European settlers in the early twentieth century. Western music was banned during the ten years of the Cultural Revolution, 1966–76. It was only with the restoration of liberties under Deng that such composers as Beethoven and Tchaikovsky, formerly denounced as running dogs of imperialism, could be played again. Conductor Han told American journalists traveling with the BSO that Beethoven's Fifth Symphony was the work the Beijing Philharmonic had performed to celebrate the return to its old repertoire. It was also the work Ozawa chose for the BSO's climactic concert in Beijing. When he went back to Beijing over the Christmas holidays in 1979 for a repeat visit with the Philharmonic, he led the Beethoven Ninth.

The BSO found interest in Western music surprisingly strong in both Shanghai and Beijing. Conservatories in both cities were swarming with students eager to listen and learn at master classes the American visitors gave. The orchestras in both cities played with obvious feeling for Western music but also, because of the years of isolation, with hand-me-down instruments and an uncertain sense of style. (BSO first clarinetist Harold Wright discovered a clarinet with a German barrel, a French top, and an American mouthpiece.) Though the BSO had been warned to expect reticent audiences, the most enthusiastic Tanglewood crowds could not have outdone the eighteen thousand Chinese who mobbed a modern Beijing sports palace to hear the final concert, given jointly by the BSO and the Peking Philharmonic. U.S. Ambassador Leonard Woodcock told BSO leaders the tour had advanced Chinese-American relations by twenty years — two-thirds of the gap that began when the Communists wrested the mainland from Chiang Kai-shek's Nationalists and the Korean War ensued.

The Chinese, perhaps prompted by a desire to please American ears, spoke freely of ten years of suffering under the Gang of Four, led by Jiang Qing, Chairman Mao's wife. Han's concertmaster was sent to a prison farm for 9½ years — a common fate for intellectuals and artists — and not allowed to touch his instrument. Pianist Liu Shikun, who played Liszt's E-flat Concerto with the BSO in Beijing and then in Boston, was jailed, his arms repeatedly beaten. Li Teh-lun, the Philharmonic's alternate conductor, incurred the wrath of Jiang Qing for giving the score of a modern Chinese piece, *Moon Reflected in the Water*, to Eugene Ormandy when the Philadelphia Orchestra visited in 1973. Jiang said the music had a melancholy ending that reflected unfavorably on revolutionary water. The officially prescribed repertoire consisted of nine or ten patriotic set pieces celebrating the revolution and exhorting the masses to work and sacrifice. Han said the Philharmonic repeated the politically inspired works until the musicians — those who were not on work farms or in jail — lost their skills and incentive. The orchestra no longer was able to "cultivate the younger generation," he lamented.

With help from visits by the Toronto, Vienna, Philadelphia, and Boston orchestras, Han said, the Philharmonic was relearning its Beethoven and Tchaikovsky; young people were again interested, and concerts sold out within two hours of their announcement.

The BSO's attempt to bring Chinese musicians to Tanglewood began with Deng's loosening of controls in 1977. In 1978 and 1979 the Chinese never said "no" but never quite said "yes." In 1980, with the good will generated by the BSO's tour and Ozawa's return visit at Christmas, the "yes" finally came. BSO officials blamed a lumbering bureaucracy rather than political obstacles for the two-year delay.

As far as the BSO knew, Han's appearance was the first by a Chinese conductor with a major American orchestra — certainly the first since the communist takeover in 1949. The musicians arrived at

Tanglewood on a Wednesday after a day of sightseeing in New York, where their jet landed on Tuesday. On Friday night the three instrumentalists played a Prelude recital for a crowd of five thousand in the Shed. The Sunday afternoon BSO concert featured all four musicians.

The Prelude offered a mixture of modern Chinese pieces and traditional Chinese music in modern arrangements, with a surprise ending — "Turkey in the Straw," which, on an erhu, pipa, and dulcimer, had a decided Chinese accent, and was all the more a hit because of it. At the main BSO concert later in the evening Ozawa led Beethoven's Fifth, his signature piece in Beijing.

Han, who was also the conductor of the Beijing Central Opera and Beijing Ballet Theater, led the BSO in Tchaikovsky's *Romeo and Juliet* overture to open the Sunday program. He worked up some big climaxes, but the star-crossed lovers seemed more refined than impassioned in his interpretation. Then, with Ozawa on the podium, the three instrumentalists shuttled on and off the stage for a series of Chinese concerto-style pieces, followed by solo encores. *Little Sisters of the Grassland* turned up again; Liu, in a neatly pressed Mao suit, coaxed a howling blizzard out of his pipa as the music spun its patriotic tale of two girls who save a commune's horses from the storm. In another picture-painting piece, *Wailful Wraith by the River,* Jiang's erhu wailed like an old woman.

The pleasantly whining or nasal sounds of the instruments had to be amplified in the Shed to be heard over the orchestra. By Western standards the music was terrible. The styles ranged from watered-down Debussy to riding-into-the-sunset movie music, and *Little Sisters,* a committee-written potboiler extolling the virtues of work and loyalty, had the subtlety of a wall poster. But musicians are musicians everywhere, and audiences are audiences. Chinese fingers flew, producing wonders of virtuosity and sensitivity on the exotic instruments. The warm ovations were both a tribute to the artists and a ratification of Chinese-American friendship. Shutters snapped all afternoon, in defiance of the ban on picture taking in the Shed, and a bird in the rafters chirped happily through the program. In short, a splendid Tanglewood afternoon.

The BSO's first three concerts in China were for invited musicians and government officials only, Deng himself attending in Beijing and sipping tea in a box in the center of the theater. The farewell concert, however, was open to anyone who could pay the ticket price (20 or 35 cents). In baggy, dull blue or green Mao suits, row on row of working Chinese gazed intently down upon the musicians arrayed across the gleaming wooden floor of the coliseum. Red and white banners streaming across the walls proclaimed the friendship of the American and Chinese peoples.

The program began with Ozawa leading the Beijing Philharmonic in the Mendelssohn Violin Concerto, with BSO concertmaster Joseph Silverstein as the soloist. Then the Philharmonic yielded the floor to the BSO, which played Verdi's *Forza del Destino* overture and a pipa concerto (Liu Dehai returned as the pipa player). For the final work the two orchestras combined — a Chinese stand partner sitting beside each American — to play the Beethoven Fifth. With the merged orchestras still before him, Ozawa swung into two encores — one from each country. The first was *The White-Haired Girl*, a Chinese story-telling piece featuring the banhu, another stringed instrument. The piece, which had also been a hit earlier in the tour, drew instant "ahhhhs" of recognition from the audience. Ozawa stopped in midstream to let cellist Martin Hoherman, the BSO's banhu expert, hand the solo instrument over to a Chinese counterpart, who finished the performance. The symbolic exchange brought the eighteen-thousand-person house down.

Is *The Stars and Stripes Forever* known in China? The last encore answered the question forever. The tweetling of the combined orchestras' nine fifes, followed by the blaring of the massed trombones swinging around to all sides of the coliseum, set off pandemonium. The audience stood, clapped in rhythm, and, at the end, shouted a delirious farewell to musicians who had become heroes. After several curtain calls alone, Ozawa took the Philharmonic's two conductors, Han and Li, and the two orchestras' concertmasters, Yang Pin Sung and Silverstein, and marched them around the floor arm-in-arm before the cheering throng. The procession wound up in front of Ambassador Woodcock, Chinese Vice Premier Fan Yi, Foreign Minister Huang Hua, Minister of Culture Huang Chen, and other officials, who presented a wreath to Ozawa for the BSO.

Forty-one microphones planted within the orchestra and eleven television cameras around the hall captured the event for other audiences around the world. The popping of flashbulbs threw Silverstein off so badly in the Mendelssohn concerto that he later said it was like playing in a Japanese subway at rush hour. In the tumult on the floor afterward, even a group of American music critics watching the scene was besieged for autographs.

Before leaving for Boston the next morning, Ozawa visited his boyhood home in Beijing. Surveying the small gray-brown house, where four families with a total of thirty-five people now lived, he recalled the previous night's concert for the assembled Chinese and American journalists and television cameras:

> When two orchestras play together, I didn't see Western guy and Oriental guy. On musical level I think they were really together. The Chinese musicians got a lot. They need to see how Western orchestra play. But we got something very pure. We are so busy sometimes — concerts, records — we forget pure importance of music. Chinese people, because of their situation — life is so simple — music is simple and pure, too.

On the eighteen-hour flight home bassist Lawrence Wolfe, recurperating from eight days crammed with teaching, rehearsing, performing, sightseeing, shopping, and twelve-course state dinners, compared the trip to the BSO's 2½-week tour of Japan a year before: "I'll tell you, when we were in Japan last year, people were friendly, but never like this. That was all sort of on the surface. But these people really meant it, and you felt something really overflowed from deep inside."

The BSO's motives for making the trip were not entirely altruistic. Ozawa wanted to help China emerge from its musical dark age, but he also wanted to show off his orchestra in the land of his birth, just as, on the Japanese tour, he had shown it off in the land of his upbringing. Then for publicity's sake management speeded up the arrival to get the BSO into Beijing ahead of the Berlin Philharmonic and a string of other American musicians planning Chinese tours later in the year. A media blitz — an eight-man CBS-TV crew and representatives of the major American newspapers, news services, and magazines went along on the chartered jet —was partly engineered to bring maximum publicity to the BSO in a time of mounting deficits.

But for a $650,000 investment (underwritten by industry) the BSO bought priceless good will for itself and its country, gave inspiration to Chinese musicians, reached millions of other Chinese who watched or heard the concerts on television or radio, and — who knows? — perhaps improved chances for world peace. On the flight home Arthur M. Rosen, president of the National Committee on

U.S.–China Relations, who accompanied the BSO on the trip and assisted in planning it, said:

> The seal of approval has been given by the highest authorities, and there is a reservoir of good feeling for the United States. Don't forget, many Chinese, both musicians and others, have connections in the United States through relatives or study. Something entirely new is releasing feelings that have existed for many years. This is the first time in history we have established one-on-one — Chinese and American musicians playing Western music together.

The BSO also bought unexpected friendships at the grassroots level, and out of sight of the cheering throngs these friendships also blossomed at Tanglewood during the summer of 1980. While Han and his comrades were making their official visit on one side of the lawn, on the other side the Music Center was hosting its first students from the People's Republic, Fu Xiao-hong, a violinist, and Chang Li-ke, her cellist husband. Unlike Han and his group, these Chinese came without government sponsorship or help.

During the rehearsals for the final Beijing concert Fu Xiao-hong had been the Philharmonic stand partner of BSO second violinist Sheila Fiekowsky. Through music, interpreters, and Fu's learner's English, the two twenty-seven-year-old women had struck up a friendship. They had exchanged gifts and gone shopping together, Fiekowsky buying a quilted Chinese jacket with Fu's clothing ration coupons.

At the farewell dinner for the two orchestras on the last night in Beijing, Fu had also befriended Marylou Speaker (later Marylou Speaker Churchill), the BSO's principal second violinist. When Beijing Philharmonic members turned out en masse at the airport the next morning to wish the BSO goodbye and exchange gifts with their new-made friends, Fiekowsky and Speaker gave Fu a battery-powered metronome, which she accepted for her orchestra. Fu presented vases to her American friends. Amid embraces, tears, and promises to write, the three women parted — who knew for how many years?

Chang Li-ke, a newly graduated cello teacher, had heard the farewell concert in the audience. Like his wife, he had been greatly impressed by the visiting orchestra. The couple wanted to stay close to the Americans and perhaps become elite musicians like them. But how? After talking it over Fu and Chang decided to go to the United States to study.

The BSO was hardly back from China when Speaker received a letter from Fu, asking for help with her plan. Speaker went to work to enroll the couple in the New England Conservatory and raise $6,000 for their initial expenses. The conservatory contributed $2,000 in student aid. On October 24, 1979, Fu and Chang landed at Boston's Logan Airport, carrying two cellos, three violins, and very few clothes, and speaking little English. They went to live with Speaker and begin their Boston studies.

At the conservatory the couple — both born to Chinese who play Western music, and both confined on labor farms during the Cultural Revolution — heard about the BSO's summer festival and school. They decided to apply. Like the other students in the fellowship program, they were accepted for the eight-week term on the basis of auditions and received full scholarship assistance.

In the Berkshires they played chamber music for the first time, making their debut in a student performance of Dvořák's Quintet, opus 77. Two weeks later, far from Beijing, Fu had a reunion with Han, her former conductor, when he and his party arrived for their three-week stay. Speaker meanwhile continued to coach the couple in reading English to supplement the conservatory's language course for foreign students. She had them study *Pinocchio, The Grouchy Lady Bug,* and other children's books that summer to ease them into the strange grammar and syntax.

Between classes at Tanglewood Fu and Chang said that since the inauguration of Deng's reforms it was no longer unusual for Chinese citizens to study in the United States. But, Fu said, Chinese studying abroad privately had to have sponsors like Marylou Speaker.

"If you want to go to another country and don't want to study," she said, "it's difficult. Chinese now need to learn. But we don't have enough money to give to students to go to another country."

"So when we come here," added Chang, grateful to Speaker, "very easy. We don't have hard time."

"I love them," Speaker herself said. "I've got a big house. I hope they can stay with me forever."

They stayed the 2½ years it took them to finish their studies and find jobs, which at first required them to live apart for two difficult years — Fu in Calgary, Canada, as a member of the orchestra, Chang at Sarah Lawrence College, where he played in a string quartet. Then they were taken into the Montreal Symphony Orchestra, Fu as a first violinist, her husband six months later in the cello section. Reunited at last, they bought and renovated a house in Montreal and applied for Canadian citizenship. They remained friends with Fiekowsky and Speaker, writing, calling, and visiting regularly. But, unlike Han and his group, they never returned to China.

After 1980 students from the People's Republic came to Tanglewood in growing numbers, and Speaker, heartened by the experience with Fu and Chang, took more Chinese students into her home and helped put them through school. Ozawa remained in touch with the musicians he had befriended in China, and the manager of the Shanghai Symphony Orchestra spent a month in 1987 as an intern in Symphony Hall during a year in the United States to study orchestra management. American musicians by the dozens poured through the gates the Bostonians had opened, but there were no more formal BSO–Chinese exchanges. The special moment in history had passed.

*   *   *

Another special moment in history, with long-range consequences for Tanglewood, occurred in 1979, five months after the China trip. The BSO flew to Europe for its first festival tour, which took in musical shrines from Salzburg to Edinburgh. Not only was the two-week trip something new in itself, but to catch the European festival season the BSO had to depart its own summer festival a week early. For the first time another orchestra would play the big weekend concerts in the Shed.

With much of the faculty departing, the Music Center had opened and closed early, too. For four days there was silence on the grounds: no rehearsals, no musicians coming and going, no chamber music floating down from the Main House or out of practice cabins in the woods. Then the New York Philharmonic, directed by Zubin Mehta, Tanglewood '58, moved in.

In a sense history had come full circle. In 1934 sixty-five members of the Philharmonic under Henry Hadley inaugurated the Berkshire Symphonic Festival (as it was then called) with a weekend of three concerts in a riding ring three miles south of today's Shed. Hadley also conducted a second summer of concerts in 1935, using a mixture of Philharmonic and other New York musicians. Dissatisfied with the quality of the programming and playing, Gertrude Robinson Smith's committee of arts patrons turned in 1936 to Koussevitzky and the BSO. A year later, with the donation of the Tanglewood estate as a permanent site, today's festival was born. Coming to Tanglewood in 1979, the Philharmonic would be returning to the Berkshires and a historic role in Tanglewood's creation. But under its Tanglewood-trained conductor the orchestra would be making a Tanglewood debut.

The debut was also a sentimental journey for Mehta, the Indian Parsee who became the orchestra's music director in 1978. He first came to the United States in 1958 as a Tanglewood conducting student in a class that also included Claudio Abbado and David Zinman. A colorful, sometimes flamboyant North American career soon followed. As success followed success, the BSO tried repeatedly to land Mehta as a guest conductor for either Boston or Tanglewood. Busy with the New York Philharmonic, the Israel Philharmonic, and guest appearances elsewhere, he had never found time.

Back at last after twenty-one years Mehta at first remembered little from his student summer except the Shed. Then, collecting his thoughts in the Green Room after a rehearsal, he recalled flying over from Vienna, where he had been studying, and getting his first glimpses of America on the train ride out from Boston to Pittsfield and then the taxi ride to Lenox. The new surroundings pleased him, he said, but "I didn't know where I was" and couldn't form any clear impressions. The heavy schedule kept him oblivious to just about everything except his work and dorm room. "What I remember, really, was the first introduction to a great American orchestra." Munch and Monteux were the conductors he most vividly remembered with it.

The invitation to the Philharmonic wrapped up history, sentiment, and business acumen in one package. The occasion arose when the BSO accepted an invitation from Herbert von Karajan to play at the 1979 Salzburg Festival. Orchestras, no less than people, like to preen and strut. For the BSO the opportunity to show itself off at Karajan's festival, before Europe's musical aristocracy, was too good to pass up. To make a tour of it, the orchestra added the Berlin, Lucerne, and Edinburgh festivals and four other cities to the itinerary. That, of course, meant missing the last week of the eight-week Tanglewood season. Management considered a variety of options, including dropping the final Tanglewood week. But, said assistant BSO manager Gideon Toeplitz, who handled most of the tour arrangements, the front office considered that option "no longer than it takes to say it." Instead, attention soon centered on the Philharmonic, for several reasons.

First was a history of friendly relations between the two orchestras' managements. More importantly, the Philharmonic was available, having no commitment to a summer festival elsewhere, as did such other major orchestras as the Cleveland — the BSO's second choice if the Philharmonic could not or would not come. Because of the summer under Hadley the Philharmonic also felt a historic attachment to the Berskshires. And Mehta, recalling his student days, was "very enthusiastic" about the idea, Toeplitz said.

There was also a nice symmetry in having Mehta stand where Ozawa normally would stand. The two conductors are only a year apart in age (Mehta was born in Bombay in 1936). Both are Asian, both came to Tanglewood from Europe to continue their conducting studies, and both rose to eminence in the United States from podiums in Canada — Ozawa in Toronto, Mehta in Montreal. Ozawa went on to San Francisco en route to Boston; Mehta spent sixteen years in Los Angeles before moving on to New York. The two men also are friendly, although too busy to see each other often. With the Tanglewood visit looming, however, Mehta attended two of Ozawa's BSO concerts in New York during the preceding winter and had dinner with Ozawa after one. Ozawa reciprocated by attending one of Mehta's Philharmonic programs.

The Philharmonic contract was signed in 1977, a year after the BSO knew it would be going to Salzburg. The Shed sold out for all three 1979 concerts. Silent during the week, the grounds buzzed with anticipation as the crowd began streaming in for the first of the weekend's concerts. What would Tanglewood be like with a strange orchestra sitting where only Koussevitzky's BSO had sat for forty-three years?

It was a different Tanglewood in many ways that weekend. Philharmonic members and their families bustled about the Shed before, during, and after rehearsals, snapping pictures. Mixed crews of BSO and Philharmonic stagehands wrestled with chairs and packing cases. The Saturday morning open rehearsal was available to the public without charge, BSO officials reasoning that they could not charge a Philharmonic audience for a program that normally benefits the BSO's pension fund. (The box office counted 4,267 listeners who took advantage of the free offer.) Mail-order ticket sales and a license plate count in the lots showed a shift in attendance at the concerts, with fewer New Englanders than usual on hand and a higher concentration from the New York–New Jersey–Connecticut area. Why would New Yorkers flock to the Berkshires to hear a New York orchestra? Mystified BSO officials could only surmise that the bucolic surroundings exerted a spell on Mehta's followers as well as on Mehta.

The Philharmonic traveled to the Berkshires on Thursday night directly from two weeks of free concerts in Central Park. All the works on the three Tanglewood programs were repeats from either the park concerts or the regular winter season. Familiar with the music and soloists, the orchestra held only two rehearsals in the Shed, one on Friday and the other the Saturday open rehearsal. Having played before audiences of up to 140,000 in Central Park, as well as at Saratoga, Wolf Trap, Hollywood Bowl, and smaller summer festivals, the musicians knew the pleasures and perils of alfresco concerts — the crying babies, the frisbees and snuggling on the lawn, the heat waves and thunderstorms. The only thing lacking at Tanglewood was jets blasting overhead.

The Mehtas arrived a day ahead of the orchestra party and stayed in the same guest cottage up the road where the Chinese would put up the next summer. The tight schedule left him little time for the sightseeing that he had missed in 1958. But the couple did enjoy Malcolm Frager's piano recital in the Theater–Concert Hall on Thursday night. The night before, they went to the Jacob's Pillow Dance Festival and saw the mother-daughter dance team of Indrani and Sukanya, from India.

"I learned something," said Mehta. He was familiar with the traditional Indian numbers, but dances from the province of Orissi were new to him.

Mehta said that as veterans of outdoor concerts he and the Philharmonic found the Shed comfortable to play in: "It sounds very mellow and nice. We're used to giving it more volume, but we can tone it down here." It was also pleasant to stay in one place and give a three-day mini-festival. "It's better than going out on tour," he said. "By the time we know the hall, the tour is over." And,

Zubin Mehta conducts the New York Philharmonic during the first appearance by a visiting orchestra in the Shed.

tossing a bouquet to the BSO in its distant musical Eden, Mehta described the Berkshire surroundings as "heavenly." In Tanglewood, he said, "the Boston Symphony has a kind of Salzburg of their own."

Seven Philharmonic members, including five principal players, presented a Telemann-Stravinsky-Mendelssohn program as the Weekend Prelude. After the usual one-hour break Mehta and the Philharmonic came on to play a program of Schubert (the Fifth and *Unfinished* symphonies) and Strauss, with Montserrat Caballé singing the final scene from *Salome* and the *Four Last Songs*. Even with a blindfold on, you could have felt that something was different at Tanglewood. The Philharmonic's sound had a distinctly darker color and texture than the BSO's, and Mehta proved a more relaxed, extroverted leader than Ozawa.

Saturday brought a Mozart-Mahler evening — the former's G Minor Symphony, K. 550, and the latter's Fifth. On Sunday afternoon the Beethoven Ninth, always a Tanglewood favorite, attracted a final-day crowd of fourteen thousand. The performances remained looser in both discipline and style than the BSO's average in the Shed. Mehta's one complaint about being back in the Berkshires was that the peaceful surroundings lulled him into drowsiness. Shortly after arriving, he said, he and his wife, the former actress Nancy Kovack, lay down for a "three-minute" nap, only to wake up four hours later. The Philharmonic, which can play as well as any other orchestra when it is so inclined, sounded as if it, too, had mellowed out in the country.

The BSO, meanwhile, played Salzburg, the first stop on its tour. The first night, with Frederica von Stade, Dietrich Fischer-Dieskau, Veriano Luchetti, and Douglas Lawrence as the soloists, it performed Berlioz's *Damnation of Faust,* the work with which it had closed its Tanglewood season a week before. The performance brought a fifteen-minute ovation for Ozawa and his players and singers. Offstage other weighty business was taking place. It was during this sojourn in Salzburg that Ozawa made his apology to the orchestra, regretting his absences and promising to work harder. They went on to meet Karajan's Berlin Philharmonic head-on, playing Strauss's *Heldenleben* — a Karajan signature piece — at the Berlin Festival. "We want the Berliners to compare two signatures," concertmaster Joseph Silverstein said dryly.

The BSO found its taste of European celebrity so heady that five years later, in 1984, it flew off to play the festival circuit again. The Tanglewood scenario was the same: the early departure, the four-day silence on the grounds, the visiting orchestra moving in and setting up camp for the final weekend.

This time, however, the BSO looked to the future rather than the past for a replacement. The visiting band was the Cleveland Orchestra, the fallback choice in 1979. The conductor was Christoph von Dohnányi, the fifty-four-year-old German (and 1952 Tanglewood graduate) who was officially to become the Cleveland's music director the next month. It was Dohnányi's first series of concerts with his new orchestra apart from a weekend at the Blossom Music

Festival, thirty-five miles outside Cleveland, earlier that summer. Tanglewood, in effect, was getting a good look at the Cleveland with its new conductor before Cleveland did.

Dohnányi (in America he drops the aristocratic *von* before his name) came to both Tanglewood and Cleveland wearing an air of mystery. Little known in the United States, he was a surprise choice to succeed his Tanglewood classmate Lorin Maazel on the Cleveland podium. Before his appointment in 1982 he had guest-conducted the Cleveland only once, and he had been back only sporadically in the two years since. On the eve of his arrival Robert Finn, music critic of the *Cleveland Plain Dealer,* called him "largely an unknown musical quantity in Cleveland." As the new man at the helm, Finn said, he would somehow have to "come to grips with the ghost of George Szell," whose legacy of tightly disciplined playing lived on fourteen years after his death.

In fluent English Dohnányi said he had a special reason for looking forward to his return to Tanglewood. He was leading a drive to establish a Tanglewood-style festival in Europe—an area near Frankfurt was later designated the site — and wanted to pick up ideas at the source. He also was coming with fond memories of the "absolutely marvelous countryside" and camaraderie with students and teachers. Unlike Mehta, Dohnányi recalled specifics of his summer, such as outings with teachers and score study in the woods. "That's what I liked so much, you know," he said. "You have very human contact to everybody."

Dohnányi bears a famous musical name. He is the grandson of the Hungarian composer Ernö Dohnányi. (His father, Hans, achieved fame in his own right. A noted German jurist and anti-Hitler conspirator, he was hanged by the Nazis in the last days of World War II.) It was the grandfather who was indirectly responsible for Christoph's going to Tanglewood to study. As a young man in Germany, Christoph had decided to give up his law studies and pursue a musical career instead. In 1951 he had come to the United States to study with his grandfather, who was teaching at Florida State University in Tallahassee.

But Christoph was a modernist, and the old man clung to the age of Brahms. After seven months Christoph struck out for the North and new ideas at Tanglewood. Although he nominally studied under Munch, Bernstein ran the conducting program that summer and was Dohnányi's principal mentor. As Mehta also discovered, Munch took only a casual interest in teaching.

Returning to Germany, Dohnányi began a conductor's traditional climb up the ladder through the opera houses. After an assistantship to Georg Solti in Frankfurt, he directed the Lübeck, Kassel, and Frankfurt companies. He climaxed his ascent by becoming chief of the Hamburg Opera in 1978 — the position he held when, after a twenty-nine-month search, the Cleveland Orchestra designated him Maazel's successor. Maazel, who had left to become the first American director of the Vienna Opera, lasted only two years of his four-year contract there. Dohnányi had not even arrived in Cleveland when Viennese politics and tastes sent the chastened Maazel back to his homeland and a job with the Pittsburgh Orchestra.

The Ohioans came to Tanglewood from concerts in Milwaukee and Detroit. Unlike the Philharmonic, which stayed in Pittsfield's glossy Berkshire Hilton, they bedded down in the rambling, Norman Rockwell–style Red Lion Inn in Stockbridge, a favorite haunt of tourists. For the Weekend Prelude the Cleveland Orchestra String Quartet played a Haydn-Brahms program. Then the full orchestra opened its stand with Brahms's Piano Concerto no. 2 (Emanuel Ax was the soloist) and Mendelssohn's *Scottish* Symphony. Again the sound was unmistakably different — darker than the BSO's, but also more compact, with a more pronounced edge to the winds. The ghost of Szell was indeed hovering in the wings.

Saturday night and Sunday afternoon brought a pair of symphonies with a bit of Dohnányi symbolism — Dvořák's G Major, the main work in the 1981 concert that had led to his appointment, and Beethoven's *Eroica,* one of his maiden recordings with his new orchestra. (The disc was just then being rushed to the stores to mark his accession.) The Saturday and Sunday soloists were Shlomo Mintz (in Lalo's *Symphonie espagnole*) and Jean-Pierre Rampal (in Mozart's Flute Concerto in G). For curtain raisers Dohnányi led Carl Ruggles's *Men and Mountains* — the weekend's only venture into the twentieth-century repertoire, for which Dohnányi is noted — and Mozart's *Magic Flute* overture.

By the time the weekend was over, it was clear that not just Tanglewood but also Cleveland had scored a coup. The extraordinary run of concerts caught a new music director and his orchestra in the full glow of their honeymoon. Dohnányi's *Eroica* had an extreme

Christoph von Dohnányi conducts the Cleveland Orchestra as it fills in for the BSO.

clarity, almost like chamber music, while his Dvořák was mellow and spacious — all play of light and shadow, where the *Eroica* had been a journey from darkness into light. He also excelled as a technician, employing a beat and gestures that were both economical and eloquent. Even before Cleveland knew exactly what it was getting, Tanglewood showed that the city had bet on a dark horse and won. To complete the triumph, Dohnányi donated $1,000 to the Tanglewood Music Center as a memento of his return.

Possibly with Rampal as a draw, the final program attracted the largest audience of the season — more than sixteen thousand. But, no matter how electric the performances, Tanglewood could not fill the Shed for the Friday and Saturday night concerts even by papering the house. Unlike New York, Cleveland apparently had little constituency in the Berkshires.

Across the Atlantic the BSO was beginning its two-week tour where the 1979 tour had left off — at the Edinburgh Festival. The reviews were mixed. From Edinburgh the orchestra moved on to London and Salzburg. In both cities the major work was Mahler's *Resurrection* Symphony, with Jessye Norman and Edith Wiens as the soloists — the same work and soloists with which the BSO had finished the Tanglewood season. A return appearance at the Berlin Festival matched the Bostonians against Karajan's Philharmonic again.

From Berlin Yo-Yo Ma, who was skipping about Europe as a soloist with the orchestra, sent back a dispatch to the *Boston Globe.*

> It is amazing to me [he wrote] how the members of the BSO are part of an international network of musicians. There is always a contingent of local friends waiting at the airport. Within minutes of arriving in the city, the best restaurants, the best boutiques, the instrument shops, the location of tennis courts, the jogging trails are known and exchanged in a kind of spoken shorthand.

If jets, hotel rooms, and irregular eating habits can be hard on musicians' nerves and stomachs, the pleasures of travel and butting heads with the competition offer compensations.

With the ground broken by the New Yorkers and the Cleveland, Tanglewood played host in later years to the Israel Philharmonic — Mehta's other orchestra, which he also conducted in the Shed — and the Academy of St. Martin-in-the-Fields under Neville Marriner. Tanglewood, for four decades the exclusive territory of the BSO, was on its way to joining Salzburg, Edinburgh, and Berlin as an international showcase for touring orchestras.

*   *   *

The trend toward an international festival was accelerated in 1980 with the return of opera, another hallmark of the Ozawa era. The audience filing in on the Saturday night of July 26 encountered a sight no Tanglewood audience had seen before: the Shed had been transformed into an opera house.

Not a real opera house, of course. The Shed has no curtain, flies, or pit. But staged opera, with sets, lighting, and a cast including Shirley Verrett and Sherrill Milnes, was returning as a Tanglewood fixture after a two-decade absence. The production was Puccini's *Tosca.* But now, instead of the student performances of the past, the cast was professional, the orchestra was the BSO, and the conductor was Ozawa.

The New York and Boston critics hated it. They called the performance a travesty and a waste of money. If the Metropolitan Opera does not play symphonies, they said, why should a symphony orchestra stage operas? But *Tosca* was the first in a series of partially staged productions under Ozawa, whose idea they were. In succeeding years he plowed ahead, through *Boris* and *Fidelio*, through *Oedipus Rex, Orfeo ed Euridice,* and *Béatrice et Bénédict,* through *Oberon* and *Elektra,* with a staged *St. Matthew Passion* for good measure. He said opera — opera staged and played not by students in the Theater–Concert Hall but by the BSO in the Shed — was a necessity. Without it, he insisted, Tanglewood would not be a complete festival nor he a complete conductor.

The *Tosca* set, made of wood and canvas, consisted of reversible panels. Turned one way, they showed the exterior of a palace with a central colonnade, stone walls, and vaulted windows. Turned the other, they showed interior palace walls hung with sconces or church interiors with frescoes. But there were no props — not even a knife for Tosca to plunge into Scarpia's ribs. The cast included Verrett as Tosca, Veriano Luchetti as Cavaradossi, Milnes as Scarpia, Italo Tajo as the sacristan, and Douglas Lawrence as Angelotti. But their costumes looked like a collection from a cocktail party. Tosca wore flowing gowns, Cavaradossi a beige sports jacket, Scarpia a tuxedo.

Other oddities cropped up: when Tosca ran Scarpia through with her nonexistent knife, he staggered offstage to die, leaving her no body around which to place her candles (which were nonexistent anyway). And the BSO, deployed across the apron of the stage and dressed in black like Scarpia's thugs in the unfolding story, looked like a branch of his police. At the front of the stage Ozawa weaved and bobbed in plain view of the audience like a black-clad mime who had popped in on the action.

The strange thing is that — in spite of what the critics said, and in its own creaking way — the production worked. It was not a *Tosca* any self-respecting opera company would have presented. But, as a *Tosca* designed specifically for the Shed, it was miles ahead of the occasional concert versions of operas given there before, even if miles short of a full staging.

Putting it another way, the production team that the BSO borrowed from the Met — director David Kneuss and designer John Michael Deegan — tailored *Tosca* to the setting as much as they tailored the setting to the opera. Their objective, Kneuss said, was "to abstract the action, bring things down to the idea of the piece, clarify the psychological conflicts by means of bold character strokes." They counted on listeners to use their imaginations to fill in details that would be visible in a 2,000-seat theater but could not be made explicit in a 5,000-seat concert pavilion, much less on the lawn, where another 5,000 people sat. The conception remained the basis for the following years' productions, though the stagings grew increasingly ambitious.

But why do *Tosca* in any form when the Shed was never designed for opera and the Theater–Concert Hall was by now too small and dilapidated to accommodate it? The idea, according to orchestra manager Gideon Toeplitz, went back to a remark by Verrett when she visited as a soloist a few years earlier. The soprano, Toeplitz said, commented that she "would love to come back and do *Tosca* with Seiji."

That did not exactly plant the seed, but in the spring of 1979, while preparing for *Tosca* performances in Japan and at La Scala, Ozawa decided that the piece might also work at Tanglewood. Verrett, as the original proponent, as well as a Tanglewood regular and Ozawa favorite, was a natural as the heroine. The BSO signed up a cast with her at the head.

The next decision was whether to do a concert opera, as in the past, or to attempt a staging. Ozawa and the staff decided to gamble. But what kind of staging, and by whom? The BSO called the Met for advice. The Met recommended Kneuss, who had staged its own new *Tosca* production that winter. And so it was that on a wintry Saturday afternoon Ozawa and Toeplitz traveled to New York to meet with Kneuss. He undertook the project and brought Deegan with him. On a February day when, Kneuss recalled, "we nearly got blown off the road by wind and snow," he and Deegan joined Toeplitz at Tanglewood to look over the silent, frigid Shed.

Deegan took photos, which he later used to build a model of the stage to work from in New York. Standing onstage, he thought the space was manageable. "But when you start designing a set," he said, "you realize how huge it is." It was just one of the problems the two men faced.

With four months in which to experiment, Kneuss and Deegan tried out a variety of ideas, beginning with screens and a color scheme employing a different hue to highlight each act. At first, said Kneuss, "we weren't really sure how specific we could be." But, becoming "more comfortable with the idea and the space, we were able to be more bold in how far we could go." They decided to go for sets.

The final production was brought in for about $20,000 — roughly a tenth of the cost of the Met production. (Later productions cost closer to $50,000 apiece.) That figure, of course, did not include artists' fees, which, with three star-class singers and two choruses, ran considerably higher than fees for an ordinary Tanglewood concert. But, Toeplitz said, the BSO regularly spends more on some programs and less on others, spreading out the expense over a season.

The performance was put together in four days, culminating in a public dress rehearsal on Thursday night. The Berkshires were flattened under a heat wave. Besides the usual run of problems afflicting an opera put together from scratch — the principals, for instance, had never before sung *Tosca* together — humidity, exhaustion, a plague of moths, beetles, and mosquitoes, and a delay in Luchetti's arrival from Italy tried everyone's endurance. Kneuss, who cuts the figure of a bantam rooster when at work, said he was used to putting tenors onstage with as little as fifteen minutes of preparation. He nevertheless worried that Luchetti would be a "basket case" when he arrived. As the hour neared for the nonexistent curtain to rise on a very real *Tosca,* it was Kneuss himself who seemed nearly ready for the basket carriers.

Opera at Tanglewood goes back to the first year of the Music Center, 1940. Considering opera as important to public enlightenment as symphonic music, Koussevitzky envisioned an amphitheater sloping down toward the lake and seating twenty-five thousand for musical pageants. Without even a theater, much less an amphitheater — the Theater–Concert Hall, equipped with a pit and flies, would not be ready until the following year — he began the program modestly. Under a department headed by Herbert Graf, with Boris Goldovsky as his assistant, the first production was *Acis and Galatea,* presented by daylight in the gardens.

The war shut down opera and nearly everything else at Tanglewood, but not before Graf and Goldovsky staged Nicolai's *Merry Wives of Windsor.* (The two performances introduced a golden-voiced tenor named Alfredo Arnold Cocozza in the minor role of Fenton. Unteachable as an opera singer, he went on to stardom of another kind under the name of Mario Lanza.) The resumption of activity in 1946 brought the American première of Britten's *Peter Grimes,* composed on a commission from the Koussevitzky Music Foundation and given its world première in London the year before. Bernstein, by now elevated to the position of Koussevitzky's assistant, was in the pit. Britten and his stage director, Eric Crozier, came over from England to assist in the preparations.

Graf, however, was not around. He opted for a temporary assignment in Hollywood, an absence that Koussevitzky soon made permanent, and in 1946 Goldovsky began his fifteen-year reign over an opera department that gave Tanglewood some of its pioneer achievements. Under his direction the next summer brought the American première of Mozart's *Idomeneo.* The first American performance of Britten's *Albert Herring* followed in 1949. Other productions included Ibert's *Le Roi d'Yvetot,* Grétry's *Richard the Lion-Hearted,* and Copland's *The Tender Land.* In 1946 an ambitious student named Sarah Caldwell appeared. She quickly became Goldovsky's assistant and, in time, his rival as a conductor and director in Boston. Singers coming out of the department in those days included Phyllis Curtin, Shirley Verrett, and Sherrill Milnes, along with Leontyne Price, Richard Cassilly, Justino Diaz, and Frank Guarrera.

Goldovsky's tenure was doomed with the appointment of Leinsdorf to the BSO podium. Leinsdorf, who had strong operatic ideas of his own, considered the opera department too much of a fiefdom within the Music Center. The BSO trustees, meanwhile, worried about the drain on the treasury. Seeing the omens, Goldovsky departed after the 1961 season.

Jessye Norman as a soloist with the BSO.

Opera continued at Tanglewood, but on something of a hit-or-miss basis. With Music Center singers and players Leinsdorf led a 1969 production of *Wozzeck* that is still talked about with awe on the grounds. With the BSO in the Shed he did a complete but unstaged *Lohengrin*, spread over an entire weekend — one act to a concert — in 1965. It did not go over so well. Even Leinsdorf, in *Cadenza*, speaks of it as a "disaster" of miscastings and miscalculations. Also with the BSO he did concert versions of *Fidelio* (in the original 1805 version), *The Abduction from the Seraglio*, and *Otello*.

In the early 1970s student opera returned in the Music Theater Project, a three-year program emphasizing small-scale, experimental productions, given in a barn. Ozawa also kept the spark alive by leading concert versions of *Eugene Onegin* and *Così fan tutte* with the BSO. When the grants for the Music Theater Project ran out, he tried to get a Goldovsky-style program going again at the Music Center. The money was not there. Opera would have to wait until 1980 and *Tosca* until it again became a regular feature of Tanglewood.

To me [Ozawa said], still this festival must concentrate on symphonic music the whole season. We have contemporary music, which is a great thing here, and a conducting class, orchestra students, piano seminar, listening-analysis seminar, and symphony concerts — so, really, everything except opera. This is why I thought we should do some opera.

It's very dangerous for me. You know, when we do opera, the whole office goes crazy, and so I have to be very careful, not extreme, because opera takes so much energy. To do that, we need a very good director, and I have to be very careful to choose the right opera and organize so we don't have a hectic week. And I have to keep the symphony program as healthy as possible.

It was 1982, the third year of Ozawa opera in the Shed. Stravinsky's *Oedipus Rex* and Beethoven's *Fidelio*, both staged, were to be the summer's productions. In 1981 Ozawa had also led two programs — a cut version of Mussorgsky's *Boris Godunov*, staged, and act 2 of Wagner's *Tristan und Isolde*, unstaged. The *Tristan* performance, with Jessye Norman and Jon Vickers in heroic voice as the fated lovers, predictably created a sensation with the audience. But it was the *Boris* production — cuts, Rimsky-Korsakoff orchestration, heavy traffic onstage, and all — that came closer to justifying Ozawa's faith.

In *Tristan* Ozawa alternately rushed and tiptoed through much of the score, leaving it to the singers to make of it what they could. In *Boris,* with Nicolai Ghiaurov as the tormented Czar, Ozawa responded at a deeper level. Despite the omission of act 2, and other cuts, the music was at once visceral in its impact and epic in its sweep. The staging also marked a step forward. There were props — golden crosses for the pilgrims, a throne for Boris — and the ebb and flow of the 19 singers and 130 chorus members added a dimension to the basically flat surface that *Tosca* had presented.

Ozawa admitted mistakes in the first two years' performances. In both *Tosca* and *Tristan,* he said, he misgauged the time it would take the singers to make entrances across the breadth of the stage. Kneuss lessened the damage in *Tosca.* But in *Tristan* Ozawa decided — to his regret — to let the singers make entrances and exits even though there was no other staging. The singers demanded it, he said, and this time he had no stage director to warn him against it. He slowed down the music too much. Tempos were thrown off. And when King Marke (Aage Haugland) came in, he distracted the audience from the lovers, who were singing beside the podium. As a result, Ozawa said, "all this moment doesn't mean anything, doesn't belong to the opera."

"So my answer is," he concluded, "either staging or a complete absence of action, as in an oratorio. There is no between. And in *Tristan* we tried between, you see. That was the biggest mistake — on my side, a mistake."

Irrepressibly cheerful, and gifted with a sense of mimicry, Ozawa strutted and thumped around the Green Room, imitating certain well-known singers who had caused him grief. "It wasn't easy to do *Tosca* here," he said, explaining that half the audience was sitting on the lawn and could not see Tosca's face and movements.

> But I don't want to limit too much, you know. Sometimes we should be able to do some Verdi opera here, which you must [be able to] see. Or, for instance, *Salome* could be done here. Again, if you sit in the grass outside, it's almost impossible to see. But you hear fantastic sounds. So it's a dilemma right there.

Another dilemma was the rehearsal schedule. In Europe, Ozawa said, he gets six weeks to prepare a production and then conduct the first eight or so performances of what might be a twenty-performance run. American houses, like the Met, allow two weeks of rehearsal. But at Tanglewood the singers arrive on a Sunday, and "rehearsal is only a few days — Monday, Tuesday, Wednesday, and Thursday is already open rehearsal," with the performance on Friday or Saturday night.

Language, too, was still a problem — not just English, in which he could at least make himself understood, but Italian, French, and German, which, Ozawa said, are "very difficult for me." To connect the words to the music, he usually works from Japanese translations, and for that "I take time, time, time, so I get it by ear." Hardest of all was *Boris,* for which he had to write out each word of the Russian text phonetically in the score. On the other hand, he said, when he did his unstaged *Così* at Tanglewood a decade earlier, he memorized the Italian words fairly quickly. But he forgets texts as easily as he learns them. "Two years later," he said, "completely gone."

Time, time, time, and problems, problems, problems. It had been seven years since the failure of his plan to bring Goldovsky-style opera back to the Music Center, yet Ozawa still spoke longingly of taking more time and using younger singers — possibly with one or two professionals in major roles — in student productions. He still spoke, too, of doing the same opera he had spoken of earlier, *Falstaff.* But then, he said, "management becomes absolutely a headache because if you get big soloists it doesn't pay" — not, at any rate, in the Theater–Concert Hall, with its 1,000 seats. Yet the productions would be too intimate for the Shed. "In opera, people want to see," he said. "We need 1,800 seats, a theater that has a pit."

Ozawa had been doing staged opera for only a decade — and then only one or two productions a year — when he began the Tanglewood series. Unlike European-born conductors such as Abravanel, Tennstedt, and Dohnányi, he did not come up through the opera houses, serving an apprenticeship as a coach and rehearsal assistant. His repertoire was small and, with his BSO obligations standing in the way, unlikely to grow at a rate of more than one or two works a year. In Europe he usually conducts one production a year at the Paris Opera or La Scala, or sometimes both. He also does opera in Japan and appears occasionally at Covent Garden and Salzburg. As of the late 1980s, however, he still had not appeared in any American opera house — again, partly because of his BSO commitments. Although the Met and he had talked, the house's schedule of staggered performances required more time than he could give. By the 1980s it became clear that if he was going to do opera in the United States, it would have to be with his own orchestra. And he was set on doing opera.

> To me [he said], to know opera is absolutely important to become a better musician and orchestra conductor. For instance, if I don't know Mozart operas—if I didn't know *Fidelio,* if I didn't know any Verdi opera, or if I didn't know Puccini, or if I didn't touch Wagner operas—it would be one big side of a great composer's work I never touched. And, sure, we could understand Mozart with the symphonies or concerti. But still lots of things for Mozart I never learn until I experience them with Mozart opera. For me to become a better musician or better conductor, I must experience through the opera. And then I realize even conducting technique — not just the arm but contact with orchestra — is different in opera. And then I realize the orchestra that plays opera becomes better in accompaniment, in hearing each other.

Opera in a place and by an orchestra that were not designed for opera: it is, as Ozawa said, a dilemma.

The 1982 *Oedipus* suffered from one set of problems, *Fidelio* from another.

Oedipus had been jinxed from the start by the dismissal of Vanessa Redgrave as the narrator for the winter run of Boston and New York performances. Beset with controversy and threats of violence stemming from her pro-Palestinian activities, the BSO canceled her engagement, paid her fee, and began looking for a different narrator. (Redgrave sued for damages and civil rights redress. The litigation dragged on for six years until the BSO won a final ruling that it had acted within its legal rights.) Then Peter Sellars, the *enfant terrible* director who was to have staged the winter production, resigned as a protest against the BSO action. The setbacks forced the cancellation of the winter programs, but Ozawa went ahead with the single performance scheduled at Tanglewood. Sam Wanamaker replaced Redgrave as both narrator and director. But now Jessye Norman, the Jocasta, canceled at the last minute because of sickness. The little-known Glenda Maurice was her replacement.

Fidelio was hobbled by one of the coldest nights in Tanglewood history — the temperature stood at 44° when the performance let out at 11:20 P.M. — and by further oddities in staging and pacing. As in Ozawa's previous operas, the first act moved cautiously, and

Kneuss's staging called attention to itself with fussy gestures that might not have been necessary or obtrusive if the music had generated more momentum on its own.

In *Oedipus* Ozawa conducted with a good ear for Stravinsky's dry sonorities but the performance and spare staging never recovered from the loss of the regal Norman as the queen. Sellars's original concept, which was to have Stravinsky's *Symphony of Psalms* follow *Oedipus* as a Christian catharsis to the Greek tragedy, also fell by the wayside. The symphony came first on the program and was not staged.

Fidelio, on the other hand, with Hildegard Behrens and James McCracken as the heroine and hero, transcended its limitations and even seemed to draw strength from them. Behrens sang Leonore's cruel part with dramatic urgency, attaining a special poignancy when she wandered through the crowd of shabby prisoners, looking for her husband. When McCracken's opening cry of *"Gott!"* echoed off the hills during the dungeon scene that begins act 2, the performance took on an irreversible momentum. Even the weather seemed a part of the experience. It was as if the fate of the audience, struggling to keep warm in sweaters, coats, and blankets, were inextricably tied to the fate of the figures onstage in their struggle to break tyranny's chains.

One listener who clearly was impressed was Luciano Berio, that summer's composer in residence. At his invitation Kneuss and Deegan restaged the production in 1984 at the Maggio Musicale festival in Florence, where Berio served as guest director. He found the minimal staging a way out of the dilemma of presenting opera in an age when productions were growing ever bigger and costlier.

The next two summers' productions voyaged on new seas of troubles. In 1983 Kneuss and Deegan staged Gluck's *Orfeo* as a kind of classical frieze, without dancing, furies, or even a lyre for Orfeo, but with a series of colored projections in abstract designs to suggest specific scenes (fiery red waves for Hades, a mottled, foliage-like green for the Elysian Fields). The program book spent eleven pages in telling how, in *Orfeo*, Gluck took the starring role away from the singers and gave it to the music. The production spent $2^{1}/_{2}$ hours in giving the music back to the singers as a star vehicle — chiefly Marilyn Horne as Orfeo but also Benita Valente as Euridice and Erie Mills as Amor.

Seiji Ozawa leads the semi-staged performance of Gluck's *Orfeo ed Euridice*. The soloists (from left) are Erie Mills as Amor, Marilyn Horne as Orfeo, and Benita Valente as Euridice. The chorus is behind a scrim, and ramps leading through the orchestra provide acting spaces for the singers.

In 1984 the staging team gave Berlioz's *Béatrice et Bénédict* a turn-of-the-century French look, far from the Messina of Shakespeare's story. The action took place on and around a carousel. The idea turned on a pun. A carousel, the program book stated in bold lettering, can be either a tournament among knights or a merry-go-round. So life became a merry-go-round and the two lovers — Frederica von Stade and Jon Garrison — did their jousting in the midst of wooden horses. Tricolor flags, balloons, banners, carnival lights, and cut-out swans and chickens lent further atmosphere.

The next year Kneuss and Deegan staged Bach's *St. Matthew Passion* — an idea Ozawa had picked up in Austria during his European *Wanderjahr,* 1959–60. Under a large blue-and-gold baroque cross suspended over the stage, Bach's double orchestra and chorus, and a new, smaller chorus of the faithful created by Kneuss, surrounded a platform on which Jesus and the other soloists enacted the story. The simple, largely stylized staging had a surprising dignity, many of the images strikingly enhancing the music. When Jesus confronted Judas, for example, the traitor, instead of standing still and singing to the audience, turned from Jesus in shame at the betrayal. Dramatically and vocally strong in the principal roles, Anthony Rolfe Johnson was the Evangelist and Benjamin Luxon the Jesus.

But a new problem cropped up. During the intermission Ozawa came down with stomach cramps and had to be rushed to a hospital. After a forty-five-minute delay John Oliver, director of the Tanglewood Festival Chorus, went on to complete the performance. It happened that, as part of the experiment with a ten-week season, the performance was to be repeated the next night. Ozawa was back, recovered from exhaustion, to do a complete *St. Matthew* on the rebound.

If in 1980 Tosca did not have a knife with which to work her vengeance, by 1986 opera at Tanglewood had not only a genuine swordfight but also a storm, complete with thunder and lightning. There were also pirates, with a peg-legged leader, and a mermaid outfitted with a tail. Soldiers' spears turned magically into rowers' oars, and Baghdad appeared as a series of gilt domes borne on poles. In one of many sight gags a passing singer handed Ozawa — who, with the orchestra, still shared the stage with the cast — a flowerpot.

The opera was Weber's *Oberon,* presented in the original English as a two-hundredth birthday party for the composer, and Kneuss and Deegan were out, at least temporarily. Instead, the Edinburgh Festival, reciprocating the BSO's 1979 and 1984 visits, and the Frankfurt Opera were co-producers; Frank Dunlop, Edinburgh's director, took personal command of the staging. From Tanglewood Ozawa, the principal singers, a group of non-singing actors, and the costumes, specially made in England, traveled to Scotland and then Germany for a further run of five performances. The Tanglewood *Oberon,* in fact, opened that year's Edinburgh Festival.

The sheer energy expended on the production could have lighted the whole of the Berkshires during a series of power failures from storms the week before. But much of that energy ended up as confusion and clutter, compounding rather than clarifying a muddle created by a silly libretto. The casting, too, was uneven. Paul Frey, a late replacement in the role of Huon, was apparently under the Berkshire weather. Elizabeth Connell, as Reiza, had the ringing high notes for the *Ocean* aria — the opera's big moment — but struck stock poses. James Robertson, a boy alto (and also a late replacement), had the impishness but not the voice for Puck. Only Philip Langridge, as Oberon, and Benjamin Luxon, as Sherasmin, made their characters more than cartoons.

The production got good reviews in Edinburgh, where an indoor theater and, presumably, the road tryout in Massachusetts helped. At Tanglewood the madcap staging put the emphasis on the story, which is feeble, at the expense of the music, much of which is great. Perhaps Tanglewood had gone big time with its Edinburgh, Frankfurt, and Florence connections. But in its seventh year opera at Tanglewood seemed to be trying not for too little, as the critics at first said, but for too much.

Unexpectedly, in the eighth year there was no opera at all. Strauss's *Elektra* had been scheduled as the production, but Hildegard Behrens, the heroine, canceled, and the production was postponed for a year. When it finally arrived in 1988, it had a new director, Behrens's husband, Seth Schneidman, a black monstrosity of a set, made of platforms projecting precariously above the orchestra, and a dramatic and musical impact more powerful than that in any of the seven previous productions. The performance also came better prepared (and more highly acclaimed) than any in the past. Before bringing the opera to Tanglewood Ozawa had led performances with Behrens in Paris and Boston. By now semi-staged opera had also come to Symphony Hall.

Despite the problems Tanglewood did as well in its casting as most major opera houses (which, of course, draw on the same international pool of singers). Behind the confusions, moreover, Ozawa showed a strong sense of drama and control of his performers; the troubles that arose came more from hasty preparation and inadequate stage facilities than from lack of musical imagination.

The most successful stagings, in retrospect, were those of *Boris, Fidelio*, the *St. Matthew Passion,* and *Elektra.* In each a few well-chosen strokes supported the singers and illuminated the action. But Ozawa was right: opera at a symphonic festival is a dilemma — not only a dilemma but an anomaly. The stagings were an improvement over concert opera; if the BSO management doubted that, it had only to listen to the audience, which whooped and whistled in the time-honored manner of opera fans everywhere. But, as the more ambitious productions proved, the Shed could never be made to do duty as a true opera house, and the Theater–Concert Hall was too small and antiquated.

As often happens, Tanglewood looked to the future by going back to its beginnings. In the late 1980s planning began for a modern Theater–Concert Hall to open in the early 1990s and replace or supplement the present theater. It would have about eighteen hundred seats — the magic number Ozawa had mentioned back in 1982 — and be equipped for fully staged productions, just as in Koussevitzky's design. As for performers, two principal options exist: BSO performances with professional casts, or student productions on the Goldovsky model.

Ozawa, however, had also learned his lessons in Europe. In the 1980s he spoke more and more about making Tanglewood an international festival, with more conductors and soloists from abroad, along the lines of Salzburg and Edinburgh. The singers from abroad were already coming, as were visiting orchestras. All that was missing was an opera house. Whatever shape opera took at Tanglewood in the 1990s, there seemed little doubt that Ozawa would be in the middle of it. But perhaps with adequate stage facilities and a pit he would not be quite so much in the middle that a passing singer could make fun of the situation by handing him a flowerpot.

*   *   *

A warm ovation went up in the Shed when Harry Ellis Dickson walked up to the microphone on Saturday morning to introduce the Verdi *Requiem* at the final open rehearsal of 1987, Tanglewood's fiftieth anniversary season. The crowd — many in it at any rate — not only recognized and applauded Dickson from countless open rehearsals and Pops programs past but knew this would be his last pre-concert talk. "Old musicians never die," Dickson responded, his voice ringing through the spaces over the public address system. "They just become legends in the Boston Symphony." The next afternoon, after the final chord of the *Requiem* had died away over the lake and hills, the BSO turned Dickson and five fellow musicians into legends.

Tanglewood opens with a tradition, the singing of the *Alleluia* at the Music Center. It closes with another tradition, the farewell ceremony at the final BSO concert for players leaving the orchestra by retirement or resignation. (Tanglewood marks the end of the BSO's contract year.) Three players depart in an average year, but 1987 produced a bumper crop of six with a total service of 218 years. While each was a veteran, none was more of a legend in his time than Harry Ellis Dickson, BSO violinist for forty-nine years, backup conductor of the Pops for the last twenty-nine of those years, author, raconteur, man about town, and father-in-law of a presidential candidate. Seiji Ozawa had told Dickson he was an institution. And so he was — an institution within an institution — as the waves of cheers that rolled through the Shed late on that Sunday afternoon demonstrated.

Ozawa, who had conducted the *Requiem,* began the post-concert ritual while the audience of eleven thousand was still on its feet, cheering the performance. One of the departing half-dozen, double bass player Leslie Martin, who was retiring after thirty years, was absent because of illness. Hot, happy, and bouncing around as if he were on the tennis court, Ozawa called the five others out of the orchestra one by one to present them to the crowd.

Violinist Cecylia Arzewski was first. An assistant concertmistress with seventeen years of service, she was leaving to become associate concertmistress of the Cleveland Orchestra — a step up. It was not, however, a happy parting. Frequently hostile to Ozawa, she seemed reluctant to come forward when he beckoned. But finally the warmth of his gestures and the roar of the crowd melted her resistance, and she came up and acknowledged the appreciation with grace. On returning to her chair, she exchanged a big hug with her stand partner, Max Hobart.

Behind Arzewski in the first violins Ozawa now singled out Dickson. Silver-haired and slightly owlish, he was a favorite with both the audience and the orchestra. As he threaded his way through his cheering colleagues, the crowd broke into clapping, shouting, and

Harry Ellis Dickson acknowledges the plaudits of the crowd after Seiji Ozawa has pushed him onto the podium.

waving that must have been heard halfway to Lenox. Ozawa pushed him onto the podium, where he waved back to the sea of hands before him like a champ in the boxing ring.

A bouquet from the audience greeted principal oboist Ralph Gomberg, who was retiring after thirty-seven years. He too mounted the podium and waved, acknowledging the tumult. Stepping down, he went around the front of the orchestra to wring the hands of his fellow first-stand players. Back at his chair he raised his bouquet high for the whole Shed to see.

Bassist John Barwicki, familiar to Pops fans for his clowning, got off a last joke. He ran offstage when his turn came. With fifty years behind him, he was retiring as the orchestra's senior member — the only still active member whose tenure went back to the original Tanglewood season. He was also, it turned out, a favorite of the Tanglewood Festival Chorus. When Ozawa summoned him back from the wings, the chorus, which was still onstage from the *Requiem,* erupted in a rattling ovation. Barwicki snatched the baton from Ozawa's hands and leapt to the podium as if to conduct.

Out from the wings, finally, came personnel manager William Moyer, in a navy blue blazer that looked formal in contrast to the players' whites. Taking early retirement to study the life of the seventeenth-century English musician and religious martyr Francis Tregian, Moyer had a tenure of thirty-five years — fourteen of them as a trombonist before he rose to the management position. He received a warm embrace from Ozawa.

That should have ended the ceremony, but the audience, reluctant to let the season or its heroes go, remained on its feet, clapping and shouting for more. Ozawa led the orchestra, chorus, and soloists in a final bow and then trooped offstage with them. Having drunk its fill, the crowd filed out into the slanting sunshine and the autumn and winter ahead.

"I've been through four stages in my life," Dickson said. "Childhood, youth, middle age, and 'You look marvelous.' "

Dickson, a marvel and a gentleman at the age of seventy-eight, began a fifth stage on that Sunday afternoon — retirement. But even if he had wanted to slip quietly off to the golf links, Ozawa was not going to let him. Back in Symphony Hall, anticipating his departure, Dickson said:

> It's forty-nine years and I'm a little bit superstitious about it. I'd rather people say, "Why didn't you wait until fifty?" than "Why did you wait till fifty?" [He smiled at his quip and explained.] There comes a time when you feel that this is it. I had a talk with Seiji last year and he said, "Well, you not leave orchestra completely." He said, "You know, you institution in Boston," which was very nice in a way. And so he said, "You will still stay here with the Pops and with the Young People's Concerts." I'll maintain my desk here and they won't get rid of me until they carry me out, I guess.

Dickson's role in the Pops, which is the BSO in informal attire and music (but without its first-chair players), became that of associate conductor laureate. He would still conduct the Pops at home and on tour but, with a newly acquired manager, he would also branch out and become a guest pops conductor with orchestras in Canada and the United States — Quebec, Edmonton, Ottawa, Florida, and New Orleans among the first. In Boston he began an expanded series with his own chamber group, the Classical Orchestra, and continued his orchestral programs for a favorite charity, the

Retina Foundation. He also continued to do some of the BSO's Young People's Concerts, which he founded.

He contemplated going out on the stump, too — how many violinists, after all, have a son-in-law who is running for president? The former Kitty Dickson is Mrs. Michael S. Dukakis. As soon as her husband's campaign got rolling in 1988, Dickson joined it, just as he had during Dukakis's last run for governor. He went to the big primary states of Florida, Iowa, New York, and California, addressing senior citizens clubs, Democratic groups, and college students on the presidential candidate's behalf. Disclaiming a politician's knack, he spoke "about Mike as I know him — as a human being and what he's done and what I think he'll do." When Dukakis won the Democratic convention's nomination, Dickson was in Atlanta to lead a convention band in a newly completed *Fanfare for Michael Dukakis* by Pops director John Williams. Afterward he continued to turn up regularly at campaign stops with Mike.

Finally, this author of two kiss-and-tell books about life in the BSO — *"Gentlemen, More Dolce Please"* and *Arthur Fiedler and the Boston Pops* — has been considering writing his memoirs. A lifelong Bostonian and one of Koussevitzky's first American appointees, he has plenty to write about. He began his career in vaudeville bands as a teenager, studied in Germany during the early Hitler years — he saw Hitler inaugurated as chancellor — and made music and conversation with everyone from Koussevitzky and Monteux to Fiedler and Danny Kaye, whose conducting sideline benefited from Dickson's coaching.

The two sides of Dickson's forty-nine BSO years are neatly bracketed by his two books. *"Gentlemen, More Dolce Please"* recounts his experiences with a succession of BSO managers, board presidents, soloists, and conductors, but chiefly the conductor who hired him and who mangled the English language as in the book's title. That, of course, was the imperious Koussevitzky.

A "strange audition" landed Dickson in Koussey's BSO. For three depression-era years Dickson had headed a Works Progress Administration project in Boston — five hundred musicians at work in two symphony orchestras, an opera company, and an assortment of other ensembles. Then a friend arranged for him to play for Koussevitzky. In the great man's Symphony Hall study, Dickson played the standard audition items — a chunk of a concerto and some orchestral parts, which he had to sight-read. He was a good sight-reader, and every time he tackled one of the unfamiliar parts Koussevitzky, as a backhanded compliment, would insist Dickson had played it before. Dickson would deny it.

Finally Koussey brought out his atom bomb — a symphony by Sergei Taneyev. The part was all but impossible to play. Dickson never knew how well he did, but "frankly, I don't think Koussevitzky did, either." He did well enough, however, for Koussey to offer him a contract. When he returned on the appointed date a few months later, he found twenty other violinists auditioning for his spot. After hearing the whole bunch go through their parts, Koussevitzky saw Dickson hanging around like the forgotten man. He said, "Oh, Dickson, I look for you. We vill come and you vill sign the contract."

Arthur Fiedler and the Boston Pops is a warts-and-all portrait of a man whom Dickson unhesitatingly calls a curmudgeon. Fiedler, who became the Pops's conductor in 1929, first asked Dickson to fill in for him at a concert in the mid-1950s. Finally the old man had to have an operation and missed almost an entire season. He designated Dickson to take over. Soon afterward Dickson became the Pops's official assistant conductor, the first and last Fiedler ever had.

Dickson describes the kindly looking Fiedler as "a very unhappy man," a man

> with no outward emotion. I knew him as well as anybody, and that wasn't too well, because I don't think his family knew him too well. In all the years I knew him, I never saw him kiss his own children. It was just foreign to him. But he was an unusual, unusual man, a fine musician. He had wonderful orchestral ears, he could hear everything, he had a great sense of balance, his records are marvelous, and he was a wonderful craftsman. But when it came to emotions, he just was embarrassed.

Dickson left the BSO with regret and affection but no unseemly nostalgia. Unlike other old-timers, he rejects criticism that Ozawa does not measure up to Koussevitzky or other titans of the past.

"There's never been another Koussevitzky, there never will be another one," he said. "Seiji may not be Koussevitzky, but he's Seiji. To me, he's one of the greatest phenomena that I've ever seen in music. I have the utmost respect and admiration for this man."

Koussevitzky, Dickson said, achieved an incomparable beauty of sound with the orchestra. But there was a price:

> Koussevitzky did a lot of that through fear. It's a different era. The orchestras have become much more democratic and have lost something because of that. But Koussevitzky was, I think, the greatest leader of musicians that I ever knew. He had the faculty for making you play better than you knew how, for playing your maximum. You didn't always agree with him in his tempi and so forth, but even if he played wrong tempi, he made them convincing.

Dickson was disappointed not to get the Pops director's job when Fiedler died in 1979. Although Dickson had asked to move up, the BSO trustees gave him a consolation prize — promotion from assistant to associate conductor. Nevertheless, he speaks well of John Williams, the Hollywood composer and conductor who moved into Fiedler's second-floor Symphony Hall office. He calls Williams "a fine musician and a wonderful human being" and says the Pops has "improved tremendously" under him. As for himself, Dickson says he was already in his seventies at the time and could not "fault the management for wanting someone younger whom they could groom."

One of Dickson's most treasured memories is the BSO's 1981 centennial concert in Symphony Hall — a "great concert," he calls it — featuring Perlman, Isaac Stern, Rostropovich, and Rudolf Serkin as soloists. He also looks back fondly on an eighty-fifth birthday concert he helped to arrange for Monteux. One of Dickson's commissions for the event was Stravinsky's *Birthday Prelude,* now an inescapable "happy birthday" serenade whenever a musician puts another year on the calendar. Dickson also savors the memory of rehearsals for the première of Bartók's *Concerto for Orchestra,* now a twentieth-century classic, which Koussevitzky commissioned when Bartók was new, down, and out in America. The composer, Dickson recalls, was sitting nervously in the balcony of Symphony Hall, calling down instructions to Koussevitzky on how the music should go. Koussevitzky, says Dickson, finally asked Bartók to please write out a list of his compaints. Koussevitzky then ignored just about all of them.

Dickson's wife, Jane, a New Yorker whom he met in Berlin as a fellow student, died in 1977. If she were still alive, he said, they would have retired to their summer and weekend home in Tyringham, in the hills a few miles east of Tanglewood. Even without her he keeps the place, which has heat, insulation, and a swimming pool, as a year-round retreat. He wrote part of the Fiedler book there during the summer and thinks it would be a "wonderful place" to work on his memoirs.

From there he will still go to Tanglewood, though now as a listener. He will still conduct, still play his "good Guadagnini" violin, and still see his daughters and their families, who live within a three-mile radius of his house in the Boston suburbs. But, he says, "there comes a time when you just have to change the direction of your life." The conductor laureate is not one to rest on his laurels.

John Barwicki recalls Tanglewood in its first season as a place where traffic jams were worse than they are today and lovers strolled arm-in-arm in the gardens, the women sometimes under parasols. Women wore evening dresses to the concerts and men wore black ties and jackets. There was no thought of the candelabra-and-blankets scene that prevails on the lawn today. There was, in fact, virtually no lawn scene at all, Barwicki says. Nearly everyone sat in a tent.

Barwicki remembers more: the BSO played only a twenty-four week winter season then, and most men in the orchestra (women members were still far off in the future) went home to Europe for the summer. Committed to the new Berkshire season, Koussevitzky personally asked each musician to stay on in America to join in the exodus to the country. Out of pride in the orchestra, each did. There were two weekends of concerts. Most players put up about eight miles to the north in a Pittsfield hotel, long ago torn down, and traveled to Lenox by chartered bus.

A trim, elfin seventy-seven, Barwicki was not the oldest member of the orchestra at his retirement. That distinction belonged to Dickson. But Barwicki had the longest tenure — the longest, in fact, since violinist Rolland Tapley's record-setting fifty-nine years, which ended in 1978. Like Tapley and Dickson, he entered the orchestra as an American amid a preponderance of Monteux and Koussevitzky appointees from Europe.

Barwicki was born and brought up near the waterfront in South Boston. As a student during the depression he began freelancing in orchestras in and around Boston. One of those gigs was the original set of Pops concerts on the Esplanade under Fiedler in 1929. Barwicki joined the Pops the following year, while still a student, and the BSO in 1937. He was one of the few BSO members who enjoyed his nights in the Pops. Audiences knew him for his funny hats and way of twirling his instrument on its peg, slapping it as it went.

Barwicki's first year in the orchestra was also Tanglewood's first year. That made him an eyewitness to the fateful 1937 thunderstorm that flooded and all but collapsed the tent in which the BSO played. The orchestra, Barwicki recalls, was protected because it was sitting in a wooden shell. But the drenching of the concertgoers in their evening attire was a "good luck omen," he says, because Gertrude Robinson Smith's festival committee rushed construction of the Shed to have it ready for the next summer. Indeed, from the opening day of the 1938 season the new pavilion provided the BSO with what Barwicki describes as a "beautiful" — and dry — summer home. The new chairs and backstage area added over the years only made it better as a place to play and hear music, Barwicki says. In the postwar years, when two weekends of Bach-Mozart concerts for small orchestra would open each season, he used to go over to the steps of the Main House to listen to programs in which he was not playing. There was no amplification on the lawn then, and even at a distance, he says, the sound "was unbelievably beautiful."

Change came on the other side of the road, though, and Barwicki did not like it. In 1956 a spectacular fire destroyed the original Shadowbrook mansion, made of stone, where the Carnegies once had lived. The Jesuits, who had turned the property into a novitiate, replaced the burnt-out mansion with what Barwicki describes as "that big monstrosity" of red brick — today the home of the Kripalu Center for Yoga and Health, visible on its hillside for miles around. But Shadowbrook's original boathouse still stands on the lakefront, now as a private home, and Barwicki can remember seeing the Carnegies taking housefuls of guests on cruises around the lake on their private steamer, the *Sheila*.

As Barwicki recalls it, his audition experience with Koussevitzky was much like Dickson's. He got the audition on the recommendation of his bass teacher, and Koussevitzky, a bassist himself, hired him on the spot. When the young man reported for duty, he found a gaggle of other bassists waiting to audition for the same vacancy. Barwicki's fears, like Dickson's, proved needless. Koussevitzky took him into the orchestra without further discussion. Those were the days when there were no committees or unions to tell a conductor whom he could or could not hire.

Barwicki recalls that Koussevitzky kept a close eye on his ten basses, lining them up in a single row across the back of the stage (they play in two rows now). "He wanted to see how we fingered, how we looked at him — oh, boy, it was a thrill to play. I tell you, we were outstanding. Outstanding."

But then the whole BSO under Koussey, Barwicki said, was outstanding in a way that conductors and orchestras no longer are. Koussevitzky, he said, was "one of the most dedicated of them all. I've never seen a conductor so much involved. He loved the music. He wanted to get all the beauty, what the composer had in mind. He wasn't satisfied with what was on the score."

Barwicki also remembers outstanding concerts under Munch, Sir Thomas Beecham, Dimitri Mitropoulos, and George Szell, as well as great solo performances by Gregor Piatigorsky and Vladimir Horowitz. But perhaps his biggest thrill was a performance of Rachmaninoff's Second Piano Concerto with Rachmaninoff as the soloist. Even the great Koussevitzky, Barwicki said, yielded when Rachmaninoff began lecturing conductor and orchestra on how he wanted his music played. It was, Barwicki said, the only time "I saw Dr. Koussevitzky — God bless his soul — I saw his baton a little bit nervous."

It is a new breed today. Unlike Koussey, who would attend BSO concerts during his vacations to see how his orchestra was playing, conductors today want only to pack the largest number of concerts into the smallest number of days, Barwicki said. Orchestra players, he said, are more concerned with time off for vacations or solo gigs than with service to the orchestra.

"Nowadays things go too fast, I think," he reflected sadly.

A widower, who for his last thirty-five Tanglewood years camped at the BSO beach on Stockbridge Bowl, Barwicki continued to swim and take out his sailboat up till his final season. He still spun from place to place on his motorscooter, winter and summer. ("They call me Reckless Driver," he said, proud of the epithet.) Musicians might change, but just about the only change at Tanglewood, he said, is that "the trees are taller."

"To me, it's just like it was yesterday — fifty years ago and just like yesterday," he said with a distant look in his eyes. He was the last Tanglewood veteran who could make that claim.

More hoopla awaited backstage after the farewells in front of the throng. Television cameras have become almost as essential to music as bass fiddles; camera crews from Boston, Albany, and points beyond jammed Ozawa's Green Room, as did radio reporters with their tape whirligigs, photographers with their guns, and newspaper reporters equipped only with pad and pen. All had been alerted by the BSO press office to a "news break" after the concert.

Green Room? It looked like a locker room after the pennant victory. Hot, noisy, and fizzing with champagne in plastic cups, the cinderblock retreat with its rugs, hangings, sofa, grand piano, and long window giving onto the lawn and woods teemed with fifty or so sweating newshounds jostling for position. Into this den the retiring musicians were shepherded with their families. Arzewski, evidently still miffed at Ozawa, was conspicuously not there. Nor, for the moment, was Ozawa. He soon emerged, however, from his dressing room. As is his custom, he had changed from his sweat-soaked concert whites into a kimono-like Japanese gown.

The BSO press staff guided Ozawa and the guests of honor through the mob to the piano. Questions, and instructions on where to stand, peppered them. Recorded for posterity were such gamely spoken lines as Gomberg's "What time does the next rehearsal begin?"

Can a son-in-law, governor, and presidential candidate resist the cameras? No more than nature can a vacuum. Dark and compact, with something of the air of an Eagle Scout about him, Mike Dukakis was right there by the piano, along with Kitty and Dickson's other daughter, Janet Peters. On the other side of the lid Ozawa's wife, Vera, and Gomberg's wife, Sydelle, stood hemmed in by the crush, looking dazed.

When the TV crews discovered a presidential candidate in their midst, the questioning touched off another round of wisecracks. Addressing the quartet of players, Dukakis said, "I think what you guys should do is get together and form a combo, and we'll bring it down to the White House."

"This is too much emotion," said the weary Ozawa. "It's a tough day."

The summer had also begun on a note of high emotion — a fiftieth birthday party for Tanglewood as a coda to the opening night's concert. The same press office that could round up fifty pushing, sweating journalists had rounded up one thousand candles and fifteen thousand cupcakes, all donated. After Ozawa had led the Brahms Fourth Symphony to end the bso program, one thousand concertgoers around the three open sides of the Shed each lighted a candle dispensed by an usher. As the candles formed a ring of light, John Oliver's Tanglewood Festival Chorus, standing just inside the Shed under its southern rim, sang Thompson's *Alleluia* to recall the distant stirrings under Koussevitzky. The tears that students can raise when they sing the piece at their opening exercises flowed afresh from those who understood what the ceremony meant. Then the crowd joined in as Ozawa led everybody in a chorus of *Happy Birthday*. At the gates each departing guest received one of the fifteen thousand Tanglewood birthday cakes.

After that opening the season had been much like any other — a few highs, a few lows, much in the middle — but with little to mark it as an anniversary year. It was not until, on the final day, Ozawa turned Verdi's prayer for the dead into an affirmation of life, just as he had the *War Requiem* the year before, that Koussevitzky's ghost stirred again in his Shed, and on the sunny afternoon the famous thunderstorm echoed again in the hills. Much had happened in the intervening half-century: new conductors, new orchestras, an international repertoire and thrust. What would the next fifty years be like?

Probably much like the first fifty — the more things change at Tanglewood, the more they have a way of staying the same. But for one day Harry Ellis Dickson, violinist, conductor, campaigner, man about town, and introducer of great music, had the last word. As the Green Room gang began dispersing to families, dinners, and vacations, he waved and called to everyone, "So we'll see you all in a year in the White House." History proved him wrong.

Chapter VI

A MISCELLANY OF VISITORS

More than 300,000 concert-goers stream through the gates at Tanglewood every summer. Not all of them are simply visitors who come to hear music. A handful — composers, patrons, critics, celebrities, and volunteers among them — come for a special reason or with a special cachet.

Perhaps foremost among these guests are composers. They come in steady numbers to hear new works — often their own — performed in the Festival of Contemporary Music and to mingle with fellow composers in a vacation setting. Over a half-century these visitors have ranged from the distinguished to the unknown (the unknown sometimes going on to become distinguished). At one end of the spectrum Aaron Copland, the original chairman of the faculty, has returned in recent years for programs in honor of his major birthdays. At the spectrum's other end Michael Gandolfi, a student in 1986, came back the following summer for the première of his first orchestral work.

Composers need patrons, and one of Tanglewood's most colorful visitors, until age restricted her travels, was Margaret Lee Crofts. For forty summers she has supported two student composers at the Music Center, even though she finds much contemporary music unspeakable. Critics regularly visit, seemingly unable to agree on anything, and actors also appear, unable to escape their public. There was the time, for instance, when Robert Redford tried to avoid the press by hiding in the press office. Robert J. Lurtsema, New England's favorite classical-music radio announcer, shows up every summer for a weekend of broadcasts. One of his visits ended a mystery over his two-month disappearance.

What would a festival in the country be without wildlife? Tanglewood enjoys visits from skunks, birds, and mosquitoes, and as concert visitors birds can be as unwelcome as skunks. The most famous incident occurred when a young skunk ambled into a contemporary music concert and made himself at home under a listener's chair. After a bit of confusion the concert proceeded amicably to its end. For four decades, however, Tanglewood fought the battle of the bird. The problem stemmed from families of starlings, grackles, and sparrows nesting in the Shed's rafters. Rasps and squawks from hungry chicks at feeding time set up a silly symphony that sometimes vied with the BSO for listeners' attention. After unsuccessful experiments with weapons ranging from wire mesh to ultrasound, inflatable plastic owls and snakes finally dislodged the visitors — for how long, no one was saying.

Tanglewood has a special group of visitors in its volunteers, who serve as ushers, distribute program books, raise funds in the community, and operate a gift shop next to the Main Gate. Along with parking attendants and ticket takers, the ushers and program handlers are Tanglewood's ambassadors to arriving concertgoers. Usually the meetings are cordial on both sides. But once in a while an unexpected crush in the lots and on the grounds, such as occurred when Isaac Stern and some friends played a chamber concert, can cause tempers as well as radiators to boil over.

In the end, however, it is the concertgoer who is Tanglewood's most influential visitor. He casts the critical vote in determining what the BSO will play, which artists will play it, and what shape a season will take. If the Tanglewood audience is more relaxed — and sometimes more noisy — than audiences in the cities, the quest for great music in a setting of great natural beauty may say something hopeful about Tanglewood and a musical democracy.

*　　*　　*　　*　　*

For more than forty years, until she was nearly ninety, Margaret Lee Crofts made the pilgrimage to Tanglewood once a summer. She would leave her home in Stamford, Connecticut, in the morning and drive for three hours to meet her "boys" for lunch. In the earlier years she sometimes stayed for the evening BSO concert, but that was not the point. She wanted to see how her protégés were doing.

The 1976 trip, Mrs. Crofts's twenty-eighth, was much like the others. In Lee, five miles short of Tanglewood, she had her driver stop at the Colonel's place to pick up a carton of Kentucky fried chicken. "No backs and wings," she ordered. "We want something to *eat.*" Amply supplied with choicer parts, she motored on for the picnic under the trees at the Tanglewood cafeteria.

Mrs. Crofts, a widow, was eighty-three that year. Her "boys" (sometimes "girls") are the two student composers she has sponsored at the Music Center each summer since 1948. She came up with the idea because other donors, including some of her friends, were supporting student pianists, conductors, and singers; composers, she decided, were less glamorous but needed help, too. After discussing the idea with Koussevitzky and Copland, who encouraged it, she established the fellowships and began the annual trips to meet the composers the Music Center had designated as Crofts fellows.

"I've been doing this since 1948 and now I've got quite a family," she told the gathering at lunch in 1976. "When I used to travel more, people would show me pictures and ask about grandchildren. Well, I say I've got all these grandsons now."

By the time Mrs. Crofts, at the age of ninety, had supported sixty-nine composers and become too frail to travel, Tanglewood decided to return the favor. In that year, 1983, the Music Center staff gave her a scrapbook of letters and brief compositions as a tribute from her protégés. Two years and four composers later Tanglewood dedicated the whole Festival of Contemporary Music to her. In the program book Daniel R. Gustin, then the Music Center's administrative director, wrote that, not "content simply to send in her donations each year," Mrs. Crofts continued to play a part in her musical sons' and daughters' careers in the life after Tanglewood. Gustin said:

> She has attended their weddings, and the birthdays and bar mitzvahs of their children; she has given them advice when they asked and sometimes (if she thought it important enough) even when they didn't; she has sent them abroad; she has helped them with residencies at the MacDowell Colony; she has helped them to pay for a recording, a book, the publication of a new work. Above all, she has treated them as she believes composers ought to be treated — as the really important people in music.

Mrs. Margaret Lee Crofts and composer George Crumb sit at the picnic table with her composition fellows, Robert Beaser (left) and Michael Kowalski. They are looking at the Tanglewood poster the students gave her.

The 1976 Crofts fellows — the fifty-fifth and fifty-sixth in the series — were Robert Beaser of Yale University and Michael Kowalski of the University of Illinois. There was also a special guest at the picnic table that year: George Crumb, forty-seven, a Crofts fellow in 1955 and, thirteen years later, the winner of the Pulitzer Prize in music. A mild-mannered West Virginian who teaches at the University of Pennsylvania, Crumb was in residence at Tanglewood for a week to hear a BSO performance of his Pulitzer Prize work *Echoes of Time and the River* and to counsel student composers. He brought his wife, Elizabeth, and their two sons, David, fourteen, and Peter, eleven, to lunch with him. So, counting Richard Ortner, the assistant administrator of the Music Center, who was the Tanglewood host, the party numbered seven.

As everybody sat at the picnic table, crunching the Colonel's best, the composers and their patron exchanged mementos. They signed Tanglewood posters for her. She gave Crumb a detailed, typewritten report from her dentist on a performance of *Echoes of Time and the River* he had heard in New York on her tickets.

The conversation turned to past composers Mrs. Crofts had helped, including one of her first pair, Charles Strouse, who went on to write the hit musical *Bye Bye, Birdie.* They all call, visit, or write sooner or later, she said.

Turning her concern to Beaser and Kowalski, Mrs. Crofts asked Crumb, "Do you think they have any gifts at all?"

"Oh, yes," he said. "I like their music. I've listened to it a lot."

"Well, I sat down the other night and played all your records," she told Crumb. "I thought I'd bring myself up to date."

At times, Mrs. Crofts said, finding the money for the two fellowships was a struggle. At times, too, she finds modern music "unforgivable." But, she said, her friends were helping singers and other musicians, and she felt she ought to be helping someone musical, too.

"When I first decided to do something like this for composers," she recalled, "Alfred Knopf, the publisher, told me, 'Forget it, you can't afford it.' I said, 'Alfred, I believe in a widow's right. If I have to sell securities, I'm still going to do it.' "

After dessert Mrs. Crofts walked over to the Theater–Concert Hall to say hello to Gunther Schuller. He was sitting in on a rehearsal of a new electronic work to be performed in the Festival of Contemporary Music. Seeing her at the door, he came out, greeted her with a kiss, and invited her to hear a sample of the music. She stepped inside and received the full force of four large loudspeakers bleeping the taped part. Shuddering and clasping her ears, she left quickly.

After buying some postcards and collecting her driver, her maid, and a friend who had come for the ride, Mrs. Crofts left for the three-hour trip back to Stamford.

She did not stay for any music. Except for the BSO concerts in the early years, she never did. But at ninety-five she was still sponsoring composers.

* * *

If a patron does not come for new-music concerts, who does? Certainly not ordinary listeners. They avoid Fromm Week — or what used to be called Fromm Week — in droves. For them it is what otherwise faithful Tanglewood habitués, in the era when Paul Fromm was still the new-music festival's chief patron, described as

Keep Away Fromm Week. For composers, however, a trip to the Festival of Contemporary Music combines the pleasures of vocation and vacation.

Tanglewood has its annual composer in residence and other faculty composers. Each year, in addition, the contemporary festival attracts an assortment of composers passing through. Many come to hear their own works performed and often to assist in preparation of those performances. Others want to hear what their colleagues are producing and perhaps attend a BSO or chamber concert. Most come to mingle, talk shop, and enjoy a few days in the country. These visitors have ranged from the distinguished to the unknown.

One of the regular guests, always received with honor, is Aaron Copland, whose recent visits have occurred at five-year intervals. Each time both the BSO and the Music Center have presented musical tributes.

In 1975, for his seventy-fifth birthday, a peppy Copland joined Olivier Messiaen, that summer's composer in residence, for performances of their works — Copland's *Connotations for Orchestra,* Messiaen's *L'Ascension* — at the festival's climactic orchestral concert, conducted by Gunther Schuller. (In honor of Pierre Boulez's fiftieth birthday, the program also included his *Rituel.*) In 1980 Copland returned for an eightieth-birthday garland. He conducted the BSO in a program of his own pieces, and the Boston Symphony Chamber Players presented a sampler of his and Roger Sessions's works to honor their contributions to American music and their long BSO associations. Frail but still greeting friends with his old affability, Copland was back in 1985 for his eighty-fifth. The BSO played his *Appalachian Spring* — now as much a part of the American landscape as the region it celebrates — and the contemporary festival presented his song cycle *Twelve Poems of Emily Dickinson.*

Besides celebrating father figures, Tanglewood introduces and attracts younger, less established composers. At the 1975 orchestral concert, for instance, Stephen Albert shared the program with Copland, Messiaen, and Boulez. The occasion was the world première of Albert's *Voices Within,* a joint Music Center–Fromm Music Foundation commission. Little known when he took his bows in the Theater–Concert Hall that night, he won the 1985 Pulitzer Prize.

Another unusual constellation of composers attended the 1981 festival's orchestral concert, also conducted by Schuller. The program brought an outpouring of four premières. All four composers were present, two of them coming from Europe.

Schuller's coup that year was the rediscovery of Igor Markevich, the European conductor-composer, whose 1937 work *Le Nouvel Age* received its first American performance. The program also included the American première of the Third Symphony by Oliver Knussen, over from England for one of his many Tanglewood visits; the world première of another Music Center–Fromm commission, *Life Dances*, by Ramon Zupko of Western Michigan University; and the first complete performance of *Fragments from Antiquity*, a work for soprano and orchestra by Yehudi Wyner, a Tanglewood composition teacher.

Considerable curiosity attended Markevich's visit, his first to the United States, according to Schuller, since his American conducting debut with the BSO in 1955. Although he was known in this country through recordings with European orchestras, his music was — and still is — seldom played. The short, trim composer, who traveled from France and was sixty-nine, added to the enigma with his elegant air, which belied an association with the postwar avant-garde in Europe.

Markevich was born in pre-revolutionary Russia but spent most of his life in Italy and Switzerland before settling in France. After serving in the Italian resistance during World War II and suffering two serious illnesses, he renounced composing. He later explained: "There is music which needs to be heard before mine, and for which the need is more urgent. Apart from that, if my works are good enough, they can wait; and if they cannot wait, it is pointless to play them." Indeed, they remained unplayed until Belgian Radio induced Markevich to conduct two selections in 1978 and Schuller brought the revival to Tanglewood. *Le Nouvel Age* proved clearly of the 1930s in its Prokofiev-like sonorities and pouring of new wine into the old bottle of the sinfonia concertante form. Tanglewood was apparently as far as the Markevich revival went in the United States. Little more was heard of him after the performance.

Elliott Carter, on the other hand, is a frequent visitor, often coaching performances of his music. On the occasion of his eightieth

Leonard Bernstein and Aaron Copland reminisce on the lawn at Seranak on the occasion of Copland's 1985 visit.

birthday in 1988, the festival brought the much-honored American composer back for a presentation of a half-dozen of his works, including the world première of *Remembrance,* an orchestral piece commissioned by the Fromm Music Foundation in memory of Paul Fromm. In connection with the celebration the BSO presented Carter with its Horblit Award, a $5,000 prize for composers. (Previous recipients included Leonard Bernstein, Gunther Schuller, and Roger Sessions.) David Del Tredici, a former Margaret Crofts Fellow who won the 1980 Pulitzer Prize, returned in 1985 for a performance of his *Happy Voices* (from *Child Alice, Part 2*). Like north and south on a compass, the two composers represent opposite poles in composing styles. Carter comes from an older generation and a cerebral, atonal tradition, while the younger Del Tredici embraces the tonal and the vernacular with his obsessive retelling of the *Alice in Wonderland* saga by a monster orchestra.

Never, however, did the contemporary festival flirt more daringly with pop trends than in the premières of three theater pieces that brought a new breed of composer to Tanglewood in 1978, 1980, and 1982. All three composers took a hand in the stagings.

First in the series came the world première of *Wake Up, It's Time to Go to Bed!* by Carson Kievman, a West Coast composer. The forty-five-minute piece, for which Kievman was a coach, told an autobiographical story of an American male (named Orpheus) jilted by his girlfriend (Eurydice). The cast of children and adults played out the action amid such pop devices as flashing strobe lights and taped speech speeded up to squeaky Minnie Mouse levels. Two years later, with Copland and his fellow composer Otto Luening in the audience, Heinz Karl Gruber of Austria was the narrator (or, as he put it, *"chansonnier"*) in the American première of his *Frankenstein!!!* The half-hour tale of vampires, werewolves, and child butchers was a musical comic strip scrambling gibberish, doggerel, jazz, cabaret, Kurt Weill, Stephen Sondheim, popping paper bags, toy saxophones, whirling plastic hoses, John Wayne and "Jimmy" Bond, Superman, Batman and Robin.

Wake Up and *Frankenstein!!!* were student productions. In 1982 an outside cast, made up mostly of Tanglewood alumni, staged the world première of *The Musical Seminar* by Gheorghe Costinescu, a Romanian-born composer living in Washington. Costinescu served as the director, producer, and pianist for his ninety-minute survey course, which recounted an apparently traumatic schooling all the way from the Renaissance polyphonists to Louis Armstrong and John Cage. The staging called for five musician-actors, two of whom, at one point, impersonated dancing dice. The scene produced a festival rarity — a protest from the audience. After executing the apparently tireless pair of dice with nimble *épée* strokes from the pit, conductor David Hoose ordered them to get up and begin the dance again. That was too much for the BSO's head librarian, Victor Alpert, who shouted a pained "No!" that resounded through the house.

The trip to Tanglewood took a different — and more typical — route for Mario Davidovsky, an Argentinian composer who first came as a student in 1958 at Copland's invitation. Tanglewood became what Davidovsky later called his "port of entry" into American musical life. He got to know two classmates from abroad, Zubin Mehta and Claudio Abbado, for whom the festival served much the same purpose. More importantly for his career, he met composer Milton Babbitt, who was then helping to found the Columbia-Princeton Electronic Music Center in New York. On Babbitt's recommendation Davidovsky returned on a Guggenheim Fellowship to study at the center. In time he became an American citizen, took up teaching, and returned to Tanglewood in a series of short visits that culminated in 1981 with a summer-long residency.

Best known for his electronic music — one of his *Synchronisms* for acoustic instruments and tape won the 1971 Pulitzer — Davidovsky also composes in traditional forms and for traditional instruments. Electronic music, he said, is a "very, very important addition to the materials available to the contemporary composer," but "did not replace anything. It just added a new dimension to music."

In 1986 another young composer followed the path Davidovsky, Del Tredici, and others like them had blazed. With a series of awards, fellowships, and performances behind him, Michael Gandolfi, a thirty-year-old native of the Boston suburb of Melrose, came to study under Knussen. Toward the end of the summer Knussen suggested that Gandolfi write a short orchestral piece for the next year's contemporary festival. Out of that suggestion came *Transfigurations,* Gandolfi's first orchestral work. The eleven-minute piece had its première in 1987, with Knussen conducting. It was the first commission awarded through the Paul Jacobs Memorial Fund, a gift from the estate of the pianist and specialist in twentieth-century music.

No longer a student but now a composer with a performance in the festival, Gandolfi returned to Tanglewood for the première. He recalled that Knussen's offer of a commission had been "a fantastic opportunity." Despite successes with chamber works, Gandolfi had been "beginning to get very depressed" about a new composer's chances of ever getting an orchestral work performed. He dedicated *Transfigurations* to Knussen.

Gandolfi shared the program with two other former Tanglewood fellows, Jay Alan Yim (his work was *Karénas,* also a première) and Gerald Levinson (the Symphony no. 1, *Anahata*). The evening's other selections were Stravinsky's *Movements for Piano and Orchestra,* with Peter Serkin as the soloist, and Alexander Goehr's *Metamorphosis-Dance.* Goehr, a Stravinsky scholar and the son of the English conductor Walter Goehr, was visiting from Cambridge University for two weeks as a Music Center lecturer. A parade of four composers — Yim, Levinson, Gandolfi, and Goehr — marched to the stage to accept applause. Only Stravinsky, dead since 1971, was missing.

The Festival of Contemporary Music can be frustrating, irritating, trivial, tiresome, maddening; rarely is it dull. A typical year will bring performances of works by thirty or more composers, perhaps ten of them, like Gandolfi, new to the festival. Half or more of these composers — the majority of the living Americans and a scattering of others — will attend. More important than numbers is the diversity. Each composer brings a new viewpoint to students, performers, listeners, and other composers.

The list of composers who have been heard in the festival is like Leporello's catalogue in *Don Giovanni*: so many from this country, so many from that, so many tonal, so many atonal, so many pop-oriented, so many minimal (but not so many as Paul Fromm might have liked), the young, the old, the famous, the obscure, and so on. Many of the names, like Del Tredici's, Albert's, and Knussen's, were unknown at first but subsequently became public property, at least within the world of music. Other names are forgotten or never gained currency in the first place. The catalogue, however, includes

Japan's best-known composer, Toru Takemitsu, who visits regularly (he is a friend not only of Ozawa but also of Knussen and Peter Serkin). Women are represented, though not in large numbers. In recent years Ellen Taaffe Zwilich, who in 1983 became the first woman to win the Pulitzer Prize in music, and Joan Tower have visited for performances. The 1987 festival included works by three women from an earlier generation, Ruth Crawford, Louise Talma, and Miriam Gideon. The eighty-year-old Gideon was in the audience for her song cycle *Creature to Creature,* which she describes as "an animalculary."

Critics, another species of visitor attracted to the contemporary festival, complain from time to time that it is unrepresentative of broader trends in American music. John Rockwell of the *New York Times* actually became embroiled in the power struggle that led to Fromm's departure as the festival's Maecenas. Although Fromm denied being influenced by the *Times*'s reviews, Rockwell's tattoo of criticism of the programming, which he found narrow and academic, incensed Schuller and probably contributed to his stiffening of the back against Fromm, his friend and supporter in the new-music trenches for two decades.

On the other hand, a new breed of composer arrived — or failed to arrive — with the advent of the "electro-acoustic preludes" instituted by Knussen in 1986 as part of the festival. Each half-hour program, which precedes a main festival concert, offers computer-generated works from the United States or abroad. Because Tanglewood has no synthesizers, each work is presented on tape. The audience (usually no more than fifty) sits in a small hall surrounded by loudspeakers. No composer is present; no performer, either. The only human touch is provided by the electronic music coordinator (composers Paul Lansky and Tod Machover so far), who gives a brief introductory talk and then turns the stage over to the machines.

This is not necessarily the wave of the future. Back in 1981, after all, Mario Davidovsky had said that electronic music did not replace anything but merely gave the composer a new instrument. Still, the Festival of Contemporary Music remains a ghetto within the musical democracy at Tanglewood. Aaron Copland, who is to Tanglewood's composing tradition what Leonard Bernstein is to its conducting tradition, once said of his time at Tanglewood: "This is a thrilling place to be for eight weeks. I don't know if I could stand it much longer. . . . I mean that in the best possible sense. It's so stimulating and so alive that after you've had eight weeks of it you want to go home and think about it for eight more weeks." It is a truth that the crowds easily discover for themselves at the BSO's Shed concerts. Composers, along with a small band of other aficionados, have to prove it anew at each contemporary festival.

* * *

Except during contemporary music week most critics (also known as "crickets" in certain Tanglewood offices) avoid Tanglewood as assiduously as other listeners avoid the contemporary festival. Critics, having heard enough Beethoven and Tchaikovsky to last them a lifetime, tend to seek out the new and different and avoid the familiar, which, of course, is precisely what pulls the crowds in. A few newspapers — the *Berkshire Eagle*, the *Boston Gobe*, the *Springfield Union* — cover each BSO concert religiously. Other nearby papers, such as those in Albany, Worcester, and Hartford, hit the high spots, and more if they can. To get the *New York Times*, the *New Yorker*, or the newsmagazines to pay attention, Tanglewood has to offer a major debut or première, celebrate an anniversary, stage an opera, or play new music. A press office with a full-time staff of five sees to it that the word gets out and that critics' needs, from tickets and photographs to coffee and bourbon, are met.

The habitual critics take a no more jaundiced view of Tanglewood than they do of other crowd-pleasing aspects of musical life. The reviews by the occasional visitors from the big city tend to fall into two camps. On one side, casehardened critics complain about the crowds, the traffic, the humidity (or chill), and the quality of performances prepared under less than Michelin four-star conditions. On the other side, refugees from the city, weary of the jostle and bustle, sometimes find the fresh air and scenery such an elixir that they spend as much of their reviews on paeans to the beauties of nature as on whatever the BSO happens to have played.

Once in a while the inducement of music and a week in the country, especially during the Festival of Contemporary Music, is enough to attract one of the institutes given by the Music Critics Association in a series across the United States and Canada for the education of critics. The BSO (which also provides hospitality for occasional conferences of music educators and other professional groups) hosted one of these powwows in connection with the 1978 contemporary festival. The ten participants, each either the chief critic on a small paper or a backup critic on a large daily, worked under a faculty made up of senior critics, editors, and scholars.

Every day for a week the group argued and thumped scores in the living room at Seranak. By night it descended from its aerie to hear the new-music concerts. The next morning, fortified by further listening, the debates at Seranak raged with renewed fury. There was no composition in the festival so roundly denounced that it did not have a defender. There was none so thoroughly esteemed that it did not have an attacker. As for the performers, some had reason for their ears to burn.

Four members of the institute hailed from California, four from the Midwest, and two from the east coast. In the same week Sir Michael Tippett came from England to conduct the BSO in a performance of his oratorio *A Child of Our Time* as a centerpiece of the festival — and therefore of the critics' discussions. The group also met with composers, aired complaints against money-pinching, space-conscious editors, and wrote and compared reviews. From time to time auditors, eavesdroppers, and kibitzers wandered in and out of the Seranak sessions.

A compendium of the faculty's advice shows that if there is little agreement among ordinary critics about music, there is even less among the experts. Michael Steinberg, the BSO's publications director (and formerly in the enemy camp as music critic of the *Boston Globe*), said to beware, in listening to new music, of confusing a bad performance with a bad composition. Seymour Peck, arts editor of the *New York Times,* said he would be suspicious of a review that used the word "ostinato," although he might admit "melisma," not because he knew what it meant but because it sounded so seductive.

Paul Jacobs, the pianist and specialist in twentieth-century music, said musicology is "intellectual welfare," its exponents in the universities "people being paid for not working." (He made an exception for professors who shed new light on performance practices.) David Hamilton, critic of the *Nation,* said that if the visitors could not understand Jean Barraqué's *Le temps restitué,* which received its first American performance as the climactic work in the contemporary festival, neither could he or anyone else, except possibly Gunther Schuller, who conducted it.

Roy Blount, a sportswriter turned humorist, said his first rule of journalism is: whenever you get a chance to go to the bathroom, do it. Paul Fromm spared the critics further advice. Taking them to lunch, he was more interested in hearing their opinions than in telling them his.

Not much in the way of a consensus emerged. Not much could. Critics have disagreed about Tanglewood — except for the glories of the setting, of course — almost from the beginning. And it is usually the experiment in bringing music to the masses that draws the sharpest criticism.

The critics transacted their business out of sight. But another species of visitor appears on the grounds from time to time, invariably sending ripples of excitement through the crowd. One year, for example, movie director Steven Spielberg made a cameo appearance with the BSO at Tanglewood on Parade, banging on percussion noise-makers to help out his Hollywood friend John Williams, who was conducting. Another time actor Paul Newman attended a Shed concert with his wife, actress Joanne Woodward. Even dark glasses were no protection against autograph seekers, who know a star when they see one. Actress Blythe Danner and other cast members from the Williamstown Theatre Festival drive down occasionally for musical interludes. Television personalities Gene Shalit and Hugh Downs, both of whom have summer homes nearby, are Tanglewood regulars. Shalit sometimes takes a bit part by introducing a pops-style number or drawing winners in a benefit raffle. Downs imported a whole ABC crew in 1988 to tape a special on the Shed's golden anniversary.

There is a legendary precedent for these incursions by show-biz folk. In the Music Center's first year, 1940, Koussevitzky escorted Tallulah Bankhead into the Shed to observe a dress rehearsal of the student orchestra. Leonard Bernstein was conducting. The actress, who was playing in summer stock in Stockbridge, was smitten. She demanded that Koussevitzky take her backstage to meet the young man. When Bernstein emerged from the rehearsal in a sweaty T-shirt, she told him she had fallen in love with his back muscles and had to take him to dinner.

What could Bernstein do? He accompanied Bankhead to her boardinghouse room in Stockbridge, got high on bourbon, and

Movie director Steven Spielberg takes a turn as a percussionist for his Hollywood friend, conductor John Williams.

suddenly realized it was less than an hour till he was to conduct. Bankhead's chauffeur rushed him back to his dormitory room, where he showered, shaved, changed into concert dress, and barely got to the podium on time. By all accounts, the performance of Constant Lambert's *Rio Grande,* an orchestral-choral work with two soloists, went splendidly.

Nothing quite so dramatic occurred when actor Robert Redford came up from New York in 1984 on one of his concertgoing jaunts, but he made his presence known in an unorthodox way. He tried to dodge the press by hiding in the press office.

There was a certain logic in Redford's strategy. The habitués of the press office are mostly critics, who tend to know Beethoven's physiognomy better than Redford's. But that was not exactly what the actor had in mind. To assure a peaceful visit, Redford's New York manager had called the press office in advance, asking its help in steering away reporters and photographers. The press office, which also handles the BSO's promotion and public relations, replied that it would do what it could, but it was in the business of helping the press to cover performers, not of protecting visiting celebrities from the press. Nevertheless, it issued Redford press tickets and parking credentials such as critics receive to smooth their access and escape at the gates.

Traveling with a woman friend, Redford arrived from New York to attend the Friday and Saturday concerts. Beethoven, who was on both nights' programs, was apparently the attraction; Redford told press office regulars that he was fond of the master's music. He picked up his tickets and was on his way. But in the busy press office, which is in the row of wooden warrens to the east of the Main Gate and offers beverages and nibbles as hospitality, he found nobody paid much attention to him. Nobody, at any rate, asked for a picture or an interview. He began to make himself at home, mingling with the staff and critics.

The Friday concert seemed to go satisfactorily, and Redford returned Saturday afternoon to stroll the grounds and shop in the Glass House, the gift shop at the Main Gate. On checking in at the press office, which was now largely deserted, he encountered R. C. Hammerich, critic of the *Springfield Union* and *Sunday Republican*, who was cleaning up a few details before he too left till the evening concert. Mistaking Hammerich for a member of the staff, Redford followed him out to his car and asked for his company as a shield against photographers.

Hammerich explained that he was a critic and his duties did not extend to providing escort service. He and Redford had a chat in the parking lot, the actor declaring his love for the Berkshire country. In the end it turned out that autograph seekers, not *paparazzi*, were the problem, just as they had been for Newman. They besieged Redford on the grounds both days. But whenever the crowd became too thick he retreated to be among his new-found friends of the press.

And then there are radio announcers. Chiefly, where classical music in New England is concerned, there is the announcer with the biggest following of them all, Robert J. Lurtsema, whose five-hour show, *Morning Pro Musica*, goes out over fourteen stations of the Eastern Public Radio network every morning of the week from the flagship station in Boston, WGBH-FM. And one weekend each summer, as faithfully as he signs on at seven A.M. every morning with bird twitterings as his theme music, Lurtsema broadcasts from Tanglewood.

Normally the first weekend in July, Tanglewood's opening weekend, provides the occasion for Lurtsema to set up shop on the lawn at Seranak, where he introduces records, reports the news, and interviews Tanglewood luminaries. But as the 1984 date neared, Lurtsema had dropped out of earshot and sight. All during May and June his deep, rolling cadences had been missing from the airwaves. The public was never told why. The network filled in with staff announcers, whose delicate references to the host's absence ("while Robert J. is away . . .") only fanned the flames of speculation. Where, fans asked, is Robert J.?

Then Robert J., as his legion of admirers knows him, made Tanglewood his reentry point. At the customary time on the customary date, from high above foggy, rainy Stockbridge Bowl, birdsong, Beethoven, and banter announced to listeners in seven states and southern Canada that Lurtsema was back. The fifty-two-year-old host, a silver-bearded bachelor with the mien of a swami, said he had been suffering from overwork, complicated by flu that turned into pneumonia. On doctor's orders he had taken the two months off to recuperate. He said it was the first time he had missed a day of work because of sickness (he occasionally tours as a narrator for concerts) during the 12½ years he had been running *Morning Pro Musica.*

Lurtsema broadcasts BSO records but not BSO concerts. The voice of the BSO is William Pierce, another bachelor with a silver beard and golden tongue, who has been announcing the BSO's broadcast concerts from both Tanglewood and Symphony Hall since 1952. Pierce's weekly programs go out over the same stations, and presumably to the same unseen audience, as Lurtsema's daily show. But while Pierce secretes himself in the backstage broadcast booth, Lurtsema takes over the front lawn, veranda, and hallway of Seranak for his visit.

Lurtsema made his 1984 reappearance in characteristic Robert J. fashion. He flew into Boston's Logan Airport the night before from a two-week trip to Scotland, where he and folksinger Jean Redpath — a frequent guest on his show — had led a tour of music festivals. He drove to his home in Wellesley, did the laundry, went through the mail, and watered the plants. After sleeping 3½ hours he climbed behind the wheel for the trip to Lenox.

At seven he was on the air. But the bird songs that introduced the show were not the canned twitterings he uses in the studio. Instead, the WGBH crew had strung microphones in the trees around the terrace and was broadcasting Seranak's robins, thrushes, and sparrows (along with the raindrops) live. The morning's selection of music also had a Tanglewood air. While Lurtsema was live from the lawn, engineers in the Boston studios spun records, including vintage BSO discs, by Tanglewood composers and performers. He had selected the music back in Boston.

Sheltered from the rain by a red-and-white striped tent set up for a benefit tea dance, Lurtsema gave eyewitness weather reports ("Things are beginning to clear up a little at Tanglewood. The fog has lifted and we can see the lake"), read the news, offered a preview of the weekend's concerts, cued in the WGBH production crew on the veranda, interviewed two Tanglewood figures, and sadly reported a bulletin on the death of playwright Lillian Hellman. During the spoken intervals microphones in the living room of the mansion picked up a student composer, Sidney Friedman, as he played background piano music ranging from Beethoven to jazz. From time to time Lurtsema broke out a pair of binoculars to check on the birds or the view.

The morning had its moments of comic relief. At ten A.M. Daniel Gustin, a professional needler as well as the Music Center's administrative chieftain, picked his way through the jungle of cables on the grass to be the first interview subject. As Leslie Warshaw, a WGBH producer, seated him at the table with Lurtsema, she gently suggested, "If you could just talk naturally to Robert . . ."

Laughing, Gustin said, "It's very difficult to talk naturally to Robert." Lurtsema, evidently used to the joshing, took it in good spirit.

For the next interview John Harbison, the summer's composer in residence, showed up in the nick of time from his summer place across the mountain. Lurtsema, occupied with other matters, did not realize that so early in the season Harbison was still having trouble in finding his way around the country roads. Casually he asked if Harbison was living at Seranak with the student composers.

"I don't live at Seranak," the composer demurred as four of his students, who did live at Seranak, hung on his words. "I live some-

Robert J. Lurtsema interviews Kenneth Haas, the BSO's managing director, and Phyllis Curtin on the terrace at Seranak.

where up in the mountains, which I can barely find, much less describe.''

Other visits and other interviews — with Phyllis Curtin, Kenneth Haas, Maurice Abravanel, and Charles Dutoit among many — followed in later years. Lurtsema was back, his cadences seemingly more rolling than ever. His fans cheered. The birds twittered.

*   *   *

Birds: strictly speaking, of course, the wildlife does not visit at all but inhabits the place. But when people come to hear music, birds, skunks, and mosquitoes can become visitors, mostly unwelcome.

Tanglewood takes a laissez faire attitude toward mosquitoes. The clouds of bug spray that rise like incense from personal dispensers on concert nights testify that where insects are concerned, it is every man for himself. Skunks, too, have the run of the place. Every now and then a skunk will scurry across the lawn or through a section of Shed en route to wherever skunks scurry — possibly one of the Dumpsters on the grounds. But, by and large, peaceful coexistence between man and beast prevails. It even prevailed on the night in 1977 when a skunk got mixed up in a concert in the Festival of Contemporary Music.

Gilbert Kalish was playing the second of five works on the program, Roger Sessions's *Pieces for Piano,* when the visitor ambled out of the woods and into the Theater–Concert Hall. He was a young skunk, with a wide, bushy stripe down his back. Like any polite latecomer, he went quietly down the aisle to his place, a chair about a third of the way back in the center section, where he began nosing around on the floor for crumbs.

The chair, of course, had someone sitting in it. And only a few chairs away sat Paul Fromm, the festival's patron. Still, most of the 750 concertgoers were unaware that they had company, and only those along the aisle began thinking about an early exit. Both the Sessions work and Yehudi Wyner's *Serenade for Seven Instruments,* the next piece, went off without disruption.

People will talk, though, and during intermission, which followed Wyner's piece, the word spread. When the gong sounded for the program to resume, listeners who had been sitting in the outer sections went peaceably back to their places, but a large block of seats in the center remained empty. Their former occupants milled about in the aisle, pointing and talking. Repeated dimmings of the house lights failed to impose decorum. Finally house manager James Whitaker went onto the stage and asked everybody to sit down.

"These things happen every summer," he pleaded, "and if we'll all be patient, everything will take care of itself."

Nature followed its course, all right — human nature. Nobody sat down.

Now head guide David Alpert was dispatched from the stage with a corrugated box to try his luck. Alpert gulped, grinned, and put on a brave face, but at the last moment he was saved from his trapper's duty. A woman near the skunk stood up and addressed the crowd.

"That skunk was under my seat the whole first half of the concert, and he minded his business," she said. "I say let's be quiet and get on with the show."

She sat down and, with hardly a murmur, so did the crowd. The concert ended with the skunk forgotten.

Birds present a different problem. Not the birds in the trees, of course: Lurtsema is not the only visitor to discover the pleasures of their music. But for years the birds that nested among the Shed's rafters and girders, just under the roof, were the bane of musicians and audiences. Their music — if the rasps and squawks of hungry baby sparrows, starlings, and grackles can be described as music — set up a cacophonous counterpoint to the harmonies coming from the stage.

Perhaps the most famous bird incident, comparable to the skunk's visit in Tanglewood's animal lore, occurred during a 1979 Weekend Prelude in which Gennady Rozhdestvensky and Viktoria Postnikova were playing a program of Russian piano music for four hands. A young sparrow, apparently just learning to fly, swooped down a minute or two before the end of Mussorgsky's Sonata in C and landed inside the piano. The husband-and-wife pianists, unaware of the problem, played on. The audience held its breath, waiting to see how the drama — or the music — would end.

It ended with the sonata finished and the chick still inside the piano. When the duo went offstage before the next number, they learned they had become a trio. It was time to have the piano debirded. Out went the BSO's stage manager, Alfred ("Al") F. Robison, a giant who wrestles pianos and risers around as if they were papier mâché. He took one look under the lid and saw the bird roosting on the frame.

In reached Robison and out came the bird, cupped in his hands. The giant carried his prey out to the woods behind the Shed, where he deposited it on a branch and watched until he was sure it could fly away.

Robison did not make much of his adventure into the animal kingdom. "He was just sitting there on the back of the piano," he said of his catch. "He was scared, or enjoying the music, or something."

Robison is just a foot soldier compared to Tanglewood's field marshal in the battle against the birds, James F. Kiley. A member of the groundskeeping staff since 1949, Kiley since 1958 has been Tanglewood's facilities manager, otherwise known as superintendent, otherwise known as "Jim." He is the man who, through a

Stage manager Alfred Robison meets the sparrow chick he rescued from the piano.

careful balance of lime, fertilizer, aeration, and mowing, sees to it that the lawn remains a magic carpet of green even through the heaviest summer traffic. Weeds, however, are easier to tame than birds. Over the years Kiley tried just about everything to get the birds out of the Shed and into the trees — wire mesh, chemical stickum, ultrasound. Nothing worked.

Summer after summer the baby birds disrupted the concerts with their gabble every time mama bird flew in with a delicious worm in her beak. In the seats below heads twisted and craned. Some concertgoers smiled, thinking the sounds a quaint addition to music in the country; others grumbled about a nuisance. BSO players became battle-hardened, but visiting artists sometimes complained. The distraction often went out over the air as an audible accompaniment to the BSO's Brahms and Beethoven.

Then in 1986 Kiley tried inflatable plastic snakes and owls, the kind you buy for the garden in the hardware store. For the first time in forty-nine years, the only music heard in the Shed was the BSO's.

Kiley had hit upon the idea the summer before, when he bought fifty great horned owls — imitations, of course — for $4 apiece and hung them on strings along the colonnade at the open end of the Shed. The experiment met with only limited success: the nesting families returned after an early scare. During the winter a salesman in Tennessee called and suggested adding plastic snakes to the zoo. Kiley invested in twenty-five snakes, along with about thirty more owls. The total cost was under $500.

The strategy was to keep the birds from getting a toehold inside. During the first week in May, as soon as the wooden panels were removed from the sides of the Shed to let it dry out from winter, Kiley and his crew spread the eighty owls and twenty-five snakes around in the rafters. The owls hung on strings, which let the crew slide, raise, and lower them day by day to make them move about as real predators would. The snakes, spotted brown and puffed up to their full three feet in length, looked frighteningly realistic as they coiled in and along the rafters.

The first test came during the school graduations held in the Shed in June. Not a bird was seen or heard. Kiley did not even have to send a worker around to wash the usual doo off the seats.

By the time concertgoers arrived, the first nesting season had passed and the Shed was still bird-free. Kiley removed most of the predators, leaving only a few snakes as a deterrent up close to the stage. But they remained on top of the ledges, rafters, and acoustical clouds, well out of sight; Kiley was taking no chances that music lovers would suffer a shock worse than bird squawks on walking into the Shed. The July nesting season also passed with the birds choosing more desirable real estate outside. Tanglewood regulars were struck by the silence overhead. Kiley said orchestra members commented that they were "amazed" by the change.

Nobody was declaring the war won. Daniel Gustin, who was the BSO's acting general manager that year, hailed Kiley's success but warned that "we're not claiming final victory." Kiley himself cautioned that owls and snakes worked this time: "But you never know. Next year the birds may be used to them and we may have to try something else."

Thomas D. Perry, Jr., also took a philosophical view of the situation during his years as the BSO's executive director. "Mankind," he once said, "cannot outwit the bird."

*   *   *

When visitors come, they come by car or tour bus. There is no other way, unless you park in the center of Lenox and walk the mile and a half down to the gates (and the mile and a half back up after the concert).

The first representatives whom these arriving concertgoers meet would probably rather listen to rock than to symphonies or chamber music. They work for a minimal wage, live in nearby towns, and stay at their stations through heat, cold, and rain. They are the parking attendants.

"You have to have the right type of disposition to take the flak those kids take out there," James Kiley said of the crew of forty and some of the drivers they encounter. "Some of these people are really obnoxious."

"You're out here all day in the heat of the sun," said parking chief Neil Merwin, mopping his brow under his visored cap. "You've got everybody and their brother giving you all kinds of excuses why they should get up to the Shed. You try to hold your temper. All in all, the patrons are courteous and friendly. We're here to try to make it enjoyable for the patrons."

Parking is a second job for Merwin and most of his crew. He is a full-time high school maintenance man, an emergency medical technician, and a volunteer ambulance driver. The attendants under him range in age from sixteen to their early thirties, with eighteen the average. Some are students whom Merwin brings over from school. Some work days as camp counselors or lawn or garden helpers. The older attendants hold year-round jobs in the area.

Kiley, who with Merwin is responsible for hiring the corps, gives each year's group a set of rules and an orientation at which he stresses that they "work for the world's greatest orchestra and the first impression is a lasting impression." That first impression in the lots, he makes it clear, had better be favorable. For their labors the attendants get a starting wage of $5 an hour, a supply of white shirts, flashlights, reflecting orange vests, raincoats, meals when they work all day, and Cokes at night.

They also get — very important, Kiley said — nametags so patrons can report any "who lose their temper or get sassy." He personally takes complaints. In a typical season he recently had to fire three parkers. That is not a bad record, Kiley said, for a year in which he had to take on seventeen new attendants.

The parking crew takes over after police officers and deputy sheriffs, supplied by the Town of Lenox and Berkshire County (but partly paid for by the BSO), have directed traffic to the festival over state and local roads. On a busy day as many as six thousand cars will funnel into the lots. By city standards that is a trickle, but on two-lane country roads the trickle can grow to a crush comparable to rush-hour lines at the Holland or Lincoln Tunnel.

One of the worst traffic jams in Tanglewood history occurred in 1986, when violinist Isaac Stern and six friends — violinist Cho-Liang Lin, violists Michael Tree and Jaime Laredo, cellists Yo-Yo Ma and Matt Haimovitz (then a sixteen-year-old prodigy), and pianist Emanuel Ax — played a pair of weekend chamber concerts. The popular Stern alone can fill Tanglewood for a concert. With seven all-stars on the bill, the opening program caused the nearest thing to a riot that Tanglewood had experienced since the rock concert era of the 1960s and 1970s.

The only times the two programs could be shoehorned into the concert schedule were Saturday afternoon and Sunday night. Sunday night was no problem; except for an occasional student concert the grounds then are dark. But for the Saturday program a crowd of five thousand — a record for the Theater–Concert Hall — descended on the grounds just as the BSO's open rehearsal in the Shed was letting out.

Tanglewood had anticipated a crunch when the two audiences collided. The strategy was to hold the crowd for the Stern concert outside the gates until the rehearsal audience left. What Tanglewood did not anticipate was just how big the Stern audience would be and how unruly it would get on the hot, sticky afternoon when it found entry to the grounds barred.

Near-chaos erupted on the roads, in the lots, and at the gates. The police and parking details were overwhelmed as masses of cars came at them from both directions. Tempers popped as ticket takers and security guards sealed the gates. Meanwhile some of the rehearsal audience simply strolled across the lawn and, without paying a second time, helped themselves to lawn space for the Stern concert. That did nothing to help the mood of the paying crowd watching at the gate.

Part of the lawn plan was to post a limit of three thousand tickets and mount two extra loudspeaker systems to carry the sound to the grounds. Given the temper of the crowd, the limit proved unenforceable. When the gates finally swung open and the throng streamed in, a sea of humanity stretched across the lawn on beach towels and chairs all the way back to the Main Gate. The scene suggested one of the BSO's bigger Shed concerts, or the Fourth of July at Atlantic City.

Inside the hall conditions were only somewhat better. Seats for both concerts had been sold out from the day in April when tickets were put on sale. Because of the crush outside, some lawn sitters tried to crash the hall and stand along the walls, take over empty seats, or just catch a glimpse of the starry assemblage onstage. When ticket holders arrived and ushers tried to evict poachers, the confusion delayed the concert, at one point forcing Stern to plead for silence. Sadder but wiser after such experiences, Kiley and Merwin began a crackdown on parking abuses.

At and inside the gates the concertgoer meets the next lines of receptionists: the ticket takers, the women who hand out program books, and the men and women who serve as ushers. The ticket takers, a group of about eighteen men, older than the parkers and mostly Tanglewood veterans, also work part-time for the pay. The program handlers and ushers — 90 to 130 of them at a concert, depending on the popularity of the attraction — are in a sense visitors themselves. Each is a volunteer, drawn from a pool of about 350 summer and year-round Berkshire residents who sign up during the spring. Like the ticket takers, most return year after year. Among this group Harry Stedman, head usher from 1955 until his death in 1984, became not only a host to a generation of concertgoers but, in time, a musical godfather to a generation of Tanglewood students.

"Stubby" Stedman was a singer in college and later in Berkshire church choirs, one of which sang at Tanglewood under Koussevitzky in the late 1930s. He worked for a time as a schoolteacher and vice principal but, for twenty-eight years until his retirement in 1968, was the personnel manager at the Crane & Company paper mills in Dalton, about fifteen miles north of Tanglewood. His Tanglewood career began in 1946, after a friend took him to a BSO concert. The friend introduced him to Willard M. Sistare, then the head usher, who signed him up for ushering duty. When Sistare moved away in 1955, Stedman succeeded him. For twenty-nine years Stedman manned the head usher's station in a busy back corner of the Shed, deploying his volunteers, answering questions, and, when necessary, handling complaints. The system remains the same under his successor, Bruce Callahan, an industrial hygienist for an ecological consulting firm.

Stedman liked to talk about Tanglewood, and one of the stories he most liked to tell was the one about the skunk at the contemporary concert. The moral of the tale, he said, was that the intruder "was a young skunk that didn't know how to use his weapon." Another favorite story concerned an usher in the 1960s who reported for duty in a Little Lord Fauntleroy costume. Stedman never did figure out why the young man did it. But the incident, he said, showed why he insisted that volunteers come properly dressed. Good dress, he would say, means good manners, among both ushers and audiences. For male volunteers that means ties and jackets. Women must wear dresses, preferably long.

The ushers and program handlers are only one arm of a large volunteer organization that serves Tanglewood. Among its many activities the Association of Volunteers also canvasses Berkshire residents and businesses for contributions, runs benefit dinners and dances, hosts student events, and stocks and staffs the Glass House, the gift shop at the Main Gate. (Yet another volunteer group, numbering about thirty, is made up of trained first aid workers who take turns manning the Red Cross station near the East Gate.) Besides visiting regularly as both helpmates and concertgoers, volunteers regularly bring new visitors to Tanglewood. An open house every June at Seranak provides an opportunity for newcomers to look around, get acquainted, and — if all goes according to plan — return as concertgoers. A series of talks and walks in the large, candy-striped tent near the Shed presents Tanglewood figures and visiting artists in informal discussions of their work, followed by tours of the grounds for newcomers. Business supporters enjoy a dinner in the tent and a student concert in appreciation for their gifts.

Unlike the moonlighting parking attendants and ticket takers, the volunteers, who include about thirty-five husband-wife teams, are true-blue classical music lovers. The only recompense for their service is free admission to the concerts they work, with two extra lawn passes for family or friends. The usher group ranges in age from the

late teens to the late eighties and runs the gamut of jobs and profes-
sions. Bankers, real estate agents, accountants, dentists, teachers —
both retired and active — and engineers of all sorts from the Pittsfield General Electric plants fill the ranks.

Stedman never stopped to figure how many concerts he had attended. For one thing, he was too busy. From 1973 on he also
worked five afternoons a week as the tour guide at the Crane &
Company papermaking museum, a Berkshire tourist attraction. He
also served as a volunteer in a variety of civic organizations, ranging
from the Salvation Army to the Bicentennial Commission in Dalton,
his hometown. At Tanglewood he also had a job that made him the
envy of children attending concerts: he was the man who, at the
beginning and intermission of each Shed concert, pulled the rope
that rises into a belfry and clanged the old railroad bell that sum-
mons listeners to their seats.

Two years before Stedman's death Tanglewood clanged a bell for
him. The ushers and program handlers got together and passed the
hat to support an annual fellowship at the Music Center, naming
it for their leader and dedicating it to a vocal student because of
Stedman's interest in singing. When Stedman died in 1984, the
fellowship became a memorial to him. Each year the volunteers
raise about $5,000 for the project by taking up a collection and
bringing past Stedman fellows back to the Berkshires during the
winter for benefit concerts. One Stedman fellow, soprano Elizabeth
Gintz, made such a hit that Berkshire musical groups began inviting
her back as a performer in their winter concert series. She became
a visitor from Tanglewood to the community.

*   *   *

In 1977, during his first term as governor, Michael S. Dukakis
proposed a medium-security prison at Shadowbrook, the former
Carnegie estate across the road and up the hill from Tanglewood.

Shadowbrook had stood vacant for seven years, ever since the
Jesuits, who acquired it from the Carnegies, closed it as a novitiate.
In all that time hardly anyone had given it two glances out of a car
window. But suddenly the air was purple with outrage. At a public
hearing on the proposal the Reverend Robert S. S. ("Steamboat")
Whitman, rector of Trinity Episcopal Church in Lenox, warned that
criminals would probably find the location so desirable they would

give their address as "the Prison Hilton of Massachusetts." Among the five hundred other protesters in the audience that night was Thomas D. Perry, Jr., the BSO's executive director. When his turn came to speak, he said BSO feeling against "the installation of a prison hovering over Tanglewood" was as strong as "anything since I've been associated with the orchestra."

The hometown opposition was predictable. What New England shire town, with or without a major music festival, wants a prison in its front yard? What was less to be expected was the hand wringing in other parts of the country. Letters poured in from all sides urging the governor and legislature to spare the writers' beloved Tanglewood. The mail became so thick at one point that Representative John J. Finnegan, chairman of the House Ways and Means Committee, complained that most of the opposition seemed to be coming from out of town — a statement he later retracted when townspeople deluged him with protests.

In a typical letter a Long Island couple, Earl and Janet Kramer, wrote to the *New York Times*:

> Tanglewood is a rare and wonderful oasis where one can go to refresh and restore one's soul and spirit. Indeed, the finest, noblest, and most artistic efforts of man and nature come together here at the magnificent music festival and its surrounding lakes, towns, and mountains. There is no question that a prison in the heart of this oasis will cast a pall over, and eventually destroy, the tranquility and peace that permeate the area. . . .

The Dukakis plan was rejected by the legislature, which regarded it as too grandiose, and in time the Kripalu Center for Yoga and Health settled at Shadowbrook, providing relief from aching muscles for visitors and musicians alike. But the opposition told a great deal about why people go to Tanglewood. "The finest, noblest, and most artistic efforts of man and nature": that, in a snapshot, is what the crowds see and hear. Why else would anyone battle lines of traffic and sit amid Atlantic City crowds to hear music he could more easily and clearly hear on an FM radio on his own balcony or lawn?

The Tanglewood audience is unlike any other. It is also the same as audiences in New York, Boston, or anywhere else in the country where symphonic music is heard.

There was, for instance, the night of a recital by cellist Jules Eskin and pianist Gilbert Kalish at the height of a heat wave. A half-hour after the program had begun, a group of about fifty listeners walked out of the Theater–Concert Hall en masse. Ushers, noticing the exodus, stopped the group outside and asked if anything was wrong.

Indeed, there was. The listeners were from Georgia, on a bus tour of New England, and could not take the Yankee heat. They were retreating to the Southern comfort of their air-conditioned bus and hotel rooms.

On another occasion a bso ensemble was playing Brahms's Clarinet Quintet at a Prelude recital in the Shed. During the pause after the first movement, a man from the second row of the audience walked up to the stage and addressed the string players. Mark Ludwig, the violist in the group, was so shocked he could remember the exact words: "Say, fellows, this is a clarinet quintet. Would you mind moving aside? We can't see the clarinetist."

Tanglewood, in other words, while it attracts its share of everyday concertgoers in search of the classics played by a famous orchestra, also attracts a large — perhaps even larger — number of browsers to whom music is only one ingredient in a salad of sightseeing, socializing, country dining, straw-hat theater, antiquing, boutiquing, and cable TV when they get back to the motel or inn. They and the fans who come out in hordes to hear a name soloist like Perlman or a name conductor like Bernstein probably make up, in fact, well over half of a typical Tanglewood audience, swelling the crowd to 10,000, 15,000, or more. Concert etiquette and traditions suffer. Sometimes they go right out the door, like those music-loving Georgians.

The bso has not done a formal profile of the Tanglewood audience. But a rough license-plate count in the parking lots in the mid-1980s found about 45 percent of the cars came from the New York metropolitan area — New York, New Jersey, and Connecticut. Conversations on the grounds tend to confirm the breakdown. (Bostonians, who can hear the bso during the winter, are more likely to spend their weekends on Cape Cod or in New Hampshire or Maine.) All together, more than 300,000 concertgoers pass through the gates in a season. The remaining 55 percent is a diverse mix from Boston and the Berkshires, the forty-six other states, and abroad (including increasing numbers of Asians). Tanglewood is a vast musical democracy catering to all kinds of tastes and all kinds of music lovers except unreconstructed pop, country, and rock fans.

The Tanglewood of the lawn sitter, with his beach chair beneath him and his picnic basket before him, is not the Tanglewood of the Shed dweller, up close to the music — close enough, at any rate, to hear it without amplification and have a sense of being in a concert hall. The Tanglewood of seasonal residents, whether affluent second-home owners, humbler owners or renters of cottages, or retired couples, is not the Tanglewood of townspeople, many of whom go to the concerts but most of whom look upon the doings on West Street as a combination of Mount Olympus and a traveling freak show. ("Snowbirds" the year-rounders call the flock that flees to Florida or Arizona at the first breath of frost.) Tourists, who stay in motels, bed-and-breakfasts, and inns, constitute another group. A tourist subspecies consists of travelers in tour-bus groups, usually senior citizens, who sit in a block and then ride off to the next New England attraction. (On a busy Sunday afternoon their chartered buses may take up half the West Lot.) And, of course, Tanglewood in the Shed or on the lawn is not backstage Tanglewood, where busy musicians fit in concerts and rehearsals between chamber music, teaching, golf or tennis, and responsibilities at home.

Families and social gatherings — office parties, class reunions, or friends on a picnic — make up a large part of the lawn audience. The Shed audience tends to be older and to take its music more seriously. But even within the Shed there are gradations. Hard-core music lovers continue to come in sizable numbers, although traffic and ticket prices, ranging up to $50 a seat, discourage many who can get their fill of symphonic music during the winter. Of enthusiasts and fans, attracted by personalities like Perlman, Ma, Bernstein, Leontyne Price, and Marilyn Horne, there are armies. A listener can tell their presence by the girder-bending ovations that greet their idols' first footsteps onstage.

A certain amount of social preening and stratification, inevitable in any concert hall or opera house, also takes place under the Shed's spacious roof. The Tanglewood of the Tent Club member, who pays $200 a year for the privilege of picnicking in the striped tent next to the Shed, is not the Tanglewood of the Seranak Supper Club member, who pays $650 a year to dine from a *prix-fixe* menu in the faded elegance of Koussevitzky's former mansion. Then there is the

Tanglewood of the *crème de la crème* — their names appear among the benefactors in the program book — who give elegant dinners in their country homes before battling traffic to get to the concert in time for the overture.

Somewhere, too, tuning their ears in the Shed's better seats, is a scattering of music professionals — managers, press agents, record company executives, critics, even a visiting performer or two (Isaac Stern, for one, will occasionally show up without his fiddle). All, in one way or another, are scouting the talent. Once in a while George Shultz, who has a country home in the hills over toward Northampton, would put aside his secretary of state's worries to sit inconspicuously in the boxes. It is easier to spot Senator Edward M. Kennedy, Dukakis, and other politicians, who play to the crowds much as some conductors will. They follow in a tradition that includes Eleanor Roosevelt, who used to drive over regularly from her summer home in Hyde Park, New York (and who once narrated Prokofiev's *Peter and the Wolf* under Koussevitzky).

In the end the Tanglewood visitor with the greatest clout is the concertgoer. Composers may write new works, critics may praise or damn what they hear, celebrities may attract or dodge crowds, volunteers may raise funds, but it is the concertgoer who buys the ticket and fills the hall. His response, as Costa Pilavachi said, determines what an orchestra can do — what works it can play, how long the season will be, how much tickets will cost, which guest artists will be booked. The response also determines in what kind of environment music will survive.

Audience behavior (or misbehavior) has changed as audiences have changed. The miscreants today are easy to spot; more than that, they are impossible to escape. They talk during performances. They pop flashbulbs. They flip through the ads in the program book, jangle bracelets, snap gum, rattle candy wrappers. They arrive late for concerts and leave early. They cough. They fuss. They fidget.

It is tempting to think these troubles began in the late 1940s, when Thomas D. Perry, Jr. — the same Thomas Perry who saw a threat in a Shadowbrook prison — saw a threat in the bared thigh and failed in his campaign to have women in shorts cover up. The gates, in effect, swung open to all sorts of sightseers and strangers. (Harry Stedman, after all, said good dress makes good manners.) But the lesson is probably the other way around. Sightseers and strangers were there all along; it was only the bared thighs that were recent. And when the culture explosion of the 1950s swept the United States and the "me" generation of the 1960s and 1970s followed, Tanglewood could no longer hold out against the tide.

It is true that at Tanglewood, where the wine flows freely and children frolic on the lawn, distractions are more numerous than they would be in Symphony Hall or Carnegie Hall. By the same token the Tanglewood audience is more enthusiastic than the Symphony Hall or Carnegie Hall audience. It claps between movements (sometimes *within* movements) and breaks into a standing ovation for nearly any soloist who can finish his part on time. Part of the response stems from the informality of the setting and a sense of relaxation difficult or impossible to feel in a concert hall. Yet the Kramers spoke for the times: Tanglewood offers the best of art and nature. The same casual behavior that reflects a culture craze or gratification of the self reflects a genuine hunger and appreciation for the nourishment of great music.

None of this, of course, makes the distractions easier for the discriminating listener to bear. But democracy always was a messy form of government. A democracy of tastes only adds to the litter. If a symphony orchestra presents summer concerts in the country for 10,000 to 15,000 people, only a minority of those listeners is going to be steeped in musical traditions or concertgoing etiquette. In fact, as the size of the audience goes up, as it has over the years, the level of sophistication is almost certain to go down. For better and worse, the day has passed when a Haydn could compose and give concerts for a family of aristocratic patrons in the quiet of its palace. When music moved out onto the lawn, it invited all kinds of nuisances in. The smallest was the mosquito.

Chapter VII

F I N A L E

O N J U L Y 1, 1988, fifty years after Koussevitzky dedicated the Music Shed, Tanglewood rededicated it in his honor. The ceremony was part of a concert re-creating the exact program with which Koussevitzky had inaugurated the Shed on August 4, 1938, the opening night of Tanglewood's second season.

This time the program inaugurated the 1988 season, the second of four in Tanglewood's fiftieth anniversary celebration. In the audience on the dank, chilly evening were twenty-five guests of honor who either had taken part in the inaugural evening fifty years before or were descended from participants. Eight retired BSO members who had played for Koussevitzky in the concert came back; so did the two surviving members of Gertrude Robinson Smith's original festival board and three of the original ushers

Speaking on the flower-decked stage, with the orchestra sitting behind him and Seiji Ozawa standing next to him, BSO president George H. Kidder told the audience of 6,500:

> This Shed was dedicated in 1938 without a commemorative name. For fifty years it has been known only as "the Music Shed." But for fifty years there has been building here the reality that was Dr. Koussevitzky's dream — a music festival of international renown and a summer music school of unsurpassed quality. It is time now, and some would say long past the time, to recognize Dr. Koussevitzky's contribution.

Kidder then announced that the BSO trustees had voted to rename the building the Serge Koussevitzky Music Shed and to place a commemorative plaque in its northwestern corner, where other plaques already honored Gertrude Robinson Smith and Joseph Franz, the engineer who saw the plans to completion. Ozawa followed Kidder to the microphone and, improvising his remarks, also paid tribute to Koussevitzky and the founders. Dreams don't always come true, Ozawa said, but Koussevitzky's did.

There was precedent for Ozawa's ad lib performance. From the NBC radio broadcast of the 1938 program Kidder played excerpts from scratchy, off-the-air tapes of the dedicatory talks by Koussevitzky and Robinson Smith. Also improvising a brief talk, Koussevitzky told why he had chosen Beethoven's Ninth Symphony as the principal work for the program. It was a typical Koussevitzky effusion, heavily accented and anticipating the war that was threatening Europe.

> Ladies and gentlemen! On this significant day in the musical life I have selected to give the Ninth Symphony not only because it is the greatest masterpiece in the musical literature, but also to hear the voices of Tanglewood repeating Schiller's great words calling all nations to brotherhood.

The Robinson Smith talk evoked the 1937 thunderstorm that had drenched the tent audience at a Wagner program and sent her onto the stage in an appeal for donations to build a concert pavilion. In British upper-class tones she declared:

> Most of you know what happened one night last summer, when the elements and Wagner got into conflict. This seemingly tragic event proved a blessing in disguise, for immediately afterward the Board of Trustees [of the Berkshire Symphonic Festival] decided to start a campaign for money to raise this Music Shed. Many of you responded most generously. A month ago, thanks to Mr. Joseph Franz, the engineer, the Shed was ready for the 1938 festival.

Fifty years later it had rained almost until concert time, the temperature stood at fifty degrees, and concertgoers, soloists, and BSO players shivered through the evening in sweaters, ponchos, or furs. (Under the wraps some listeners, who had come from a black-tie fund-raising dinner — Tanglewood's first — in the newly acquired Highwood mansion next door, were in evening dress.) As in 1938, the program began with the opening chorus from Bach's Cantata no. 80, *A Mighty Fortress Is Our God.* Then came the rededication ceremony, falling in the program where the original dedication had. Again it was followed by the singing of the Lutheran chorale that ends the Bach cantata, with the audience joining in as the 1938 audience had. After intermission Ozawa led the BSO, Tanglewood Festival Chorus, and four soloists in the commemorative Beethoven Ninth. As so often happens, the fickle Berkshire weather intervened. Chilled fingers and instruments could not do the music justice, no matter how hard Ozawa exhorted his musicians onward.

Earlier in the day the BSO had hosted a luncheon at Seranak for the guests from the Shed's inaugural night. Among the crowd assembled in Koussevitzky's living room were the two members of the original festival board, Emilia Franz of Stockbridge (Joseph Franz's widow), and Alice Edman of Pittsfield. Also from Pittsfield came the three original ushers, Janet Bitensky and Benjamin Bowers, both of whom were still on active ushering duty, and Harry Brundige, who had become head of the ticket takers. The BSO veterans from the opening were there. David B. Stow of Huntsville, Texas, Gertrude Robinson Smith's nephew, stood in on her behalf.

Amid a babble of reacquaintances and reminiscences in the room the two board members recounted key moments from the founding years. Mrs. Franz described Koussevitzky's reaction on first hearing music played in his Shed. At the first BSO rehearsal, she said, he turned over his baton to concertmaster Richard Burgin and walked around the outer perimeter of the building with Joseph Franz to sample the sound.

"As he walked he said, 'It's marvelous, it's marvelous. Do you think the atmosphere has anything to do with it?' My husband said, 'It might have something to do with it.' "

Mrs. Edman, who served as executive vice president of the festival organization and ran its business from an office above the drugstore in Stockbridge, recalled that it was her husband, George, who in 1935 had placed the call that brought Koussevitzky to the Berkshires. It happened after a meeting at which the festival board, amid dissatisfaction with the first two seasons' concerts under Henry Hadley, decided to replace him and his New York players. It fell to George Edman, as the board clerk, to extend the invitation to Koussevitzky and the BSO as the successors. Over opposition from Robinson Smith, who favored other orchestras, he called Boston and spoke to BSO manager George Judd. Koussevitzky was vacationing in the Soviet Union, but Judd promised to mention the idea when he returned. When Judd called back, he said Koussevitzky "was much interested," Alice Edman recalled. The next year the BSO played its first season in the Berkshires.

Over lunch in the Seranak dining room Thomas D. Perry, Jr., speaking as the emeritus manager, welcomed the fifty-year guests back. He called the gathering "one of the most exclusive clubs in the world — we happy few who have been connected with this organization from the beginning, particularly the Shed." For any who, after a half-century, still doubted Tanglewood's future, Perry concluded: "We are going to keep it up as long as we can!"

The festivities brought another round of reminiscences at a volunteer-sponsored talk in the tent by Roger Voisin, the BSO's retired principal trumpeter and one of the eight returning veterans. He too recalled the initial rehearsal in the Shed. BSO members "were enamored" of the Berkshires from the start, he said, but at the first rehearsal "we were all rather apprehensive" about how the music would sound. From the first moment, however, it became clear that the pavilion had been designed "extremely well" for acoustics. But there was a hitch. Koussevitzky, who feared drafts, complained of unwanted air currents that reached him on the podium.

"They haven't fixed that to this day," Voisin said. It is one of many things that have not changed, even as change has blossomed all around.

*   *   *   *   *

In their letter to the *Times* the Kramers spoke of Tanglewood as an oasis. The image is perhaps truer than they intended. Just as an oasis can be destroyed or poisoned by outside forces, the same pressures that threaten the Berkshires threaten Tanglewood.

Since World War II the Berkshires' manufacturing economy, based primarily on the electrical and paper industries, has slipped as jobs have gone to lower-priced places, especially the South and Japan. Money from tourism and second-home development has rushed in to fill the vacuum. The view from Tanglewood remains pristine, but just over the horizon the condominiums are rising as rapidly as they can be built and bought. Preceding and following them, commercial development has brought burger heavens, outlet stores, bed-and-breakfasts, glossy conference centers, and all the other paraphernalia of America on the go. Perhaps it is only a coincidence, but it was not until 1988, amid this boom, that the Berkshires got their first enclosed shopping mall. A second one was proposed almost simultaneously, not fifteen miles to the north of

The lawn scene at Tanglewood on Parade.

Tanglewood like the first, but in Lenox, on the main highway three miles from the Main Gate.

Tanglewood and the Berkshires' other summer cultural attractions — the Jacob's Pillow Dance Festival, the Williamstown and Berkshire theater festivals, the Lenox Arts Center, Shakespeare & Company, and the assortment of smaller concert series — have benefited from the new audience, of course. Indeed, it was this cultural platter, along with the wooded vistas, clean air, and relatively crime-free surroundings, that attracted the newcomers in the first place, just as they did Seiji Ozawa a decade earlier. But the pressures on both the natural and the artistic environment have been intense. Unlike year-rounders, who must somehow earn a living in an increasingly tourist-dependent economy, weekenders and summer residents seek leisure, entertainment, and boutique-style shopping. With a large minority — perhaps even a majority — of the influx coming from the New York metropolitan area, the newcomers sometimes demand these things in a hurry and as their due. It is a situation made for friction with Yankee town fathers and others who thought they had discovered the Berkshires first.

Townspeople may play their games of soak-the-tourist, and town-gown spats between Tanglewood and the Lenox and Stockbridge selectmen erupt periodically about sewers, zoning, traffic, and police assistance. But the Berkshires have come to depend on Tanglewood and the culture industry that has grown up around it. A mid-1980s study used by the BSO found that Tanglewood generates $25 million in tourist-related business each year, apart from whatever the BSO might spend. No wonder demands still break out among innkeepers and merchants for a longer Tanglewood season — at least until Labor Day.

The BSO can resist those pressures, if only because budgets, logistics, and union contracts will not permit more concerts. The more insidious pressures are those for more pops, more superstars, more galas, more television, hoopla, and hype, at ever-escalating prices. (Already Tanglewood has a two-tier ticket pricing system, in which the more popular attractions — the Boston Pops, Bernstein, Perlman, Ma, and the like — command higher prices than other performers no less worthy. Meanwhile ticket prices, at all levels, doubled in the ten years from 1978 to 1988.) As Tanglewood's popularity suggests, the culture boom of the 1980s suffers from simultaneous obesity and anemia; the audience for art is swollen, the understanding of it often no more than skin-deep. Many of the newcomers, of course, bring serious listening habits and long concert experience with them. Others, who came to the Berkshires to get away from crowds, avoid Tanglewood altogether. All, whatever their tastes, have helped to give the region a cachet as a place to vacation and have sun, fun, and culture all in one gulp. It is an image carefully cultivated in the tourist industry's advertising. More and more listeners come expecting to see the clarinetist, whether they can hear him properly or not.

Amid spiraling costs the pressures to capture both kinds of audiences — the casual and the educated, the lawn and the Shed — build. Meanwhile the pressures on the land by those who come for open space leave less and less open space for others. Each new Berkshire resident, each visitor, contributes a mite to killing the thing he loves.

Critics sometimes call Tanglewood a music factory and tourist trap. Indeed, a leading critic like Andrew Porter of the *New Yorker* will come to Tanglewood only when new music is being played or a distinguished artist is venturing into new ground, as Jon Vickers, primarily an opera singer, did in 1980 when he tried out Schubert's song cycle *Die Winterreise* in a recital.

The charge of pandering and commercialism is hard to deny, at least on the BSO side of the lawn. Yet the danger was present from the beginning. Koussevitzky himself recognized it, warning in his 1947 address at the Music Center's opening exercises:

> In music, we have reached a dangerous impasse. From the beginning of the twentieth century, music, once the privilege of the "initiated," became accessible to wide layers of society, bringing about a "mass initiation" of the listener into the sphere of musical art. This spreading of music in the masses, at too rapid a pace, resulted in a profound misconception of music as a means of "entertainment" and "enjoyment" to be passively consumed by the listener. Music must be listened to creatively. Only active love can lead to the understanding of art and of its lasting value.

In 1941, even before Koussevitzky's warning, Robert Lawrence of the *New York Herald Tribune* was complaining about the quantity of chestnuts — even when "beautifully roasted" — on the Tanglewood programs. Critics who repeat the charge today, escalating it into an attack on commercial programming and slick promotion, are working in a long tradition.

But Tanglewood, for all its rich heritage and international aspirations, merely reflects the world outside its gates. The demand for chestnuts is even stronger today than it was when Gertrude Robinson Smith and her followers decided to create an American Salzburg in their mountains. In fact, the trend Koussevitzky cautioned against — the misconception of music as entertainment rather than an art requiring the listener's active participation — has grown into a juggernaut, fed by television, the leisure industry, and the age of the superstar. The Beethoven Ninth remains a Tanglewood favorite, but it no longer means — nor can it mean — what it meant when Koussevitzky chose it to inaugurate his Music Shed and summon enemy nations to brotherhood. At Tanglewood as on radios and in concert halls throughout the land, it is merely one of the chestnuts.

Despite Koussevitzky's support of living composers, Tanglewood has rarely been on the cutting edge of new music where the BSO's concerts are concerned (and only sporadically in the Festival of Contemporary Music, as Paul Fromm complained). Over the entire span of the festival, the only premières of historic significance have been the first American performances of Mozart's *Idomeneo* and Britten's *Peter Grimes, Albert Herring,* and *War Requiem.* Other twentieth-century pieces turn up from time to time on BSO programs, of course, but they are in a minority, and those by living composers are in a minority smaller yet, subordinated to largely accepted works by composers from the first half of the century, such as Stravinsky, Bartók, Shostakovich, and Prokofiev. In the last few years Ozawa has made a good-faith effort to program more new music, but the exigencies of limited rehearsal time and trying to attract and please large crowds keep the results to a sprinkling of works, mostly short, in any given season.

Tanglewood's greatest legacy, in fact, is probably not the BSO concerts, popular as they are, but the student program. The roster of well-known conductors and other noted musicians among Music Center alumni tells only half the story. The other half is that, according to BSO records, 20 percent of the players in the major American symphony orchestras — and 30 percent of the first-chair players — have gone through Tanglewood. The school has been so successful in raising performance levels that Cleveland's Blossom

Seiji Ozawa in his Tanglewood whites.

Festival, Chicago's Ravinia, and the Los Angeles Philharmonic have modeled summer training programs on it.

Another way of looking at Tanglewood is provided by the growth in concerts and audiences. From six programs on two weekends in 1937, the festival grew to an all-time high of thirty BSO concerts in 1985, the first of the two experimental ten-week seasons. In those same years attendance increased tenfold, from 30,000 to 328,000 — also a record. This success, too, has provided a model for later festivals, such as Blossom, Wolf Trap, Saratoga, and Great Woods, which — with distinctive variations, of course — have patterned their pavilions and symphonic programming on Tanglewood's.

In feeding this taste for music Tanglewood has made inevitable compromises. If there is a malaise abroad in American symphony orchestras, as Gunther Schuller said in his widely quoted 1979 speech, the BSO at Tanglewood is both a villain and a victim. In order to draw the crowds to pay the bills, Tanglewood, in common with other orchestras and festivals, accentuates the big hits, in both music and performers. But in accentuating the hits Tanglewood and the other institutions only confirm audiences in the laziness of their listening habits. Wall-to-wall Mozart, Beethoven, and Tchaikovsky by celebrity artists, in other words, breeds more celebrity Mozart, Beethoven, and Tchaikovsky for larger audiences. At times it seems Tanglewood has to run faster and faster just to keep up with itself.

But, to Tanglewood's honor, it has never gone the rock, pop, and pap route of such performing arts centers as Saratoga and Great Woods. There have been and still are experiments with popular-artist concerts but the programs number only a few each season, and the emphasis now is on soft rock, folk, and old-timers like Barry Manilow. The worst damage is not musical rot but the mountain of trash that awaits the grounds crew on the mornings after. Tanglewood is no longer a pioneer in American musical life, as it was when Koussevitzky launched his great adventure, but neither does it run with the pack. If it embodies some of the less desirable aspects of today's superstar-chasing concert scene, it remains, imperturbably, a great institution and the summer home of a great orchestra, dedicated to the nurturing of a great tradition.

INDEX

142 y

6++?++